# VICTORIO ACOSTA VELASCO

## *An American Life*

**Michael S. Brown**

**Hamilton Books**
A member of
The Rowman & Littlefield Publishing Group
Lanham · Boulder · New York · Toronto · Plymouth, UK

**Hamilton Books**
4501 Forbes Boulevard
Suite 200
Lanham, Maryland 20706
Hamilton Books Acquisitions Department (301) 459-3366

Estover Road
Plymouth PL6 7PY
United Kingdom


Printed in the United States of America
British Library Cataloging in Publication Information Available

Library of Congress Control Number: 2007925218
ISBN-13: 978-0-7618-3800-5 (paperback : alk. paper)
ISBN-10: 0-7618-3800-7 (paperback : alk. paper)

∞™ The paper used in this publication meets the minimum requirements of American National Standard for Information Sciences—Permanence of Paper for Printed Library Materials, ANSI Z39.48—1984

To my late father, Winfield Ritchie Brown:

Loving father; best friend; companion; tutor; and guide for living, until we meet again. World War Two hero; a man of all trades; world traveler; and, though never finishing college, about the smartest person I have ever known in or out of school. Who continues to live in my memory; who has inspired not only high academic goals, but also an appreciation for humanity in all its beauty and foibles. I dedicate this work to him, for he has shaped it in innumerable ways, and he proudly awaits its completion.

August 31, 2006
Seattle

# Contents

# Acknowledgements

I would like to acknowledge the help of some very important people who made this work possible. First and foremost, I would like to express my deepest appreciation for the guidance that the chair of my dissertation committee, Dr. LeRoy Ashby, provided. His comments helped immensely in integrating Velasco's life into the broader themes of his times. When my own arguments were not as clear as they might have been, he suggested revisions that made the points clearer. He also managed incredible feats time and again, such as reading and commenting upon 40-page chapters and final drafts overnight and yet read thoroughly enough to catch anything from the logic of arguments to typographical errors. Throughout my program here at Washington State University, he has also provided me with extensive support in my efforts to gain funding for the project, without which it would have been very difficult to conduct the oftentimes expensive gathering of information from archives across the state of Washington.

I wish also to thank other members of my committee who have contributed significantly to this project. Dr. Noriko Kawamura was the one who, in a graduate seminar prior to the time I chose Victorio Velasco's life as my dissertation topic, first took an interest in him and encouraged further research on his life. Dr. Kawamura has also been supportive in other ways: working with me for an entire semester via telephone when circumstances forced me to remain in Seattle rather than in Pullman even as I was preparing for my preliminary examinations. She has also been instrumental in providing support and recommendations for the funding I sought and received. Dr. Orlan Svingen taught me how to conduct in-depth research of legislative materials, which aided me greatly in the sections about anti-immigration and anti-miscegenation laws both at the federal and the state level.

Other people in the History Department have contributed significantly to the completion of this study. Professor Thomas Kennedy supported me in my quest to learn about Asian culture, in my applications for funding, and in my efforts to find employment. Above all, he was, and will remain for me, a model of personal integrity. Dr. John Kicza encouraged me to continue my studies during a hiatus about halfway through my program and aided me in maneuvering around red tape so that I could remain enrolled in spite of my absence from Pullman and under the most challenging of circumstances. Others, including Dwayne Dehlbom, Marci Ballard, and Barbara O'Donnel always provided a congenial and friendly atmosphere that enhanced my stay here. The admissions committee of 1998, too, have my most sincere gratitude. It is no exaggeration to say that, without its members' willingness to admit an Asian man into its doctoral program to study Asian Americans, this biography would never have existed; without their decision, in the spring of 1998, to offer admission to an Oriental man, I may never have had the opportunity to pursue doctoral studies in an American university at this time in our history, at the turn of the twenty-first century.

There are others to whom I wish to express my gratitude and appreciation. Even though they were not officially involved with my Ph.D. program, they provided me with insights about which I have mulled over on many occasions while trying to assemble the immense wealth of information at my disposal into a story that is believable and interesting to broad audiences. First of all is my dear and loving father, Winfield Ritchie Brown, whose memory and spirit continue to encourage my progress at every step of the way and endured my sometimes impatient desire to get answers quickly. He was one of the most intelligent and knowledgeable people I have ever met, and I took full advantage of his expertise over countless dinners at Hong's Chinese Restaurant in the rural hideaway of Milton-Freewater, Oregon—my home, as my father has always reminded me. I will sorely miss his interest, help, feedback, and friendship, both in and out of scholarly endeavors. He will always be the soul who stood—and continues to stand—by me in everything I ever did or do, both in and out of school. Others include my mother, who has exercised the utmost of patience, eagerly awaiting the end of her son's ventures in books. My late uncle Danny will always be in my memory as a kind, giving man, always sensitive to others' needs. My Aunt Isa has provided me with some of the most incredible meals in recent memory. Priscilla Wegars gave me the opportunity to study the presence of Asians in the eastern Washington and western Idaho region through an internship during the summer of 2001. Nellie Zamora altruistically and selflessly helped me in obtaining the almost impossibly hard-to-get translations of letters between Velasco and family members, letters which go a long way towards explaining some of the social pressures that affected his relationship with Sixta Aquino. Lea Javier, whom I have never met except on the internet, nevertheless generously gave her time and effort while working with Nellie Zamora in painstakingly translating the letters between Velasco and family members. Fred and Dorothy Cordova, who run the extensive Filipino American Historical Society in Seattle, shared with me personal insights into the psychology of Velasco and others of his generation, invaluable information without which I would have not gained a balanced understanding of my topic and which no amount of extant documentation, however comprehensive, could ever fill. I wish also to acknowledge the assistance of librarians across the state of Washington. My discovery of the Velasco collection and my effort to bring to light, for the first time, the details of his life, would have never occurred had it not been for the help of the archivists at the Manuscripts and Archives section of the Suzzallo and Allen Libraries at the University of Washington in Seattle. Archivists at Western Washington University directed my attention towards a wealth of unexpected information about Velasco's experience in Bellingham. Dr. Lawrence Stark of the Manuscripts, Archives, and Special Collections of Washington State University's Holland Library helped me fill in gaps about Velasco and other Filipinos' experiences in Pullman. Lou Vyhnanek of the Social Sciences Collection, also of the Holland New Library, guided me through mazes of legislative documents in my research on the Cable Act. Archival staff of the Northwest Room of the Spokane Public Library directed me towards materials on Chinese and Japanese in the Spokane area. Robert Fisher of the Wing Luke Museum in Seattle directed my attention to various private and public collections of materials in the Seattle area and introduced me to Dorothy and Fred Cordova. Cecil Williams and Zoltan Porga, who have maintained the computer equipment in the lab where I wrote and assembled this biography, assisted in countless ways, including dealing with thorny technological issues and providing a congenial work atmosphere. Only small parts of Velasco's story would have survived, however, without the efforts of Josefina Querebin, his widow. Were it not for her efforts to preserve and make available to the public the details of her deceased husband's life, I may never have even heard of his name. Her determination to preserve materials covering all facets of his life made possible my endeavor to create a well-rounded portrait of this fascinating, pioneering Asian man's life.

I am indebted to others, too, who have, in one way or another, helped completing of the program or made its pursuit meaningful. Barb, Brenda, and Jonalea courageously stepped forward and provided moral support and encouragement when both were in short supply and, in so doing, helped me keep an open perspective on racial issues, both in this work and in my personal life. Yvonne, Carmel and Kristi and others at Festival Dance gave me many fond, memorable and much-needed distractions. Larry, Father Joe, and others associated with the Lilac City Figure Skating Club in Spokane similarly left me with many cherished memories of mixing studies with diversions. Regan, through sheer decency, provided hope for a United States that may someday be able to put aside racial divisions. Shelly, my pairs skating partner, has provided incalculable hours of welcome respite from the books during our early morning practices. Bonnie, in spite of differences in personal views, will always remain among the handful of people in my life whom I will always respect and hold in the deepest regard. And Ellen courageously tried to reach, for a brief moment in time, an impossible dream.

The invaluable assistance financial backing provided in making possible my many trips all across the state of Washington, securing funds for thousands of pages of photocopying, numerous long distance phone calls, and the presentation of my research at a variety of local, regional, and national conferences came from, among other sources, the following (in chronological order): Aiken Travel Grant, History Department, Washington State University (2002); Evelyn W. Hacker-Colonial Dames of XVII Century Scholarship, College of Liberal Arts, Washington State University (2002); Evelyn W. Hacker Scholarship, Eliza Hart Spalding Chapter of the Daughters of the American Revolution, College of Liberal Arts, Washington State University (2002); Rockie Family Scholarship, College of Liberal Arts, Washington State University; Pettyjohn Fund Travel Grant, History Department, Washington State University (2001 and 2002); Herman J. Deutsch Memorial Fellowship, History Department, Washington State University (2002); Claudius O. and Mary W. Johnson Graduate Fellowship, History Department, Washington State University (2002); Graduate School Travel Grant, Graduate School, Washington State University (2001 and 2002); Viola Vestal Coulter Fellowship, Washington State University (2001); Joel E. Ferris Award, Eastern Washington State Historical Society (2001); Thomas S. Foley/Burlington Northern Graduate Fellowship, Thomas S. Foley Institute, Washington State University (2001); John C. Kassebaum and Loella Kay Kassebaum Scholarship, Washington State University (2001); and the Phi Kappa Phi Scholarship, Washington State University (2001).

I wish to acknowledge also the various forums that made it possible for me to present my research on Velasco and related topics (in chronological order): "Race, Gender, and the Cable Act," at the Joint Asian Pacific American American Law Faculty/Law Teachers of Color Conference, Seattle, March 22, 2003; "Boundaries in the World of Victorio Velasco," at the Pacific Northwest History Conference, Seattle, April 4-6, 2002; "Race and Gender in the World of Victorio Velasco: Dominance, Subordination, and Changes in Context" in the following forums: William Wiley Exposition, Washington State University, Pullman, February 22, 2002 and March 12, 2003; Asian Studies on the Pacific Coast Conference, Western Washington University, Bellingham, June 21, 2002; as guest speaker for HIST 301, "East Meets West," Washington State University, Pullman, Feb. 22, 2002; Utah Humanities Council Graduate Students' Conference, Salt Lake City, Oct. 27, 2001; and the History Colloquium Series, Washington State University, Pullman, Oct. 11, 2001.

Lastly, I would like to thank Victorio Velasco. Somehow, his journalist and writer's instincts must have let him known that his life was worth documenting. Indeed, as early as 1929, within a handful of years of his arrival in the United States, he made his awareness of his own historical role apparent when he confided to his diary that it is up to "future novelists" to tell the story of his life. By preserving for posterity not only the things that flattered his image, but also place him in a less-than-favorable light, he made a contribution that, decades after his death, rebut popular American notions that all Asian men are kung fu experts, computer nerds, and asexual math whizzes, pervasive racial stereotypes intent on persisting into and shaping the twenty-first century United States.

It goes without saying that any errors or omissions are solely my responsibility.

# Abbreviations for Manuscript Collections Frequently Referenced in this Volume

| | |
|---|---|
| VVC | Victorio Velasco Collection, Manuscripts and Archives, Suzzallo and Allen Libraries, University of Washington, Seattle, Washington. |
| CWFLUC | Cannery Workers' and Farm Laborers' Union Local No. 7 Collection, Manuscripts and University Archives, Suzzallo and Allen Libraries, University of Washington, Seattle, Washington. |
| WWUC | Special Collections, Western Washington University, Bellingham, Washington. |
| FANHS | Filipino American National Historical Society, Seattle, Washington. |
| WSUC | Holland Library, Manuscripts and Special Collections, Washington State University, Pullman, Washington, 37. |

# Introduction

One day in primary school in Pangasinan, in the southern part of the Philippines, Victorio Acosta Velasco (1902-1968) became irritated because one of his Filipino classmates seemed so intent on his studies and completely oblivious to everyone around him that Velasco decided to play a trick on him. He tied a piece of cord to one end of his classmate's coat and the other to his bench so that, when the teacher asked him a question, the boy stood up, ripping his jacket in front of the entire class and causing an uproar of boisterous laughter. Velasco may have remembered the incident years later, though, not only for the fun it brought him, but also for the discipline the teacher imposed to remind him of the proper boundaries of his conduct.

The incident amounted to perhaps only a few minutes of Velasco's sixty-five years, yet it encapsulated some of the things that would affect him for the remainder of his life, most of it in the United States, as a scholar, writer, editor, and union leader. The mere fact that Velasco happened to be in a classroom that day was due to changes in the world around him in his native Philippines, in particular, the ouster of the Spanish from his homeland, the coming of the Americans, and the establishment of a new way of life, which included the beginning of widespread education and the breaking down of rigid social barriers. Velasco's presence in the classroom also revealed that he was able to take advantage of the new opportunities. Yet, the trick he played upon his classmate revealed something else: a propensity for mixing the pursuit of studies with amusements. Both of the personal traits that he showed in the classroom would play significant roles in shaping the remainder of his life, for he overcame numerous obstacles in order to reach educational levels that were rare even for Caucasians. At the same time, he never let himself forget worldly pleasures, as not only his frequent social excursions, but his numerous flirtations revealed later in his life. The fact that Velasco received discipline for acting out of line, too, was significant, for it conveyed to him that it was not only his own conduct, but also the willingness of those around him to tolerate how he acted, that shaped his experiences. The incident symbolized his place in a new world taking shape; his desire and capacity to pursue the opportunities that world provided him; his refusal to pursue work at the exclusion of other pleasures; and his encounter with limitations that the world around him imposed, something that became particularly significant in his later efforts to seek employment and a marital life in the United States.[1]

Victorio Velasco's life between his birth in 1902 and the beginning of 1947, when he came full circle in terms of no longer just helping, but fighting his kinsmen, illustrates the twists and turns in the life of one Asian man, and it also provides a way for understanding both the interracial and intra-racial tensions of his times. Many of the tensions, particularly after his arrival in the United States in April of 1924, stemmed from the widespread racial hostility against Asians in the United States. From the time he first set foot on a Seattle pier in 1924, he learned that the only employment open to him was in domestic work and manual labor. He also began experiencing his first romantic rejections from white women. This, too, was a harbinger of the future, for he never formed a permanent relationship with a white woman. Yet, his relationships with white women—although limited generally to friendships—were important for another reason: they represented the only part of his personal life in which he had meaningful relationships with whites. During the period of this study, he never had a friendship with a white male. It was not because he was a loner, for his calendars were consistently filled with engagements with male Filipino friends to attend movies, social events, parties, dinners, lunches, and countless club activities. Rather, the fact that he never had a white male as a friend indicated that, ironically, even though white women generally did not take the final step of accepting him as a romantic partner, there may nevertheless have been a curiosity across racial lines that facilitated, at the very least, some kind of initial attraction, even if it rarely led to anything beyond flirtation. On the other hand, the fact that he was able to form such friendships may have been, if nothing else, a testament to his gregarious personality and social skills, especially since he succeeded—at least in friendships—in crossing racial boundaries in spite of widespread anti-Filipino prejudice.

Whatever the sources of his difficulties, his life, in contrast to the standard portrayal of Asians' lives in the United States, hardly fit into any easily definable mold. The degree of political sophistication he attained and his use of *realpolitik* by the beginning of 1947, in particular, underscore the error of accepting without question the decades-long stereotypes about Asian men continuing into our own time.

Velasco was born in Pangasinan in the Philippines in 1902. Upon finishing high school in 1919, he became a teacher and a newspaper reporter in Manila. Soon thereafter, he met Sixta Aquino, who became one of the greatest loves of his life. They never married, but they lived together, and she gave birth to a baby girl who died in infancy. In 1922, Velasco began studies at the College of the Philippines in Sampaluc, where he spent much of his time until the spring of 1924. He then decided to leave for the United States in order to pursue his education. Full of patriotic feelings toward Americans, he felt that the United States was the best place for an aspiring poet like himself to finish his education before returning to his native land. In April, 1924, he took leave of friends, his beloved grandmother, sister, other relatives, and Aquino. He boarded a ship for Seattle, Washington via a circuitous route through Hong Kong and Tokyo. Upon arriving, he found work as a houseboy. Almost immediately, he began studies at the University of Washington towards a bachelor's degree. Between 1924 and the late 1930s, he finished his undergraduate education and started the university's graduate program in education. Along the way, he lost Aquino's love when, in 1925, she forbade him from ever contacting her again. By the early 1930s, he managed to publish some of his poetry. It was also between 1930 and 1937 that he had an affair with Delphine Brooks, a young white woman from the central Washington farm town of Wapato. What had started as a casual friendship in the classrooms of the Washington State Normal School in Ellensburg became a passionate, romantic relationship set against the backdrop of racial hostility. By the late 1930s, he had also become heavily involved in Filipino issues in the United States, the Filipino press, and unionization efforts among Alaskan salmon cannery workers. By the end of the Second World War, he was one of the most important Filipino leaders in the cannery workers' union.[2]

Ironically, by the end of the Second World War, what had begun as his journalistic efforts to work with and help fellow Filipinos in America had become a means of gaining personal political power. By 1947, when this study ends, he was working against them. Yet, the tensions he encountered in intra-racial activities by the end of the war were not necessarily surprising. Even though his relationships with other Filipinos provided him with opportunities not available to him among whites, intra-racial relationships caused conflicts and tensions. As a journalist, he eventually used his position to denigrate Filipinos who were his political enemies, particularly in the union election campaigns of the 1940s. As a member of a large network of family and friends, he enjoyed strong personal relationships, but he also endured frequent demands from family members who, unaware of racial restrictions on employment in the United States, assumed that his education and qualifications would lead to a good job and thus often asked him to send gifts and money. Moreover, in the intra-racial relationship that affected him the most profoundly, his affair with Aquino, he enjoyed not only love and trust, but also some of the greatest pain of his life. Velasco's experiences with Filipinos, like those with Caucasians, therefore, were neither simple nor predictable, and both were filled with pleasures and disappointments.

Velasco's life between his birth and the mid-1940s contributes to an understanding of Asian American history in a way that few other works have done. There are several impediments to the understanding of Asian Americans in the extant literature. One is that there is next to nothing published about the lives of individual Asian Americans. The one notable exception has been in autobiographical works. John Okada's *No No Boy* (1976) provides a glimpse into the life of a Japanese American man. Monica Sone's *Nisei Daughter* (1979) describes the author's experiences in Seattle in the early and mid-twentieth century. Jade Snow Wong's *Fifth Chinese Daughter* (1950) is about the life of an early twentieth century Chinese immigrant's life in the United States. As the editors of the first anthology of Asian American literature, *Aiiieeee!: An Anthology of Asian American Writers* (1991), argue, however, some autobiographies seem to accomplish little more than repeating stereotypes. According to them, Wong's autobiography, for example, presumes that Asian immigrants are somehow exotic. Autobiographical works, moreover, generally do not provide sufficient distance between the writers and their worlds in order to place the subjects' lives within a broader, historical context. Thus, they do not fill the gap that only historical biography can provide.[3]

Another problem is that the extant works are not commonly available or accessible. The small amount of literature on the lives of individual Asian Americans is often difficult to access because the works are often unpublished and available only in archives, university collections, and occasional articles in a limited number of academic journals. Alice Y. Chai's "A Picture Bride from Korea: The Life History of a Korean American Woman in Hawaii," for example, is an unpublished paper whose only public appearance was at a conference in the late 1970s. Another example of a semi-biographical work on an Asian American's experiences in the United States, Lowell Chun-Hom's "Jade Snow Wong and the Fate of Chinese-American Identity," appeared only in a single issue of *Amerasia Journal* in the early 1970s.[4]

The absence of detailed studies on the lives of individuals impedes a complete understanding of Asians in the United States. Some works, such as Ronald Takaki's *Strangers from a Different Shore* (1989), attempt to incorporate the stories of specific individuals in broad narratives. When he and others make the attempt, they permit their audiences to understand and appreciate the lives of individual Asian Americans. In his description of Filipinos' experience with the anti-Filipino riots of the late 1920s and early 1930s, Takaki tries to treat them as individuals rather than as anonymous masses. Other scholars, such as Sucheng Chan, similarly make notable efforts to bring out the experiences of individuals.[5]

Generally, however, in spite of the efforts of scholars like Takaki and Chan to incorporate details from real people's lives into their full-length works, there is all too little biographical information. Moreover, in the literature specifically on Filipinos, none is a book-length work on an individual's life. Among works on Filipinos, one that makes an attempt to tell the stories of individuals is Yen Le Espiritu's *Filipino American Lives* (1995). It does an admirable job in providing details about specific Filipinos' experiences in the United States. Yet, the stories are firsthand accounts, and the individuals telling their own stories do not necessarily see their experiences as belonging within a broader historical context. The absence of contextualized works can lead to the mistaken impression that Asians, in contrast to other races about whom many biographies are available, are anonymous, monolithic hordes lacking individuality and leading lives that fit neatly into specific, narrow bounds and categories.[6]

One of the goals of this study, therefore, is to help fill the gaps in writings about individual Asian Americans. It does so by taking an in-depth look at two decades in the life of an Asian man's life in the United States, illuminating his experiences in a way that shorter works cannot do. It does so also by examining the central themes in his life during different periods.

Chapter One introduces the themes in his life prior to his departure from the Philippines and his arrival in the United States in April of 1924. His departure was particularly painful because of his parting from Aquino and his beloved grandmother. At the same time, it was the logical culmination of his past several years, when he had tried to pursue his education beyond what was available in the Philippines. Another theme was the beginning of his seemingly endless flirtations. He had hardly set foot aboard the ship taking him to the United States when he began to notice other women. Among them were Japanese he saw when his ship docked in Japan en route to Seattle.

Chapter Two, covering the period between his arrival in Seattle in April of 1924 and the end of his second summer in the canneries in August of 1926, argues that his first two years in the United States was a period during which he experimented with different ways of adapting to his new world. He continued flirting with the women he met, and he began the first steps towards gaining an American education and beginning a life-long avocation as a journalist and writer. He also continued—unsuccessfully—to find work commensurate with his qualifications.

Chapter Three covers the period between August of 1926 and April of 1927 and argues that, within limits, Velasco's own determination led to notable achievements even among Caucasians. While attending the Washington State Normal School in Bellingham, he made one of the few, sustained efforts in his life to assimilate among whites. As a result, his experience in Bellingham was one of the most fruitful in terms of the respect he gained among them. At the same time, he continued to encounter boundaries because of his race. The clearest indication appeared in his efforts to pursue white women. These efforts often led to friendships, but it was nearly impossible for him to cross the line between even the deepest of friendships and romantic intimacy. Possibly because of his realization that race posed boundaries regardless of his personal merits, he increasingly withdrew from Caucasians and became involved with the Filipino ethnic press and Filipino nationalism.

Chapter Four, covering the period between May of 1927 and December of 1931, argues that the persistent but unsuccessful efforts he made to have a romantic relationship with a white woman and the limited successes he began enjoying as a published writer contrasted sharply with his increasing involvement in Filipino nationalism. He flirted with and pursued more women than in any other period in his life and enjoyed meaningful friendships with several of them. He also began publishing some of his first works with major American publishers, who included some of his poetry in anthologies of American poets. As in Bellingham, however, he found that his efforts alone did not guarantee success. In no other context was this clearer than in his attempts at romance. None of the women he pursued, including those who considered him a close and dear friend, accepted him as a permanent lover or mate. As a result, he became even more involved in exclusively Filipino issues, began enjoying prestige among his compatriots, and launched the capstone achievement of his stay in the United States, the *Filipino Forum*, a newspaper that endured for four decades and eventually became an indelible fixture of Seattle's Chinatown.

Chapter Five, which describes Velasco's life between 1932 and 1938, emphasizes his increasingly exclusive involvement with Filipinos and his last attempt to find a white woman as a mate. His breakup with Delphine Brooks, the only white woman who ever accepted him as her lover, not only marked the end of his serious efforts to seek a Caucasian woman as a mate, but also symbolized the end of his striving to fully assimilate into the world of the whites. At the same time, his increasingly exclusive involvement with Filipinos was not trouble-free. Even as he gained stature among his compatriots, he began forming political alliances that put him at odds with other Pinoys.

The final chapter argues that the period between 1939 and 1947 was full of ironies. By the beginning of 1947, Velasco had largely succeeded in making a name for himself among Filipinos and furthering his education by earning a Bachelor and a Master's degree from an American university and beginning a Ph.D. program in education. At the same time, although he had come to the United States with dreams of helping fellow Filipinos, he found himself fighting them. Racism had blocked his aspirations to find an American wife and work as a professional in the United States. Yet, his cooperation with white cannery supervisors during the war years in order to obtain draft exemptions for Filipino cannery workers led to a degree of rapprochement between him and Caucasians. Paradoxically, it was also a period which marked not only the height of his prestige among Filipinos, but also its nadir. It was during this period when he became adept at *realpolitik* and wielded his influence against other Filipinos.

Each chapter uses Velasco's life as a way to understand the myriad facets of one Asian man's life. Each places him in the broader historical context. Most importantly, each chapter shows the various aspects of an Asian individual's personality and experiences. He was a hero in some respects, and a villain in others. His aspiration to become the "Wordsworth of the Philippines" excites the admiration of anyone who has ever dreamt of, and made a lifelong effort to, achieve greatness as a writer. His role in establishing the ethnic press in Seattle and in inaugurating the efforts of other Asian journalists have also elicited admiration and respect.

Velasco's persistent efforts to find a woman in a strange land who would accept him as her mate can similarly evoke a sense of both pathos and respect. Yet, he was not always a hero, and he was not always admirable. His efforts to become a famed poet were often flawed. They were flawed not only because of the pedantic tone of many of his writings, but also because of a rigidness in structure and a lack of imagination that he never overcame. On occasion, there were signs of talent, but he never fulfilled his potential. Similarly, his efforts as a journalist were also tainted. He used his influence in the Filipino press and his political alliance with Filipino strongman Pio De Cano to fight other Filipinos. During the war years, he achieved a rapprochement with his former adversaries, salmon cannery owners and managers, in order to keep Filipino workers in the canneries and, concomitantly, safeguard his own position and influence in the union. During the late 1940s, he again used his position as a journalist to disparage political rivals within the cannery workers' union. In at least some of his personal relationships, he treated women not as individuals but as prizes to pursue indiscriminately. Sometimes, as in in his relationship with Aquino, he was cruel, manipulative, demanding and untrustworthy. The dual nature of his efforts notwithstanding, his life was undeniably multi-faceted.[7]

Above all, Velasco was not just an historical object whose life course depended solely on the events around him. He was also an historical actor; it was not only the limitations the world forced upon him, but also his own goals and actions that shaped his experiences. His inability to control the course of his life was the result not only of external factors, but also of traits, both admirable and not-so-admirable, within himself. This biography, therefore, portrays Velasco as possessing all the complexities and inconsistencies apparent in any human being; his life was the product of free will, restrictions the world around him imposed, and inherent flaws and traits in his own character. His life was hardly that of an anonymous object mixed up among an endless number of other, anonymous and inert automatons. This portrait of an Asian man's life in the United States as something other than a one-dimensional representation based on stereotypes and racial prejudices is all too rare in the United States today in both the academic and popular literature.

# 1

# Life in the Philippines (1902 to 1924)

Between 1902, when he was born, and 1924, when he arrived in Seattle, Velasco's life reflected his innate abilities as well as the momentous changes shaping his world. On the one hand, his strong will power, early aspirations, and talents foretold a future in which he could make something of himself. On the other, the world in which he lived not only provided new opportunities, but also imposed limitations.

## I. Educational and Career Aspirations

From the time he was a child, Velasco held high ambitions for himself, and he was able to realize many of them. Even when he was still in grade school, he decided that, some day, he would have a high school diploma. He also made his ambitions clear when his grandmother made the mistake of bragging to the neighbors that he would some day become a policeman. He had already decided that he would be a doctor, a lawyer, or some other professional, so he publicly rebuked her. The work of American teachers, who had started shaping the Filipino school system a few years before Velasco's birth, encouraged him to seek an education beyond his primary school years. Consequently, even at a young age, he had become aware of the spread of an American-style education in the Philippines and wished to take advantage of it.[1]

In spite of his ambitions, Velasco had to face and overcome various obstacles. One was the English language. When he entered the primary grades, he did not know a word of English, and it took weeks for him to learn a handful of words like "boy," "girl," and "cat." Other potential obstacles to Velasco's ambitions included his inability to earn the highest marks in school. In 1918-1919, during his junior year in high school, for example, he earned a cumulative average of 79. The following year, his averages ranged around 78, reflecting a high of 81 in spelling and a low of 75 in arithmetic and bookkeeping. Moreover, during his first two years of high school, his average grades in English and composition were as low as the mid-70s, a disappointing score for someone aspiring to a career as a writer and teacher, his new goal. During his last year, he barely passed arithmetic with an average of 61. His highest grades all year were in biology, in which he had a 90 average, and in literature and composition, in which he had an 86. The average of 79, the best he had achieved across all subjects, may have been respectable in comparison to the grades of his peers, but it was hardly a harbinger of academic promise.[2]

Even outside of school, in his first steps towards his chosen vocation as a writer, he faced an uphill battle because of his own limitations, some of which appeared in a compilation of poems that he had written in English. Although the Mission Press of Manila published the collection, *Lingyen and Other Poems*, the event did not necessarily bode well for his future as a poet. Even at a young age, persistent traits, including lack of imagination and excess rigidity, were becoming evident. In one of the poems, "Ode to a Tree," he seemed unable to go beyond a literal description of his subject. Other poems in the volume showed an inability to vary structure for either the sake of displaying technical virtuosity or for revealing different levels of meaning. Each also varied only in the slightest in meter from line to line. "Ode to a Tree" also illustrated another problem, a lack of comfort in his use of the English language that came through in outdated, archaic choices of words such as "thy," "thou," and "thee," a trait that afflicted other poems in the collection as well. Although it was possible that the clumsy phrasing was due to English not being his native tongue, the more likely reason was that, perhaps, his teachers in the Philippines taught their pupils outdated expressions.[3]

In spite of his limited talent, Velasco made notable progress, partly because of his determination. Notwithstanding the low grades he received, his gained some academic recognition. In his first year in high school, he received the highest grade in a composition class of forty students. During his sophomore year, he entered a poetry contest, won first place in his section, and ranked fourth in his class. That year, his English teacher bestowed upon him the honor of correcting freshman English papers, an honor that none of his peers enjoyed. While still in high school, he published a poem in an American newsmagazine in Manila. For a sixteen-year-old, average high school student writing in a language that he had begun to learn barely a decade earlier, finding his work in its pages was an immense encouragement. Thereafter, he went beyond writing simply for his classes and began to write short stories and study Shakespeare on his own. His efforts came to fruition, for he won a prize in a short story writing contest and had his work published in the school paper. His successes, along with his study of American poets such as Longfellow, Bryant, Emerson, and others, inspired thoughts of becoming, in his own words, the "Longfellow of the Philippines."[4]

There were successes in his journalistic efforts as well. In 1920, when Velasco was a high school senior, he got a job as a reporter with an American newspaper in Manila, the *Manila Times*, earning a salary of $25 a month. He also contributed to two other publications, the Philippines Free Press's the *Integridad*, and a weekly, the *Independent*, and became one of fifteen writers who gained national recognition in a poetry contest.[5]

His successes came at least partly because of his innate intelligence. His mediocre academic performance obscured the mature thought processes of which he was capable and belied what he would achieve as a pioneering journalist in the American ethnic press later in life. "In Phantasy," one of the poems appearing in *Lingyen and Other Poems*, for example, Velasco experimented with varying the aesthetic distance between the speaker and the author, revealing Velasco's ability to convey different levels of meaning through changes in literary structure. The same ability appeared, albeit inconsistently, in other poems in the collection.[6]

Yet, it was not only Velasco's intelligence and determination, but also events in the broader context that affected his early life. He undoubtedly benefited from the growth of education in the Philippines after the Americans arrived. In 1898, there was only one teacher for every 4,179 individuals in the islands because, during the previous three-and-a-half centuries, Christian churches, under Spanish colonial rule, ran the educational system almost exclusively to indoctrinate a small number of students in religion. As a result, the literacy rate among Filipinos was dismal, amounting to only 5-8 percent of the population. During the first several decades following the end of the Spanish-American War, the Americans rapidly improved education in the islands. The Americans quickly put a new educational system in place, supplied books, pencils, and other supplies, and made primary school education compulsory. Between 1901 and 1902, the Americans sent 1,074 teachers to the Philippines. Within the first decade of their effort, the Americans established over 4,000 schools, enrolling 355,722 elementary grade children and 3,404 high school students. Scarcely two decades following the Americans' arrival, there were nearly a million students attending elementary grades and 17,335 students in high schools. The results were impressive; in 1918, the national literacy rate had risen to 49.2 percent.[7]

Consequently, when Velasco and others of his generation entered the primary school system around 1910, they enjoyed both the establishment of a modern, large-scale educational system in the islands and its incidental effects, including the spread of the English language, which acted as a social leveler, breaking down racial, class, and gender barriers and creating cultural unity, unheard of in the past because of the dozens of different dialects. During the Spanish period, the small number of pupils in church schools within limited areas such as Manila had the effect of creating a social elite versed in the Spanish language and culture and thus distinguishable from indigenous peoples, a consequence of which was not only the maintenance of a rigid hierarchy based on race and language, but also separation of one indigenous language group from another. For Velasco and his Filipina sweetheart Sixta Aquino, the bounties that the new school system provided included not only a good education, but also opportunities to teach. After completing his senior year, Velasco taught English to pupils barely younger than himself at the Philippine Central Institute in Manila, a private high school, and Aquino worked as a teacher in Davao at least as early as 1925.[8]

Moreover, Velasco's education beyond high school offered additional opportunities. He was able to take advantage of post-graduate education with future leaders of the Philippines when he matriculated in the School of Journalism at the National University in Manila. Among his classmates who, like Velasco, used the opportunity to establish a base for the future, were Mauro Mendez, who became Secretary of the Department of Foreign Affairs in the Philippines, Modesto Farolan, publisher of the *Philippines Herald* and eventual Consul General in Honolulu, and Narciso Ramos, ultimately the ambassador to Taipei. Moreover, Velasco combined his education with practical experience outside the classroom. He was a reporter on the School of Journalism's paper, the *Varsity News,* and, between 1921 and 1922, he was associate editor of another of the school's publications, the *Varsity Herald.* It was in this setting that Velasco began a newfound interest in journalism, continued pursuing his dream of becoming a famous poet and, in the fall of 1924, graduated from the College of Education at the National University.[9]

As in his education, the start that Velasco made in journalism was possible largely because of historical events. When he entered the School of Journalism, he and his peers were among the pioneers of a new generation of Filipino journalists. The *Philippine Herald* released its first issue in 1920, and another mainstay in the Philippine press, the *Manila Tribune*, came into being in 1925. Both papers joined a host of others that began to crop up after the end of the first decade of American occupation largely as the result of the increasing influence of the English language and the return to the Philippines of the first Filipinos who had completed studies in the United States and turned to journalism and writing.[10]

Velasco and other Filipino journalists owed a debt to recent historical trends in other ways, too. One was the political role of the press, which began with the *Kalayaan*, a newspaper that appeared in only one edition, in January, 1896, but was directly responsible for spreading ideas about rebelling against Spanish rule and thereby increasing the membership in the Filipino resistance movement against the Spaniards from the hundreds to around 30,000. In a more general sense, too, the written word as a medium for political change may have had its source in artists' subsequent resistance to the American occupation. Filipino playwrights, for example, staged plays with nationalistic themes. By the time Velasco began studying at the National University, the notion that the press shapes political events had already taken root.[11]

Another facet of Velasco's work reflected the growth of Philippine nationalism. The revolution against the Spanish, which ultimately led to the end of Spanish rule and the coming of the Americans, was the fruit of earlier insurrectionary efforts between the mid-1500s and the end of the nineteenth century. The rebellions stemmed from many reasons, including personal feuds between Filipinos and Spaniards, protests against economic conditions, and resistance against the Catholic Church's control over rice, forced labor, and monopolies on liquor and tobacco. Other grounds for Filipino dissatisfaction with Spanish rule came as a result of the strict racial hierarchy under the Spaniards, with Spaniards at the top, mestizos next, and natives at the bottom; the highest civil positions that Filipino or Chinese mestizos of mixed Spanish blood could attain, for example, were in municipal government because their race precluded them from obtaining government employment above the local level. After the beginning of American rule, there was also resistance against the Americans. Battles between

American colonialists and Filipino freedom fighters between 1901 and 1913 led to the slaughter of tens of thousands of natives, many of whom were civilians, and the wholesale destruction of countless villages. Velasco's faith in politics and the value of ideas in bringing about change may have been the legacy of not only these events, but also of the appearance of a Filipino middle class after the mid-nineteenth century, when European liberalism, based on the work of men such as Rousseau and Locke, entered the islands. The rise of the bourgeoisie led also to reformist ideas among Filipino intellectuals during the 1880s and 1890s, just prior to the insurrection of 1896-1898, and the growth of organizations like the Hispano-Filipino Association and the Masons.[12]

Velasco's decision to continue his education in the United States reflected, too, the choices young Filipino men were making after the end of Spanish rule to study among Americans in cities across the American continent. By 1920, there were more than 5,000 Filipinos in the United States. When Velasco arrived in Seattle in 1924, there was already a significant Filipino community in the King Street area in Seattle's Chinatown. Funding for his education in the United States likewise reflected trends that other young Filipinos had set. Velasco's main source of income, cannery work, was one that earlier groups of Filipinos had begun at least as early as 1911 and resulted in Filipinos outnumbering and replacing the traditional workers in canneries, the Japanese and the Chinese. In Seattle and other cities along the West coast, businesses such as the L.V.M. Hotel, where Velasco often stayed, responded to the influx of Filipinos by hosting labor contractors mediating between canneries and the new arrivals. Even Velasco's pursuit of white women soon after he came to Seattle reflected patterns of earlier Filipino immigration.[13]

Economically, too, historical events affected Velasco's world. The Americans' easing of tariffs upon Philippine imports to the United States helped strengthen the Philippine economy. A broad array of industries, such as sawmills, coconut oil mills, cordage factories, and the fish industry, benefited from American trade. Velasco's own province of Mindanao and his hometown of Davao, in particular, gained from American economic policies, including American investments in agriculture, which aided them financially and created political stability, thereby neutralizing indigenous resistance against Americans.[14]

In other ways, Filipinos, including possibly Velasco, benefited from the changes. During the United States' occupation of the Philippines, the Americans gradually lifted sanctions against basic freedoms such as worship, assembly, and speech. By the time Velasco reached adulthood, Filipinos had gained additional opportunities that encouraged their personal and professional ambitions. In 1901, Filipinos gained the right to hold elective positions at the provincial level, and the supreme court seated its first Filipino chief justice. By 1907, Filipinos served in both the legislative and executive branches of the National Assembly. By the early 1920s, Americans in the Philippine civil service occupied only about 6 percent of the available posts, and Filipinos held offices at every level of government except for the highest position, that of the Governor-General, which

Americans occupied. By the time that Velasco enrolled at the National University's School of Journalism, he had good reason, therefore, to be optimistic about his future.[15]

In quality of life, too, Velasco and his generation were beneficiaries of American rule. In 1905, the Americans introduced the first telephone lines in Manila, and, by the 1930s, telephones, radio stations, post offices, bridges, and railways linked together even small municipalities. In 1901, the United States established the Board of Public Health and a variety of dispensaries, hospitals, and asylums. Among the results of the Americans' efforts was a decrease in mortality rates from 30.5 per 1000 in 1898 to 21.29 per thousand in 1907.[16]

Yet, the Filipinos, including possibly Velasco, were not entirely satisfied with the American presence. For one thing, many continued hoping for a Philippines free of any external control. In 1919, a delegation of Filipino leaders traveled to the United States to lobby for Philippine independence, and it became the first of a number of such missions over the next two decades. During the interim, moreover, Filipinos contested American hegemony for a variety of reasons. In November of 1927, Manuel Roxas, the Speaker of the House in the Philippine government, traveled to Washington, D.C. to present a list of grievances against then-Governor-General of the Philippines, Leonard Wood (1921-1927). Velasco was an heir to the nationalistic ideas circulating among leaders of his generation, as his work in journalism and as a writer and political activist later revealed.[17]

Nor did all American reforms end positively. After around 1916, for example, the electoral democracy that the United States brought became riddled with corruption, bribery, and favoritism. The administration of Governor-General Wood, too, caused tension because he insisted on actively running the Philippine government, vetoing 46 of 217 bills that the Philippine legislature passed between October of 1923 and February of 1924. The years between 1922 and 1925 became among the most contentious politically as Filipino leaders increasingly criticized Wood and called for Philippine independence. Also, although the Americans brought democracy in theory, not many Filipinos benefited because literacy and property requirements for those seeking government offices ruled out most Filipinos except the best-educated. Nor was it easy for Filipinos to forget the Americans' brutal suppression of Filipino resistance to American colonial rule, which cost the islands approximately 300,000 lives and involved numerous instances in which American soldiers, dehumanizing the natives as "niggers," "goo goos" and "little brown monkeys," indiscriminately slaughtered the civilian populations of entire villages. Incidents such as the massacre of 900 Filipinos at Mount Dajo, after which young whites stood smiling for the camera above a ditch filled to the brim with the bullet-riddled bodies of half naked women and children, remained deeply-etched in Filipinos' consciousness.[18]

The world in which Velasco was born was thus one in which broad changes were taking place, ranging from the Philippine Revolution against Spanish rule between 1896 and 1897 to the Spanish-American War of 1898, ending Spanish rule and ensuring the United States' victory over Filipino patriots during the first decade of American occupation. Because Velasco and members of his generation were born within a few years of the United States' victory over Spain, the events invariably shaped their lives in the Philippines and, later, in the United States.[19]

## II. Personal Life

In Velasco's personal life, events reflected the confluence of the old and the new. It was in his relationship with Sixta Aquino, his Filipina sweetheart, where the intersection was particularly clear. Aquino, like Velasco, was a product of the new world the Americans created, and, just as the changes that the Americans brought with them affected Velasco, so did they affect her and the relationship she had with him.

On one hand, the relationship seemed to reflect the Spanish legacy, especially female subordination to males. Velasco seemed to dominate the relationship in some ways, such as in her apparent and constant efforts to seek his approval. In early January, 1922, for example, when he was in Manila at the University of the Philippines and she in Davao, at the other end of the islands, she wrote to him about receiving her appointment as a regular teacher, having the honor of delivering the opening remarks for a school program, judging compositions in a writing competition, and training other teachers. "You must be proud then of me, Dearie, being elected to give [a] short address among my fellow teachers . . . . You will find your Dearie being a popular one here in the town of Davao," she told him. She also often compared herself to other teachers. For instance, she told him that her colleagues did not receive honors as she did, and she criticized another teacher because of his unpopularity among his pupils.[20]

She sought his attention in other ways as well. In early 1922, she offered to send him some handkerchiefs as gifts. She sometimes expressed her determination to gain his grandmother's love. Often, she reminded him of her ill health and told him that she faithfully took time to write to him even when she was too weak to carry on other activities and was under her doctor's orders to cease staying up until midnight grading papers and to endure a strict regimen of taking quinine, iron, and strychnine tablets. Yet, she continued expending her energy corresponding with Velasco even as she suffered from additional illnesses, including malaria, and she kept reminding him that she was writing to him in spite of her weakened condition because she knew that he wanted to hear from her.[21]

Aquino may also have been insecure about his love for her because of concerns she imagined that he had about her. Consequently, she often felt the need to justify any lag in her correspondence with him. In December of 1922, for example, she explained to him that she could not write as often as she would have liked because of her work schedule, and she reminded him that she had to correct 150 notebooks every week. She sometimes mixed boasts of her accomplishments with expressions of longing for his company. She also felt that she needed to justify to Velasco why she had signed a two-year contract. She had done so, she claimed, to help him in his studies; she had felt that doing so would help her become an experienced teacher, gain an advantage when seeking future teaching positions, and, presumably, better enable her to build a future for the two of them. She tried, too, to excuse her decision by telling him that a sister of hers, who was about to give birth, needed help taking care of the newborn. Additionally, she told him, she was helping her brother in law with expenses related to his marriage. Often, too, she reminded him of how much she valued him. On 13 January 1922, for example, she told him, "This first letter of yours gave me sweet memories of the past, and reminds me to realize how faithful and kind my lover is."[22]

In a variety of ways, Aquino's letters implied that Velasco, the male partner, dominated the relationship. Yet, the world in which they lived was one in which vestiges of the Spanish legacy were breaking down, and it was not only in the disintegration of old social barriers, but also in gender roles, where there were signs of change.

In spite of her sometimes servile posture, Aquino was willing to challenge Velasco and to question their relationship. In early 1922, she scolded him for an incident in which he had torn up a photograph of himself that she had adored. Another time, she told a mutual acquaintance that he was her cousin and hid the fact that he was her lover. At least once, she blamed him for her ill health, possibly by causing her worries. On other occasions, she compared herself to fading leaves, rebuked him for making her feel that he did not wish to see her, reminded him of the health effects of her job as a teacher, and, at least once, melodramatically told Velasco that she did not care if she died. She also asked him to quit asking her cruel questions about what she would do if he married another woman. Throughout 1922, she castigated him when she did not hear from him as often as she would have liked, and she accused him of returning a letter of hers unopened. Between the beginning of 1922 and April of 1924, when he left the Philippines, she vacillated constantly between reminding him of her love and expressing her discomfort at the way he treated her. She seemed to be on the cusp of two conflicting tendencies: seeking Velasco's love and returning her love for him, yet openly challenging him and not willing to suppress the doubts she had about him.[23]

There were various reasons behind Aquino's questioning of Velasco. One was undoubtedly her strength of character. Another was the rise of women's status because of the expulsion of the Spanish and the resurgence of traditional, female-centered values. Traditionally, Malay society was a matriarchy in which women, not men, served in important posts such as spirit mediums; and in marriage, it was the wife who was the decision-maker, controlled the family's economy, and determined the future of the children. It was only during the Spanish colonial period that there was a nadir in women's activities outside the home because of the patriarchal values of Spanish culture. However, with the ouster of Spanish rule in 1898, native practices, including the strong position of women, again came to the fore. In 1921, during the heyday of Velasco's relationship with Aquino, Filipinas were beginning to enjoy a significant enough role in activities outside the home to prompt Governor-General Wood to proclaim, "The best Filipino woman is the best 'man' in the Philippines."[24]

Another challenge to the Filipino male arose from the importation of American, Progressive Era values. Among them were women's increased participation in education and civic and political roles. The clearest link between American ideas of gender equality and their effect on gender relations in the Philippines appeared in 1912 during the visit of the American suffragist Mrs. Carrie Chapman Catt. She, with the help of American Governors-General Francis Burton Harrison and Leonard Wood, encouraged the establishment of the National Federation of Women's Clubs, as well as the Philippine Association of University Women. During the 1920s, she worked for female suffrage. Among the consequences was Filipinas' involvement in political activities like making speeches, running for office, and engaging in debates. In the professions, too, new opportunities for Filipinas arose, such as in nursing. As one Filipina who eventually emigrated to and worked as a nurse in the United States recalled a half century later, Filipinas were able to work in the nursing profession in the Philippines without even completing high school. Women could teach in primary schools—as Aquino did. It was not just Filipino men like Velasco, therefore, who were enjoying the benefits of an American educational system and American, Progressive Era ideas, but also Filipinas like Aquino.[25]

Thus, Aquino, like Velasco, was a product of her times, and she was not one who simply complied meekly with her beau. Unlike Filipinas who, with rare exceptions prior to the American colonial period, had little opportunity to receive an education above the primary grades, Aquino had not only completed her own training, but was a teacher herself. Aquino was a young woman, therefore, who, barely out of her teen years, was conscious of her own position and the opportunities she had. Accordingly, her correspondence with Velasco revealed not only her insecurities, but also her self-conscious awareness of her own accomplishments, abilities, and opportunities for a career, and it revealed her willingness and ability to challenge her male partner.

In all likelihood, Velasco may have been undecided about how to behave towards Aquino. Her protests against specific acts of cruelty he had shown towards her and the frequent appeals she made to him for solace revealed that, at the very least, he may have consciously tested his own powers over her. If this had been the case, it may have reflected the subordination of women during the Spanish period. Yet, as his relationship with his grandmother—and, later—sisters revealed, at least within his family, he held a deep respect and affection for women who were close to him. It was possible, therefore, as in many other aspects of his life, that his relationships with Filipinas represented a mixture of the old and the new.

Velasco's early life, his decision to leave the Philippines to pursue his education in the United States, and the values he brought with him were the products of his own character and the times in which he lived. He possessed experiences, talents and aptitudes that prepared him for his departure to the United States for additional study. Among them were his education, determination, and accomplishments in literature and journalism. However, what shaped his outlook and encouraged him to go to the United States was not only who he was as an individual, but also the broad changes taking place in the Philippines and in the United States. Even though many of the events had proven their worth to him—in providing him with a good education in the Philippines, for instance—in other ways, they served as harbingers of limitations that would block his way once he was in America. Among them was the inferior racial status of Filipinos in the United States. Such ideas prevented Americans from granting the Philippines complete independence and shaped the experiences of Filipinos, including Velasco, once they set foot upon the American continent. Consequently, the formative years in Velasco's life revealed myriad contrasts between both the promises his new world offered and the limited extent to which he would be able to realize them.

# 2

# A New World (April 1924 to August 1926)

Velasco's departure from the Philippines and his first two years in the United States forced him to deal with a variety of challenges. They were the result of leaving the Philippines and of adjusting to life in the United States, and he responded in various ways. He used humor, worked, wrote, and looked for an American girlfriend. Yet, for all his efforts, he had only mixed successes in trying to adjust to his new home.

## I. Challenges

Leaving his home in the Philippines was a sorrowful event. On 11 April 1924, referring to his parting from Aquino, he wrote in his diary, "Forbid it, Oh Lord! . . . The God-willed engagement to find its doom after three happy years well spent! . . . Last kisses to her cheeks and lips . . . . " Nor was leaving other loved ones any easier. The next day, his grandmother wept as his ship began its journey to the United States. Once he departed, Velasco constantly thought of those he had left behind. On the 20th, he arrived in Hong Kong, and, although he enjoyed walking around the city, he spent much of his time writing letters to Aquino and his family. On 23 April, as his ship sailed across the East China Sea for Japan, he daydreamed about Aquino. Two days later, he wrote letters to her, his father, stepmother, grandmother, and an uncle. On the 27th, in Kobe, Japan, he mailed more letters to Aquino and his family. Several days later, in Yokohama, he took a stroll through the city streets, but he still could not take his mind off Aquino or his family.[1]

In May, Velasco set foot on a Seattle pier and encountered new surroundings in the city's Chinatown, his new home. Nihonmachi, the center of the district, was redolent with the aroma of Japanese noodles and the sounds of wooden slippers against the pavement. During festive occasions, such as the Bon Odori Festival, music, dancing, and the display of Japanese lanterns outside business establishments filled the streets. Yet, it was not an area just for the Japanese; by 1901, Filipinos had arrived. By 1920, four years before Velasco came, there were five hundred Filipinos in the city and five thousand in the entire United States, many of whom, like Velasco, had come to study. However, Seattle was not a place where young Filipino males could always stay out of trouble, for there was widespread prostitution, gambling, and drinking, all of which distracted those who had supposedly come for an education.[2]

Velasco also had to find a way to put food on the table. Unlike the *pensionados* and *pensionadas*, Filipino students who had received scholarships from the Philippine government and therefore did not have to pay for their stay in the United States, he had to support himself. Moreover, his employment options were limited and, like many of his kinsmen, he found that work as a houseboy was one of the few occupations open to him. And Velasco quickly learned that such work did not guarantee economic security. On 1 December 1924, he found work doing chores in a private home. Just three days later, however, his boss fired him. It was an unsettling experience not only because he lost his only source of income, but also because he was unsure about why the family matriarch had summarily dismissed him. His unemployment affected him immediately. The day after he lost his job, he spent all of his time trying to find another job. The following day, he was broke, unable to find work, and wrote in his diary that he had a "swell dinner by myself alone." He spent the remainder of the week trying to find a new job.[3]

Even when he did find work, he faced disappointments. Between 12 December and 25 January 1925, he cooked and cleaned at another private home. After the 25th, though, he again had trouble keeping a job. During the last week of the month, he worked sporadically at a factory, but his supervisor fired him within days. Until 14 March, when he briefly found a job at a saw mill, Velasco did not have regular work again. He also learned, during his first summer in the United States, that cannery employment was also less than ideal because of the contract wage system and the abuses that characterized it. According to economist Gerald Gold, it was a system rife with corruption. Before job seekers received contracts for summer employment, they had to purchase merchandise and goods from company stores because offers of employment depended on the amount of goods prospective employees purchased. Often, because those seeking jobs had no money, they had to make their purchases on credit at prices far above market value and repay debts with deductions from wages. Adding insult to injury was the fact that the goods were frequently substandard. Moreover, laborers often never received the items they had purchased, and even when they did get them, the products were not particularly useful; suits and dress shoes, which the company forced laborers to purchase, were useless in canneries where the men spent ten to fourteen hours a day packing fish.[4]

Even after signing contracts, workers faced difficulties. Contracting firms, for example, provided boarding houses where the men could eat and sleep while awaiting departure to the canneries. However, there might be no beds, and laborers awaiting departure slept on benches, floors, and tables. Still, the firms reduced the laborers' wages by charging them for the meager accommodations. Once aboard ship, armed guards, whose pay came from deductions out of the laborers' wages, prevented men from leaving. En route, the men slept in steel bunks in rows two or three feet high and four or five feet apart and ate boiled rice, seaweed, and tea.[5]

Nor were conditions at the canneries any more pleasant. Typical meals consisted of fish heads and, on special occasions and holidays, tripe. Laborers could buy other foods, but only at exorbitant prices from foremen's private stockpiles. Foremen fleeced their charges in other ways, too. They ran card games and other gambling operations, demanded a percentage of the pot, deducted workers' gaming losses from their wages, and recruited male prostitutes who masqueraded as women and sold company goods like candy, cigarettes, and liquor. To quell unrest, guards with guns and clubs kept a vigilant eye on the men.[6]

The abuses did not end with the season. One problem lay in deductions the company made from workers' wages at the end of the summer. When the men returned to Seattle or other embarkation points at the summer's end, the company deducted from their wages debts they had supposedly incurred in places they had never been for things they had never done. One man learned that he had incurred debts for items he had never purchased at a cannery he had never visited. Another problem lay in the men's inability to collect overtime pay. Theoretically, they collected their pay at the end of the season. In practice, the system worked differently. According to Gerald Gold, who studied the cannery contract system in the 1940s, overtime wages typically were available for any work the men performed after 6 p.m. Work times began as early as 3:30 a.m., however, and there might be only one fifteen-minute break before 6 p.m. As a result, laborers worked fourteen-and-a-half hours almost non-stop before qualifying for overtime. Sometimes after a fresh haul of salmon, men worked twenty hours or more in a single shift. This was an experience with which Velasco was probably familiar. On 19 July 1924, he worked thirteen hours of overtime. On 27 July, he worked eleven hours of overtime. Yet, for all the overtime hours he worked, he gained little. On 29 August, he received the paltry sum of $20.90 of overtime pay for the entire season, an amount that was less than one month's salary at his high school job as a reporter for an English language newspaper in Manila several years previously. Nor could workers do anything about the abuses. For more than a decade, Gold asserts, a Deputy Labor Commissioner refused to halt deductions for whiskey and gambling debts and threatened to throw whistleblowers in jail.[7]

Velasco, no less than his peers, was unhappy with cannery work. In May of 1926, while working in Port Althorp, Alaska, he wrote disconsolately to Jane Garrott, an American friend in Seattle. He told her that his day consisted of working amidst the deafening noises of machines, the unpleasant odors of gas, and clouds of smoke:

> The rainy and dreary days that we have here most of the time only add to the gloomy depression of our spirits. Day in and day out we tread the self-same old beaten path-from our bunk house to the cannery, and back. The rattle of the cans that we make, the deafening noise of the machines, the unpleasant odor of gas, the clouds of suffocating smoke . . . all these are ours to endure . . . .[8]

Moreover, when he was not working, he was too tired to do anything other than confine himself to his quarters and brood about being far from friends and family.[9]

Between 1924 and 1926, Velasco faced challenges not only because of the pain of leaving his home and adjusting to his new environment, but also because of the limitations in the type of work he could find. The fact that his main source of income depended on summer employment in canneries at a time when such work verged on peonage made his life even more difficult.

## II. Responses

However difficult Velasco's circumstances were, he responded in a variety of ways. Sometimes he tried to deny the harsh realities he faced. One example appeared in his work as a houseboy. On 4 December 1924, after one family fired him, he wrote in his diary, "Was dismissed when I returned home at 1:30 p.m. . . . Cannot understand reason for my dismissal. Something remote I know, but won't put down here, just now." He seemed to be aware of the reasons behind the dismissal but was unwilling to admit them openly or acknowledge them to himself. Another example appeared in cannery work. From his first season in Alaska, he succinctly recorded events in his diary in a matter-of-fact tone without describing his suffering. On 4 July 1924, he simply recorded that it was a national holiday. He made no effort to describe what his day had been like. About a week later, he tersely recorded that he had worked overtime for ten hours. During the following week, he again noted only that he had worked overtime. In the following month, he resumed the same pattern of mechanically and impassively recording what he had done. On 19 August, he wrote that he had worked overtime for thirteen hours. His brief recording of events contrasted sharply with his expression of loneliness and frustration to his friend Garrott.[10] Velasco had not lost his sense of humor, however. He told Garrott that his supervisor was a "good ol' boy'" who knew that "when the cat is away the mice will play." He also told her that a co-worker who was always sleepy at work was not sleepy when he counted his money. When he described the work of another colleague, whose job was discarding flawed salmon tins into a recycling machine, Velasco remarked that he would have been "heroic" if he had been feeding the "hungry of Europe" instead of feeding a "noisy machine that throws away all that it eats." Describing impromptu concerts among his co-workers, Velasco remarked that, when one worker sang, he wished for a different version of a different song; he was apparently not impressed with the man's singing. Commenting upon a colleague's efforts to share his poetry with other workers, Velasco told Garrott that his "love, pathos, lamentation, and profuse outpourings of vows of sincerity and devotion" could not bear up to the "dramatic readings of a sweet, little sister," Garrott's teenaged daughter Jean.[11]

Despite the harsh economic conditions, Velasco eked out moments of fun and leisure. On 4 July 1924, he had a "supper with beer and cigars." From his first season in Alaska, he played blackjack, danced with native Alaskan women, and went on berry-picking and picture-taking excursions in the wilds. After returning to Seattle at the end of the summers, he often went to theaters. By the winter of 1924/1925, he had resumed writing poetry and working with newspapers. In June of 1925, he published an article in the *Colonist,* a Filipino newspaper. In January and February of 1926, he edited at least three issues of the *Symposium*, another newspaper. Towards the end of February, he contributed an article to the *Filipino Student Bulletin*, a nationally-circulating journal for Filipino students. When he went to Alaska in the summer of 1926, he became involved with a Filipino cannery workers' news bulletin, the *Sea Gull News.*[12]

Velasco also continued his friendship with Garrott, who remained his confidante, gave him moral support, and encouraged his ambitions as a writer. On 30 March 1926, she urged him to enter a writing contest and praised his involvement with another cannery workers' newspaper, the *Cannery Courier.* Two months later, when he was back in Alaska, she told him how much she and the other residents of Seattle's International House, where she was housemother to Filipino and Chinese students at the University of Washington, enjoyed reading the *Sea Gull News*. In late June, she praised him for publishing a poem in a journal, the *Philippine Republic*. Meanwhile, Velasco reciprocated by confiding to her and sending her sketches.[13]

Another way in which Velasco responded to his new life was by trying to find a white girlfriend. Between April of 1924 and August of 1926, as his correspondence relationship with Sixta Aquino waned and finally ended in 1925, he pursued several white women. The first was Katheryne Brown of Olympia, Washington, whom he met on 13 October 1924, possibly at the Spanish Club meeting at the University of Washington campus that day. After they met, they often spoke on the telephone; sometimes, he called her twice a day and, at least once, invited her to the University of Washington's Filipino Club meeting. She also became a part of his dreams and correspondence.[14]

To some extent, Brown responded to Velasco's attentions. On 14 February 1925, she praised him for the poem he had dedicated to her and gave him permission to publish it. At other times, she tried to be his friend. When he decided not to attend classes in Seattle during the spring 1925 quarter, she tried to console him by telling him that the newspaper he was editing, the *Philippine Seattle Colonist,* might not survive his absence. While he was in Alaska, she teased him about missing the beauty of the University of Washington campus in springtime. In turn, he gave her moral support when she became frustrated from carrying a heavy academic load. They were close enough so that, when Velasco returned to Seattle on 20 May, one of the first things he did was arrange a meeting with her. After booking a room at the L.V.M. Hotel in Chinatown and attending to other personal business, he arranged to meet her on campus the following afternoon. Ironically, the meeting that he had been in such haste to arrange, and to which he had looked forward immediately upon his return from Alaska, provided one of the first indications that there were boundaries in his relationships with white women that he could almost never cross. She showed him her engagement ring, and he realized that he would never be her boyfriend. When he went home that night, he wrote in his diary that "her frank confession of her engagement was a dagger that pierced my heart . . . ." Velasco had managed to find a friend in Brown, but their relationship never became intimate.[15]

During the last half of 1925, Velasco made a second attempt to begin a romantic relationship with a white woman, Ruth Marsh, whom he had met during the 1925 cannery season on an island near Bellingham, Washington. He pursued her unabashedly. In his first letter to her following the cannery season, Velasco told her, "Should our engagement begin here . . . I could not but be deeply grateful for what you have done for me . . . and all my life I should be a man worthy of your love." Velasco had completely fallen in love with her.[16] Like Brown, Marsh initially responded to his attentions. At one point, she even requited his profession of love. "Victorio," she wrote, "I love you and have loved you for a long time but didn't let you know." During the next several months, she frequently reminded him that she wanted his picture and wished that he could accompany her to dances. The affair, however, lasted only a few months and only in their correspondence. It was over well before the beginning of the 1926 cannery season.[17]

The third attempt Velasco made to have a romantic relationship with a white woman was with Eleanor Multmueller, whom he met on 23 February 1926, probably either at the University of Washington campus where he was taking classes or at International House, where she was a frequent visitor. Yet, although Multmueller accepted Velasco and the International House's Filipino and Chinese student residents as her friends, the main reason for her involvement with them was probably her liberal political views. International House was often the forum for discussions about domestic and world events. In July of 1926, for example, an attorney gave a talk about American imperialism, an African American man described his experiences living in France, and a professor spoke about ethnocentrism. Multmueller's participation in International House activities and her meeting with Velasco, therefore, was probably the result of a broader effort to pursue her education and political interests; it was not necessarily because she found him attractive or someone she would consider as a romantic partner.[18]

The various difficulties Velasco faced in leaving the Philippines, making his way in Seattle, and trying to become involved in a romantic relationship characterized his first two years in the United States. He was beginning to learn that the extent to which he was successful in various endeavors depended not only on his own merits and efforts, but also on the events and people around him.

## III. Mixed Results

The ambiguous results Velasco experienced during his first two years in the United States were particularly apparent in his attempts to find romance. One fact hindering him was his inability to forget his former sweetheart, Sixta

Aquino. He constantly thought and dreamt about her, and, even when he was busy doing other things, she entered his thoughts. In early July of 1924, for example, he delivered a speech about the Philippines on a radio show, stayed up until 4 o'clock the next morning editing the *Symposium* newspaper, went to an International Council Meeting, looked for a weekend job, and then went to a show at a theater. Yet, when he went to bed the next night, it was not the hectic series of recent events that occupied his mind, but Aquino. Even while busy at work in Alaska, he thought constantly about her. One July evening in 1924, he enjoyed a good dinner but went to bed dreaming of her. Two weeks later, he again dreamt about her, imagining that she had married another man. The following week, as he was busy working overtime and playing blackjack, she was still on his mind, and he again wrote to her and dreamt of her. Even when his ship headed back to Seattle at the end of the season, he kept thinking of her. Nearly two years later, while he was pursuing other women, she remained in his thoughts. In early February of 1926, as he developed an infatuation for Katheryne Brown, he still dreamt of Aquino.[19]

Velasco filled his diary with memories of Aquino. On 5 March 1926, he wrote that, no matter where he went or what he did, he always came across something that reminded him of her, and even when he sought escape by sleeping, she appeared in his dreams. He wished that, someday, she would understand how much she continued to mean to him even though they were separated by seven thousand miles and she had forbidden him to contact her. He wrote, " . . . if this humble message of my heart could not reach her as I intend to, I shall trust it to the future perusal of future novelists who may be hunting for real events to weave the fabric of their plot."[20]

He also explained, "How cruel is fate! When the wound is at its worst, and the sufferer takes the greatest care that it shall not be touched, something, somehow, finds its way and makes the body feel once more half forgotten pains. 'And the worst is yet to come.' Can time completely heal or temper agonies, heart aches, unsatisfied longings, and bitter memories of happy thoughts brought to a tragic end? Or, does it only help to fan to a consuming and merciless flame the dying embers of a deserted love?" Presciently, Velasco anticipated the years of heartache he would suffer as a result of losing Aquino. She remained in his thoughts even years later as he pursued other women.[21]

Another factor behind Velasco's lack of success in having a romantic relationship lay in personal differences, something that was particularly apparent in his pursuit of Ruth Marsh. Marsh, in contrast to Velasco, had poor relationships with her family and, during the time she knew him, the only significant adults in her life were her father and mother, who were divorced and lived in different households. Moreover, because her father had remarried, his household was separate from that of her mother, and Marsh had to split her time between his home and hers. Her efforts to stay in touch with both caused additional difficulties. Marsh did not enjoy visits with her father because she did not get along with his second wife, and her time with her own mother was no more pleasant. On one Christmas, for example, her mother forced her to stay at home while she took Marsh's two sisters to an aunt's home for a family reunion and dinner. Marsh's relationship to her family contrasted sharply with the esteem in which Velasco held members of his family.[22]

Personal interests and ambitions also distinguished Velasco from Marsh. During the time he knew her, he pursued education and writing as avidly as he had ever done. Marsh, on the other hand, did not enjoy school, and she told Velasco that she might not finish high school or even think about going to college. Velasco, in contrast, had received a university degree in the Philippines before he even set foot on American soil and was pursuing his second college degree. Nor did she have high career goals. One time, she told him about maybe attending hairdressing school, but even that modest goal may have involved too much study for her; there was no indication that she actually began such a course. The most rewarding career experience she had was working as a theater usher; there was little comparison between Marsh's goals and Velasco's, which consisted of becoming a journalist and writer.[23]

Another difference lay in their outlook and priorities. Although Velasco enjoyed socializing and going to dances and parties, he tempered such leisure with hard work, studies, and writing. Marsh, on the other hand, knew no such moderation and went dancing almost every night. She also had no regular boyfriend and often enjoyed going with a different date simply to make other men jealous. Her activities often kept her out until early morning, sleep away half the following day, and have only enough time left to plan for more dances and more parties. Other facets of their relationship told the same story. While Velasco stayed with his summer job in Alaskan salmon canneries in spite of its abuses and physical demands, Marsh was capricious, leaving a new job after a week because, as she told Velasco, someone had been mean to her. The age difference was another drawback. When they first met, he was twenty-four, and she seventeen; and, while Velasco took pride in his appearance, she thought of herself as "funny looking." In contrast to Velasco, too, she refused to think even a year ahead because, in her words, "I might be dead by then."[24]

The two were ill-matched from the beginning. Velasco's balancing of his social activities with academic endeavors clashed with Marsh's haphazard, happy-go-lucky lifestyle, and, although Velasco may have thought of her as a prize because of her race, in reality, there was little comparison between the two in terms of maturity or intellect. Ultimately, his pursuit of her revealed much about the level to which he might sink in order to find a white woman as a mate. Ironically, it was not the superior of the two in objective terms, Velasco, but the one who enjoyed superiority by virtue of race, who ended the relationship.[25]

Velasco's pursuit of Eleanor Multmueller was also unsuccessful. At least one reason was the fact that she was devoted to her studies, regularly stayed at school until about five o'clock during the week, and conscientiously spent time with family, friends, and relatives, sometimes spending weeks in Oregon on visits. She also had a wide range of interests, including playing the violin and going on picnics and, like Velasco, balancing activities with studies. In the spring of 1926, for example, she went to a picnic at a park with residents of

International House and was one of the few daring enough to go for a swim in a cold river—a feat of bravado which only two of the men were willing to imitate. Another fact acting against Velasco's efforts to have a romantic relationship with Multmueller was her initial, formal approach towards him. During at least the first few months after she met him, she consistently addressed him as "Mr. Velasco" even though he, at the age of twenty-four, could not have been more than two or three years older than she. Even when their friendship grew deeper, she addressed him only as "Dear Friend."[26]

Although personality traits and individual differences may have undermined Velasco's romantic relationships, there was another factor involved, one over which Velasco had no control: the widespread racial attitudes of the time and their impact on the way the women he pursued felt about having a relationship with him. Nativism and prejudice against Asians were widespread throughout the Pacific Northwest both before and after Velasco's arrival in Seattle. In the Dalles, Oregon in late 1919, the local Farmers' Educational and Cooperative Union of America adopted a resolution prohibiting Japanese from holding land and voting in favor of barring the immigration of all Asians into the United States. After formation of the Washington Territory in 1863, the territorial government denied voting rights to the Chinese. Later, it imposed a $6 "Chinese Police Tax." In 1885, a white mob expelled hundreds of Chinese from Tacoma. A year later, whites in Seattle forced Chinese residents out of the city. In the western Washington farm communities of Issaquah, Coal Creek, and Black Diamond, whites attacked and murdered several Chinese. In 1886, whites in Log Cabin, Oregon lynched more Chinese. After statehood, the Washington legislature enacted an alien land law making it difficult for Japanese to own land. In 1887, a small group of renegades shot and hacked to death 31 Chinese along the Snake River on the border between Idaho and Oregon. During the first decade of the twentieth century in the northeastern Washington city of Spokane, the Chinese and the Japanese became victims of violence and the targets of organized resistance. In 1913, western Washington labor unions barred all Japanese and Chinese from membership and, sometimes, immigration officials arrested Japanese for no evident reason.[27]

During the first decades of the twentieth century, Asians also faced difficulties in employment. Race was the only reason preventing Japanese immigrant Takuji Yamashita from becoming an attorney in Washington. Although he passed the bar examination, the Washington State Bar Association refused to grant him a license and, on two separate occasions—in 1902 and again in 1922—the state supreme court affirmed the bar association's refusal, basing its decision upon a state law preventing "aliens ineligible to citizenship" from practicing law. Because the only "aliens ineligible to citizenship" at the time were Japanese and Chinese, the bar association and the state were able to prevent members of both groups from joining the legal profession. Race prejudice, consequently, forced Velasco to narrow his employment goals to performing manual labor in spite of his qualifications, which ironically, even before his departure from the Philippines, surpassed those of most Caucasians.[28]

The widespread racial prejudice and assumptions of racial hierarchies affected not only Velasco's efforts to find a white girlfriend, but even his ability to develop complete trust in the closest of friendships with intelligent and articulate Americans like Jane Garrott. Whereas Velasco saw himself as an American, Garrott always thought of him as a foreigner. In one instance, she told Velasco about a ten year old Euro-American boy who missed his "foreign friends." She seemed oblivious to the fact that Filipinos were not foreigners but American nationals. However well-meaning the little boy and Garrott may have been, their belief that Filipinos were "foreign" displayed an inaccurate, yet basic assumption that Filipinos did not really belong in the United States and that their home was in the Philippines, not in America.[29]

Although there were a variety of factors affecting Velasco's ability to find romance with a white woman, at least two of the women Velasco courted probably spurned him because of his race. Both Multmueller and Marsh were aware of racial differences. From the beginning of her acquaintance with Velasco, Multmueller made it clear that she would never consider having a romantic relationship with him. On 30 April 1925, just over two months after they met, she told him, "we are and I hope ever will be good, sincere friends, pero nada mas o menos." She also apparently felt it necessary to tell him, "I am not offended at your writing me"; she seemed to assume that there was some potential impropriety in him communicating with her. It was an ironic, albeit implicit, revelation that something other than his qualities as an individual shaped her reaction towards him.[30]

Marsh, too, may have never seriously considered Velasco as her mate in spite of their intimate, albeit short-lived, correspondence. At first, she seemed intentionally to sidestep his avowal of love. When he told her that he loved her, she responded by saying, "Those pictures you sent were pretty good but nothing to brag about" and "I'm working in the corn now I like it much better than the fish. What are you doing?" Her words completely skirted the profession of love that he had made to her. When she finally seemed to requite his profession of love, she did so only after she had found time in between "running around to a dance about every nite." Moreover, she did so guardedly, as when she wondered if it was "alright" for the two of them to be in love with each other; although she was only a teenager, she had imbibed enough of the racial prejudices of the time to question the propriety of having an affair with a Filipino man. Her awareness of racial difference came across in unintentional ways, such as when she told him that she might have an affair with him "regardless of whatever other people say." She assumed that having a romantic relationship with him could lead to ostracism because of his race. Another time, she told him that she was glad that he was popular among "your countrymen," implicitly making a distinction between those she considered her people and those she considered to be his. In the end, on 18 December 1925, she told him without equivocation that she would never see him again and that she forbade him from ever attempting to contact her. Perhaps she had been trying, for some time and in various ways, to dissuade him from pursuing her as a romantic interest but, after finding that he might not have been listening to the more subtle ways in which she had been trying to tell him that she did not want him, finally decided that she would leave no doubts about the way she really felt.[31]

Yet, the existence of racial obstacles to Velasco's romantic relationships with white women were not surprising. In the years leading up to Velasco's arrival in the United States, Americans had long enjoyed a history of prohibiting interracial romance, beginning at least as early as the mid-seventeenth century when the House of Burgesses in Virginia outlawed marriage between black men and white women. Throughout the eighteenth and nineteenth centuries, anti-miscegenation restrictions became increasingly widespread, lasting decades after Velasco's arrival in the United States.[32]

In Washington, official sanctions against intermarriage had a long history. In 1897, six years before Velasco was born, the state supreme court affirmed a territorial anti-miscegenation law. The court declared that an 1868 marriage between a white and an Indian was void by noting that, prior to statehood, Washington Territory prohibited interracial marriage. In the fall of 1901, as Velasco began his primary school education in the Philippines, not a single minister in the southeastern Washington town of Walla Walla would marry a white woman to her Japanese fiancé. On 12 January 1911, when Velasco was just one month past his tenth birthday, a legislator in the Washington House of Representatives introduced a bill "making it unlawful for white persons to intermarry with Negroes, Japanese, Chinese, Hindus, or persons of the Mongolian race, or to have carnal intercourse with Japanese, Chinese, Hindus or persons of the Mongolian race, prescribing the penalty for a violation thereof, and declaring an emergency." On 13 January, another legislator introduced a bill "prohibiting marriage between white and colored races." Before Velasco had reached his eleventh birthday, a committee in the state legislature introduced a bill stipulating that "any marriage hereafter entered into between any white person and any person of the opposite sex who is of negro, Chinese, Japanese or Mongolian blood . . . of any race other than the white race . . . shall be guilty of gross misdemeanor and punished accordingly." On 24 January 1917, just after Velasco's fourteenth birthday, there was another bill "prohibiting intermarriage between white persons and Negroes, Chinese and Japanese and providing a penalty for its violation." On 19 January 1921, one month after Velasco had celebrated his eighteenth birthday and just under three years from the time he would first set foot in the state, white legislators considered a bill providing that "no marriage license shall be issued where one of the parties is of the white or Caucasian race and the other of the yellow or Mongolian race." Although the state, after its territorial stage, never enacted an anti-miscegenation law, the repeated efforts indicated that Washingtonians persistently looked askance at interracial marriage for decades, well into Velasco's life time. Their efforts symbolized the racial prejudices of many whites and probably fostered the reluctance of white women, including those whom Velasco pursued, to have an interracial romantic relationship with him.[33]

When Velasco arrived in Seattle in the spring of 1924, he came with high hopes for a bright future. He dreamed of finding a place where he could pursue his education, gain experience and new skills as a writer, and find friendships among Americans. Yet, as soon as he arrived, he found numerous obstacles blocking his way. He met them head on but learned, even in his first three years in the United States, that his ability to overcome them were limited.

Some of the difficulties Velasco experienced were the result of his own decisions, such as leaving behind people of his own race and coming to a land that had long enjoyed a racially hierarchical system and a history of antagonism towards non-Europeans. His break from Sixta Aquino in 1925, too, continued to haunt him, and his pursuit of Ruth Marsh suggested that he had become so desperate to have a white girlfriend that he would settle for anyone, even someone who was clearly his inferior in every objective measure other than race.

Yet, what made the effects of the challenges he faced more forceful than they might otherwise have been was something over which he had no control: his dark skin. Race prevented him from being able to find work other than as a houseboy, an errand boy, or cannery laborer, and it consigned him, along with the Japanese and the Chinese, to the abuses of the salmon cannery industry. In his personal life, race prevented him from being able to develop any long-term romantic relationship in the United States. Moreover, even friendships with whites, including Jane Garrott, were based upon presumptions of his racial inferiority. Because racial attitudes of the time were not something he could control, it was preordained that the successes he would enjoy would be limited.

# 3

# Assimilation (August 1926 to March 1927)

The period between the fall of 1926 and the spring of 1927 was one of milestones for Velasco. In no other period in his life did he accomplish as much as he did in Bellingham, Washington, where he lived and excelled in a world of Caucasians while studying at the Washington State Normal School. Yet, even though he achieved many things, he again had to face challenges because of his race. Consequently, even as he tried to fit in, he became increasingly involved with Filipino nationalism.

## I. Velasco's Accomplishments among Whites

Velasco accomplished much at Bellingham, including holding leadership positions in spite of his race, such as the presidency of a literary club, the Scribes Club, and the editorship of its literary journal, *The Red Arrow*. His elevation to the presidency of the Scribes Club also indicated the respect in which his white colleagues held him. On 6 January 1927, when he called the first meeting of the club, for example, his Caucasian colleagues responded by electing him their acting president. The following day, the organizers held another election, and his peers unanimously elected him their president. Eight days later, they selected him as the first managing editor of *The Red Arrow*. Velasco's accomplishments, however, came only by facing and overcoming many obstacles and did not extend to all aspects of his personal life.[1]

Circumstances hardly favored a lone Asian man in a world of whites. In both the town and the Washington State Normal School, there were few, if any Asians, and town residents nursed lurid stereotypes about Orientals. In August of 1926, when Velasco arrived in Bellingham to register at the college, he was probably a curiosity, especially because much of the residents' knowledge of Asians came from sensational headlines in the town newspaper. On 3 January 1927, for example, the *Bellingham Herald* flashed across its front page in two-inch, block letters, "Chinese Mob British at Hankow," informing readers that "thousands of Chinese coolies" had attacked the British in China. Nor did Chinese run amuck only in the Orient, according to the newspaper. The next day, locals learned that a Chinese male with a meat cleaver had attacked a white citizen in Seattle. The same kinds of horror stories involving Orientals persisted throughout Velasco's stay. The month before Velasco left, the citizenry learned about hordes of Orientals succumbing to an earthquake in Japan. Moreover, calamity followed upon calamity in the Far East, according to Bellingham reporters; on 18 March, they reported that upwards of a hundred people drowned in a river in China. Luckily, the newspaper informed its readers, Asian women were trying to make up for the ills of their brethren; in the spring of 1927, there was a Chinese "Joan of Arc" fighting the political corruption of Chinese males. During Velasco's stay in Bellingham, therefore, local residents' knowledge of Asians consisted of unimaginable inhuman tragedies, temperamental and violent Oriental men, and altruistic and saintly—when not passive and demure—Asian women.[2]

Somewhat paradoxically, though, the residents nursed lurid stories only when it came to racial issues. White residents' fears about wild Chinese brandishing meat cleavers in city streets were not a symptom of general paranoia. In non-racial matters, the town residents were unremarkable and sober. On 3 January 1927, for example, they debated a street-widening project that could cost $5,000. The next day, the issues they faced included a highway construction project, baseball scores, and a traffic citation for a highway patrolman. Several days later, other issues confronting the local citizens included a waltzing contest, the selection of photographers, and shopping for dresses. During Velasco's stay, Bellingham citizens also debated the development of thick hair, the use of fans, and the control of acne. In March of 1927, as Velasco was getting ready to leave town, residents learned about cooking fried chicken and serving warm sausage rolls. The most controversial issues during his stay were debates about the proper way to dress hair and the cost of a sewer project, poor matches for stories about wild Chinese men or the deaths of hordes of Asiatics. On 28 September 1926, while local headlines focused on traffic patrolmen gone astray, the maintenance of a full head of hair, and the best way to serve warm sausage rolls, an Asian man—Velasco—carrying books rather than a meat cleaver, made his entrance and stayed until March of 1927. It was in this setting replete with stories about massive losses of human life in the Far East, the violent tendencies of Oriental males, and the efforts of virginal Asian women to put their chaotic world aright that he tried to assimilate.[3]

Nor were those at the college much more knowledgeable than the locals when it came to Asians. As in the town itself, there was little, if any, Asian presence except in racial stereotypes. Velasco was one of only two Filipino students at the school, and there were no Filipinos, Japanese, or Chinese among the staff, administrators, or faculty. Like the locals, members of the college community learned racially-charged stories about Orientals. The 1927 yearbook, for example, contained a farcical translation of rules of the road in Japan and Korea and lampooned both countries in unflattering terms. In the same yearbook, there were aphorisms supposedly reflecting Oriental wisdom and a sketch of a little Chinese man with a pigtail. The world that Velasco encountered in Bellingham was full of stilted racial images.[4]

Yet, the period showed not only that he could achieve much in spite of his race, but also that he could do so despite additional challenges. One of these was the competition that he faced in his quest for leadership positions. The best example of the tough competition facing him appeared in the form of a precocious seventeen-year old, June Wetherell, who was his potential rival for the top leadership position on the Scribes Club as well as on the *Red Arrow*. As a leader she was dynamic; as a writer in the Scribes Club, she was without peer. The young poet showed, for instance, a remarkable capacity for creating striking imagery. In her poem "Song of a Science Class," describing a mundane topic, her experience in a science laboratory, she wrote:

> They slipped a bit of glass into my hand . . . I held it to the window . . . and I saw the dull brown hill become a fairyland./the alders dripped a magic beauty, and the long, dry grass became the orchid/and the fleur-de-lis. The clouds were fairy pillows, stitched in mauve and rosebud/And a rainbow road danced away over the hills/to lands unknown."[5]

As a writer, she surpassed Velasco. As Velasco had done in *Lingyen and Other Poems*, Wetherell used images from nature as her motifs, but she did so much more successfully than he had ever done. Whereas his all-too-obvious efforts to maintain consistency in meter generally made his work rigid, her creative mind, free of such constraints, allowed her to draw her reader into her own, imaginary panoramas. If Velasco had written about clouds, for instance, he probably would have done so by describing their physical appearance. For Wetherell, however, clouds were "fairly pillows," and a rainbow was not merely a reflection of the sun's rays upon moisture in the atmosphere; rather, it was a "road that dances away over the hills/To lands unknown." Her flight of imagination, moreover, had as its starting place nothing more remarkable than a "bit of glass" in "science class." The imagery she created, and the startling meanings she attached to them, went far beyond what Velasco was capable of in his own work. Her creativity, absent in Velasco's oeuvre, appeared in another poem, too, one in which she adopted the voice of a dead bird. In "A Bird's Dream of Heaven," the bird mused, upon its arrival in heaven, "I'll build my nest of a downy cloud/And sing my songs to a piping crowd/Of little birds, all perched below/ . . . The silvery song of a heavenly bird." She wrote of things that Velasco could probably have never even imagined: of stepping outside of one's own body and seeing the world as it might have appeared to another living creature. Even when writing prose, her words seemed to sing. In an article she wrote about a meeting with Carl Sandburg, she wrote, "For a long while he slumped down in his chair with his shaggy, gray hair falling over his eyes . . . Bits of song and story, reminiscences of the days when he was a milkman . . . fell from his lips naturally and easily as he and his old friend recalled days gone by." It was not only in her poetry, but in her prose, in which the seventeen-year-old girl made the world seem limitless in appearances and meanings.[6]

Another testament to Wetherell's talent came from Velasco himself. In December, 1926, he told his readers in his own, regular column in the student newspaper, the *Weekly Messenger*, about the beginnings of her desire to write, which occurred one winter morning when, as a nine-year old girl on Washington's Whidbey Island, she woke up in astonishment to find her world covered in white. She then became determined to write poetry; she was a poet, Velasco stated, who preferred to "starve to death rather than go into business . . . " and resolved "never to get married until [she] is rich and famous." The extent to which Velasco respected her talent may have appeared, too, in the fact that, during his stint as a columnist on the *Weekly Messenger,* his article on Wetherell was the only one he ever wrote about one of his peers.[7]

Velasco's recognition of Wetherell's talent appeared, too, in his own interaction with her. He may have found her intimidating. Although he had, almost from the moment he boarded a ship for the United States, pursued numerous women, he never pursued her. Even though women of high intellect—among whom Eleanor Multmueller was the best example—did not intimidate him, Wetherell's precocious talent may have. He admired her, but he kept his distance. In the spring of 1927, the guarded fascination he held towards her appeared in a letter in which he congratulated her on getting a job as a writer on the *Seattle Daily Times.* He began in a self-deprecating manner; "Dear Miss Wetherell," he wrote, "Excuse me for my audacity in addressing you this letter." He then said in a servile manner, "May I first extend to you my belated congratulations for the promotion, if promotion it may be properly called, which you meritoriously deserve, and which tout le monde at the Normal silently expected of you." What made Velasco's words to Wetherell unusual was the extreme formality in tone, which belied the fact that only weeks earlier, they had been colleagues on the *Red Arrow.*[8]

Whatever their personal relationship, Wetherell's literary talents were starkly clear during her short tenure at the college, which ended before Velasco left Bellingham. Velasco's position as her superior on the Scribes Club and on the *Red Arrow* indicated the extent to which his peers believed in him even over Caucasian competitors, including Wetherell. It was a testament to the extent of his achievements in a setting in which he was a racial outsider.[9]

Still, that Velasco deserved his colleagues' respect was clear from his qualifications, which none of his white peers could probably have equaled. By the time he arrived at the school, he had already worked as a professional reporter for one of the major English language newspapers in Manila, the *Manila Times*, and he had published a volume of his own verse in 1924, three years before he even arrived in Bellingham. At the same time that he wrote for the *Weekly Messenger* and edited the *Red Arrow,* he was editor of two other journals, the *Varsity Philippine Weekly* and the *Philippine Seattle Colonist.* He also brought drive and determination; well before he and the other founders formally established the Scribes Club, Velasco was calling for such an organization in his *Weekly Messenger* column.[10]

Velasco also displayed a capacity for hard work. One two-week period provided an example. On 15 January 1927, he attended Carl Sandburg's lecture in the college auditorium and met with and interviewed him for his *Weekly Messenger* column. Three days later, he corresponded with a professor at the University of Washington about judging submissions to the Scribes Club's poetry contest. On 19 January, he sorted through the numerous applications for membership in the club. The next day, he interviewed another guest lecturer, poet

Tom Skeyhill, for another article. During the last week of the month, he called a meeting of the club and participated in the initiation of new members. At the same time, he busied himself by trying to obtain a club pennant. He committed himself to all the work on the club, moreover, while taking classes full time, editing the *Red Arrow*, writing his weekly column for the *Weekly Messenger*, joining the World Politics Club, writing for two Filipino newspapers, and accumulating more college credits than he did in any other comparably short period.[11]

It was not just the leadership roles he played, but also his departure, that highlighted his accomplishments. After Velasco left Bellingham, the *Red Arrow* only occasionally showed the sparkle that he had brought to it. In 1928, the editor of the third volume continued the idealistic tradition of the journal's founders, including Velasco, when she stated in the journal's preface, "The one who writes is a blazer of trails. He has found some pleasant thought, some lovely rhythm, some beautiful picture which he must share, and with his writing he makes a path so that others may find the same pleasure, the same beauty." She followed Velasco's example of taking the *Red Arrow* seriously as a literary endeavor with high-minded ideals. In general, however, the quality of leadership declined precipitously following his departure. Standing in stark contrast to the idealism in Velasco's work was the last editor's statement. In the journal's preface, he said, "Here is the new Red Arrow all dressed up in a 'Whoopee' make-up . . . even a 'Whoopee' number has its limitations, and it is sometimes necessary to relegate to the waste paper basket material [which] . . . would result in too extensive a movement of elevated eye-brows." Velasco, in spite of his capacity for irreverence, would never have descended into the transparently self-conscious worldliness that the journal's last editor so unsuccessfully made a pretense at adopting. Likewise, June Wetherell would have been unlikely to have lapsed into the populistic jargon appearing in the last issue. There were few clues other than the final issue's editorial statement that so clearly suggested the reasons for the journal's demise after Velasco's departure.[12]

Velasco's feats, furthermore, were important not only because they showed that he was capable of transcending his status as an outsider due to race, but also because they illustrated that, in spite of a racially unfriendly environment, some factors, such as common grounds he shared with his white colleagues, may have ameliorated some of the potentially adverse effects. Like them, he endured living and studying in a highly-regimented environment and participated fully in school activities. The school encouraged students to work as much as other people their age who were not in college—forty hours a week at a minimum—and claimed that such discipline "establishes regularity of habit in work, recreation, rest and sleep . . . essential if they are to do their best work." It also told students what to do and when: every day of the week, except Sunday, rise at 6:30 a.m. and eat breakfast at 7:15; every day except Saturday and Sunday, work from 8 a.m. to 12 noon and from 1 to 4; on Mondays through Thursdays, go to recreation between 4 and 6; on Fridays, go to recreation from 7:30 to 9:30 p.m.; and turn the lights out at 9:30 p.m. on Sunday nights, 10:00 on school nights, and 11 on Friday and Saturday nights. The college's regimen made no distinctions based on race; regardless of skin color, all were subject to the same, regimented routine, a fact which created commonalities, possibly downplaying the effects of racial differences.[13]

Moreover, Velasco became involved in a variety of student activities, of which the college offered many choices. There were intramural basketball games, such as the one pitting Benedicts Cops against Durr's Dummies, or talks that featured people such as the poet Carl Sandburg. During Velasco's second quarter on campus, there was an Interclub Council Banquet, at least one dance at the school gym, and a variety of events such as a pajama party at Edens Hall—the women's dormitory—elections for hall residents' positions, and dance classes. For someone like Velasco, who had become accustomed to attending dances and theatre performances from the time he had first set foot in Seattle, the college was a lively place.[14]

By participating in activities, Velasco probably contributed significantly to building bonds with his white counterparts. On 7 January 1927, for example, he went to a social event in which he met and danced with Olive Hardan, whom he knew from their mutual involvement in the World Politics Club. Their common interests may had led to further social contact, as he met with her on a number of other occasions throughout his stay in Bellingham. It was through his participation in various events, including ice cream and milkshake parties, that he also met another colleague, Irene Schagel, with whom he worked in the Scribes Club.[15]

Not only by meeting and socializing with new people, but also by keeping in touch with old friends, Velasco made conscious efforts to bond with whites. During his stay in Bellingham, he kept up his friendship with Eleanor Multmueller, who was still in Seattle and corresponded regularly with him. One time, she told him about absent-mindedly writing out his name on a tag for someone else at a party because she happened to be thinking of him instead. On another occasion, although she was worried about a difficult exam in chemistry the next day, she wrote him a long letter saying that she missed him and wished for his return.[16]

During his six months in Bellingham, although Velasco was a rare Asian in a world full of distorted images about Asiatics, he experienced one of the most productive periods of his life. He built friendships with whites in spite of racial differences, led the busy life of a dedicated student, participated in numerous activities, and, moreover, began the project that became one of his crowning achievements, launching the Scribes Club and the *Red Arrow*. Velasco's attempt to fit in among whites, therefore, was remarkable not only because he made the effort, but also because he largely succeeded.[17]

## II. Inerasable Differences

Velasco's Bellingham period was important for another reason: the successes he enjoyed came at the cost of self-consciously straddling opposing racial worlds. His efforts to assimilate showed that, no matter how successful he could be in achieving some goals, race was a factor that would never disappear regardless of how hard he tried to fit in and what kinds of personal merits he brought.

One context in which he performed the racial juggling act was in his writing. He made a conscious effort to subsume his own racial identity when writing for one audience, Caucasians, while embracing it when writing for another, Filipinos. In Bellingham, Velasco wrote for a white audience, and he employed various techniques to downplay his racial identity. One was adopting a self-righteous voice. On one occasion, in his *Weekly Messenger* column, he criticized a teacher for having dismissed her class early; the risk the cold weather posed to health, he argued, was something that each student should decide for him or herself because the consequence was losing "an hour of an invaluable lecture." In another essay, he announced that the alumni had a moral duty to contribute to their alma mater. He stated, "To the serious-minded alumnus this day should sound the signal of a moral challenge. The history of this institution has been, and is still being, and always will be, made by the alumni." In a discussion about independent thought, he stated, "The long, dark and brilliant pages of history offer innumerable examples of leaders who stuck to their own opinion." In a piece ironically extolling original thought, he did little more than repeat the commonplace both in ideas and in the manner in which he expressed them.[18]

Another facet of his effort to deemphasize his racial identity involved writing about topics other than race. The efforts resulted in strained, apolitical, and trite results. On 21 January 1927, he criticized the old library facilities. Referring to the them as "our book-stuffed reading room-I don't call it library," he commented, "there must be lenient mercy on those who rather prefer to sit and read, or stand and whisper. You know what I mean of course. Don't you?" The paragraph seemed to be a waste of words; it achieved nothing beyond giving vent to his opinion on what was probably a well-known topic. In other issues, too, his contributions seemed to have little purpose other than filling space in his column. On 22 January 1927, he urged students to sing the college song at the end of assemblies: "They inspire and contribute to the beauty of the program," he wrote. In the same edition, he wrote an entire paragraph criticizing the immorality of eating lunch before the official beginning of the noon hour.[19]

At other times, he used humor, again probably in a conscious effort to avoid racial issues. On 5 November, he wryly commented on the posting of grades. "Students," he wrote, "look at them as they would at a mirror," for "the grades reflect the image of the night life of the students." Commenting on a course on library work, he started, "the assignments being given by Miss Wilson in her class in Library instruction, which formerly seemed long, tedious and boresom to many, are not really so." Another example was an editorial in which he criticized people who did not act independently; he commented, "these are for those whose range of vision do not extend beyond their steaming dinner." About a month later, he wrote humorously about topics that he otherwise took seriously: poetry and romance. Springtime, the inspiration for poets, had come; "The youths will lightly turn to thoughts of love," he announced, implying that the change in seasons provided inspiration for poetry about romance. Even when writing about topics close to his heart, he mustered his skills as a writer to treat them with a sense of humor not often apparent in his work in the Filipino press. Although the range of techniques he employed could have been the result of his efforts to address simply issues familiar to his fellow students, their apolitical and non-racial tone contrasted starkly with his persistent treatment of such issues, at the same time, when writing for Filipinos.[20]

There were only two instances during his six-month stay in Bellingham when he discussed racial issues. In December of 1926, he wrote about Japanese people by naively declaring that, when matrimonial arrangements between a prospective couple failed, the national practice was for the couple to kill themselves. A month later, he reflected upon a young Native-American woman's reading at the school auditorium the previous day and observed, "She must be somewhere within the boundary that demarcates the ways of the present day from those of the primeval." Moreover, the race-neutral persona he adopted as a writer on the *Weekly Messenger* came across in his pen name. Only near the end of his stay did he sign any of his columns as anything other than "V.A.V." He did not reveal his full name—Victorio Velasco, with its Latin-sounding origins—until near the end of his tenure, thereby engaging in a practice common even today among Asians, who try to hide or disguise their ethnic-sounding names for practical reasons such as seeking employment, gaining admissions to elite universities, or simply trying to fit in among whites.[21]

When he wrote for a Filipino audience, in contrast, he dealt with racial, ethnic, and nationalistic issues on a regular basis. Like other Filipino poets, he extolled the virtues of Filipino women as a means of expressing Filipino nationalism. "Ave Regina," a poem he dedicated to "A lovely rose of the Malayan race," described the subject of the poem, the winner of the 1926 Rizal Day Beauty Pageant, as a symbol of the Filipino people. He wrote, "Thy power-gifted scepter stately sway/Over thy kingdom, born on foreign strand." The words "thy kingdom, born on foreign strand" implied that the kingdom over which the beauty queen reigned was one comprised of people on foreign soil, the American continent, among foreign people, Euro-Americans. The primacy of Filipinos and the portrayal of Americans as the "other" indicated that Velasco, in spite of his successes among whites, remained supremely conscious of racial distinctions.[22]

That Velasco was very much a participant in the Filipino nationalist press was evident in other ways as well. In an article for the *Philippine American Colonist*, Velasco looked back on the progress the paper had made during its short existence and asserted that it had become increasingly effective in expressing "the national aspiration" of the Filipino people. Then, describing early efforts he had made to reach a racially-integrated audience of Filipinos and whites, he commented that they represented a "temporary fall of the thermometer"; he may have been implying that race-mixing was a mistake. That he not only knew of, but also actively encouraged, Filipino ethnic, cultural, political, and racial unity came across when he wrote, "The [*Colonist*] has indeed strengthened its [s]ervice in bringing together the harmony and unity of the Filipino community in the Pacific Northwest." That he was an active participant in the propagation of Filipino nationalism was also apparent in the fact that he continued to write for the Filipino press, including the *Philippine Seattle Colonist*, the University of Washington Cosmopolitan Club paper, and the *Philippine Republic* even while adopting a race-neutral persona in Bellingham.[23]

He remained aware of racial issues partly because of their ubiquity. Among stories appearing in the *Philippine Seattle Colonist* were those about Philippine independence, Filipino journalism in California, Rizal Day celebrations, and the American presence in the Philippines. Clearly, he was also familiar with Filipino journals that routinely published articles on Filipino-American relations. He personally corresponded with other Filipino journalists, such as the staff of the *Philippine Seattle Colonist* and the *Philippine Republic* when they were publishing stories about tensions between Filipinos and Euro-Americans. One example of such a story appeared in the November 1926 issue of the *Varsity Filipino Weekly* and accused American policymakers of exploiting the Philippines economically.[24]

The difference between the apolitical persona Velasco adopted in Bellingham and the racially—and nationalistically—conscious voice he assumed at the same time in the Filipino press attested to the uneasy and constant tension between Velasco's two worlds: one constituted of whites; the other, of Filipinos. Nevertheless, he was hardly the first non-white to make conscious choices about how to act and what to say depending on which race he was among. One of the clearest expositions of a member of a racial minority tailoring his public persona to meet the realities of his time appeared in Booker T. Washington's efforts to secure funding for the Tuskegee Institute in the late nineteenth century. According to his supporters, he purposely feigned a subordinate position in front of whites because he felt that doing so was the most effective way to get them to help African Americans' quest for education and careers. A more militant stance appeared in the work of W.E.B. DuBois, who, unlike Washington, never feigned servility and never avoided the race issue. To the contrary, DuBois criticized Washington and assertively fought for racial equality. Velasco was thus not unique in creating and manipulating his public persona depending on the racial circumstances.[25]

The tension between Velasco's two worlds also made clear the reality that, no matter what his personal merits, he faced boundaries because of his race. The line was sadly clear even in the deepest of personal friendships, his relationship with Eleanor Multmueller. Even though they remained close friends, she continued to remind him that there was a line that she would never let him cross. On 8 December 1926, even as she told him how much she would like to see him during the upcoming Christmas recess, she emphasized that she "must refuse you."

On 10 February, even when she told him that she missed him, she reinforced the boundaries of their relationship by asking him to explain the meaning of the phrase "Platonic friendship"; her words provided another reminder that he could never be more than her friend.[26]

Velasco's efforts to pursue a romantic relationship with Multmueller were unsuccessful because she could never forget that he was not white. This reality was in spite of her intelligence, her liberal—almost radical—beliefs, and the fact that she spent much of her time with Filipino, Chinese, and Japanese students at Seattle's International House. Neither her intelligence nor her political leanings could completely erase the racial divide that she saw between herself and Velasco. On 6 November 1926, for example, she praised Velasco for a poem he had written, but she did so not by recognizing her friend as a unique and talented individual, but by falling back upon a trite stereotype into which she pigeonholed him—a supposed racial trait, "such genius as you people possess." Presumably, "you people" were not whites, but Filipinos, who were somehow distinct from those she considered her own people. Later in the same letter, she told him how much she would like to have a picture of him, and then explained her statement by stating, "I just love to see how many of my various friends I can get in my album." As if making sure that it was clear what she meant by "various" friends, she explained, "That last sentence sounds peculiar but you know what I mean." No matter how close they were as friends, she may have valued his friendship at least partly because she saw him not as an individual human being, but as an exotic specimen to add to her collection of ethnic acquaintances. To Mulmueller, Velasco was never a real man as a white man could be. As historian Gail Bederman has argued, perhaps she simply could not conceive of Velasco, a dark-skinned male, as a bona fide member of the masculine sex. Were this the case, she was not unique, as the words of the female attorney and women's rights advocate, Ellen Mussey, illustrated during congressional hearings on a bill punishing white women who married Japanese or Chinese women. On 13 December, 1917 the House Committee on Immigration and Naturalization convened, and Mussey unequivocally stated that she supported intermarriage as a way to encourage world harmony. She qualified her statement just as unequivocally, however, by explaining that she did not believe in marriages between white women and Japanese or Chinese. If Multmueller thought of herself as being in the vanguard of liberalism and reform and yet drew clear boundaries when it came to race, she was in good company; she was hardly the only liberal-thinking white female to hold perhaps unconscious, yet deeply-ingrained racial prejudices.[27]

Velasco's Bellingham period was a milestone in the sense that, even as he gained a foothold among Caucasians, he increasingly became involved with Filipino nationalism, which put him at odds with whites. In spite of the tension, he made headway in both worlds. He was able to balance precariously two racially-opposed worlds by adopting a different voice in each. Still, the tension persisted because, even though he achieved much among whites, the world he entered never completely let him forget that he was a racial outsider. Regardless of his efforts, his personal merits, and his other, objective qualifications—which almost always eclipsed those of his white counterparts in a wide range of contexts—he never gained full entrance into the world of whites. Tragically, he found again—as he had in his relationship with Jane Garrott during his first year in Seattle—that even those like Eleanor Multmueller, a liberal, intelligent and articulate young woman who cared for him deeply, were incapable of looking beyond skin color.[28]

# 4

# Two Worlds (May 1927 to December 1931)

During the four years after Velasco left Bellingham, the tension between his two worlds increased. The gap became increasingly apparent in both his personal life and in his avocation as a journalist and writer. On one side were the white women with whom he sought relationships. On the other were Velasco's ties to his Filipino racial and cultural heritage.

## I. Women and Assimilation

One aspect of Velasco's effort to assimilate lay in his continuing efforts to have a romantic relationship with a white woman. Between May of 1927 and the end of 1931, he pursued relationships with several, but none of his efforts succeeded.

Velasco continued unsuccessfully to seek a romantic relationship with Eleanor Multmueller. He had often kept her company during social activities sponsored by the University of Washington chapter of the Cosmopolitan Club, part of a national organization fostering understanding across national and racial lines. At various times, he expressed his feelings for her and flirted by asking her whether she was incapable of romantic love. He also tried to be direct, as in May of 1927 when he told her of his affections.[1]

Yet, Multmueller continued to keep him at a distance. Even before he left Bellingham in April of 1927, she had tried to deflect his attentions by reminding him that theirs was a Platonic relationship. She tried, for instance, to tell him directly that she had no romantic interest in him, sensing, perhaps, that he had not been listening to what she had tried to tell him. In early May of 1927, she again emphasized that she was not interested in romance. She had even tried—although he may not have heard—to ward off his attentions by hinting strongly that "a woman does not covet the attention of even a good man if she is not attracted to him."[2]

In addition to her inability to forget that he was a Filipino, another possible reason for her continuing refusal to consider Velasco as a romantic partner was that she was an independent, bright, talented woman intent on her studies. As a student at the University of Washington, her outlook may have reflected the increased freedom and independence of other Seattle women of her time. At least since the beginning of the previous decade, women in Seattle had become more aware of their personal and political independence as a result of Progressive Era values. During the first two decades of the twentieth century, female reformers across the United States had sought more equality with men, and the women in the Pacific Northwest were no exception. By 1910, women in Washington had won the suffrage, and, by the time that Multmueller met Velasco, Seattle women were heirs to two decades of female activism in the city. Leaders in the movement had gained renown by linking suffrage to other social and political reforms in Seattle, and female activists mounted large-scale efforts building broad coalitions across social classes with activities like tea and card parties in private homes and plays and balls. Among the Seattle activists' greatest political victories was the recall of a mayor during the decade before Velasco and Multmueller met and the election in the 1920s of the nation's first big-city female mayor.[3]

Consequently, Velasco may have misunderstood the climate of activist fervor and its effects upon Multmueller. In May of 1927, she apparently found it necessary, for instance, to tell him that she would never marry until she had attained her career goals. Her college education, the seriousness with which she approached her studies and other responsibilities, several years of teaching, and the medical school training that she would complete within the next two years seemed to confirm her ambitions. Emphasizing her personal independence, she also told him that she would do nothing to encourage the attention of young men.[4]

Another young woman with whom Velasco unsuccessfully sought a romantic relationship was Annie Lincoln of Snohomish, Washington. Velasco may have misinterpreted her willingness to be his friend as an opportunity to become her romantic partner. Velasco had met her sometime in 1927—possibly at the Cosmopolitan Club clubhouse where he may have also met Multmueller—and had begun correspondence with her by June of that year, inviting her to accompany him to social events such as dances. He also sent her gifts, including copies of newspapers with which he was involved.[5]

As in his relationship with Multmueller, though, even though Velasco succeeded in having Lincoln as a friend, he never became intimate with her. When she visited him at the Cosmopolitan Club's clubhouse, it was not just a visit with him. Instead, it was a group visit with all of its residents; and she socialized not only with Velasco, but also with everybody else there. When Lincoln wrote a letter to Velasco, too, it was not because he held some special place in her heart; he was only one of perhaps dozens of people with whom she corresponded. The contents of her letters, too, indicated that a romantic relationship with him was not her goal. In late September of 1927, for example, she wrote about the weather and picking hops; in December, she told him about her job at the Puget Sound Telephone Company. Lincoln's contact with him, too, was sporadic. Although she wrote to him several times in December, she did not do so again until nearly the end of the following year and, then, mainly to discuss the weather, an automobile accident involving the family car, and Thanksgiving.[6]

The relationship between Lincoln and Velasco, moreover, was one that her mother seemed to control. As Christmas approached in 1927, Lincoln told Velasco about her plans to visit him but, as in other instances, she intended to bring her mother. Furthermore, when she visited him with her mother, it was typically only one stop in a series of other social calls; she and her mother saw

Velasco in March of 1928, but it was just one part of a visit with other family friends and a sightseeing trip. Invariably, too, when the possibility of Lincoln visiting Velasco in Seattle arose, it was not only she, but her mother, who informed Velasco. Even when Lincoln accompanied Velasco to dances, she did so with her mother. That her plans invariably depended on her mother was particularly clear when she once planned to visit him but could not because of her mother's ill health.[7]

Her mother controlled the relationship in other ways. When Velasco sent gifts to Lincoln, her mother treated them as though they were for the entire family. When he sent a box of coconut candy to Lincoln in April of 1928, it was the mother, not the daughter, who thanked him. When Lincoln was having a difficult time in her personal life, it was not the daughter, but the mother, who informed Velasco. When the daughter went on vacation to San Francisco, it was the mother who told him. The elder Lincoln had been involved in the relationship from an early stage, and it was she, not her daughter, who, in March of 1927, first began correspondence with him.[8]

As in his relationship with Multmueller, Velasco was never romantic with Lincoln. For one thing, he may have been ambivalent about doing so. Even though he invited her to dances, in his diaries he never described her in amorous terms. For another, Lincoln's mother may have prevented a close relationship. In May of 1929, when Velasco was living in Seattle's Chinatown, the younger Lincoln told him that she was reluctant about visiting him there because she was uncomfortable being around the area's residents. Contact between them ceased and never again resumed.[9]

Following the end of the correspondence with Annie Lincoln and her mother, Velasco unsuccessfully pursued other women. The first was Hope Tyler, with whom he carried on a brief correspondence after he sent her a card in June of 1929. Initially, she seemed to welcome the beginning of correspondence with him, but there was no indication of intimacy. Then, at the end of June, after she told him about another man who had given her gifts, there was no further correspondence.[10] In October of 1929, Velasco sought the attention of another young woman, Edith Wechel, whom he may have met while picking hops in the Yakima valley during the previous summer. Between October of 1929 and the spring of 1930, he wrote her letters and sent copies of his newspaper. However, Wechel may have never considered a romantic relationship with Velasco for several reasons, one of which was their age difference: she was still in high school, and he was twenty-five. Also, when she wrote to him, there was no hint of her thinking of their relationship in romantic terms. In her first letter to him in October, 1929, she described the glee club, classes in chemistry, English, and sociology, and her involvement in student government. In November, she told him about trying out for the girls' high school basketball team, and her plans for Christmas consisted of coasting down hills on a bobsled. In January of 1930, she wrote to him about her high school basketball team's victories in tournaments. When she received a yo-yo from him in March of 1930, the only significance she attached to it was that her classmates enjoyed playing with it. To her, the friendship she had with Velasco was nothing special; her sister Dorothy also considered him a friend.[11]

There were other flirtations. Early in the summer of 1928 en route to a cannery in Alaska, he accompanied a "white girl" on a walk through downtown Ketchikan, Alaska where they had dinner together. The following day, he wrote a poem, which he dedicated to a young woman, Clare Love, whom he had watched play the violin on board ship. Over the next several days, he expressed his admiration for her in his diary and then gave her the poem that he had dedicated to her; but after they met, he never saw her again. Later during the summer, he flirted with several women in Alaska. He briefly sought the attention of a "married woman" whom he occasionally visited over several weeks. Between December of 1928 and January of 1929, he renewed his friendship with Irene Schagel, with whom he had worked on the Scribes Club at the Bellingham Normal School. During the summer of 1930, he tried to attract another young woman, Evelyn Peterson. Although contact between them was brief, he told her that she was "the sweetest girl" he had ever met. Yet, Velasco was no more successful in his romantic efforts in Alaska than he had been elsewhere.[12]

Although the reasons for his unsuccessful efforts varied in each case, race, as in the past, was almost always a factor, especially because of the widespread hostility against Filipinos. The period between the late 1920s and the early 1930s was an inauspicious time for Filipino males to pursue white women in most of the places where Velasco sought their attention. In 1928 in Edith Wechel's home in the Yakima valley, a mob of about one hundred and fifty whites drove out Filipinos who had come to work on local farms. In and around Seattle, where Velasco pursued relationships with Multmueller and Lincoln, white policemen harassed Filipino men who accompanied white women. In the mid-1920s, one white woman who had married a Filipino feared her neighbors and, even before she married him, did not often accompany him to dances, movies, or restaurants because of the risk of violence. During one twelve-month period, they moved their residence thirteen times because of hostile landlords and neighbors. At the University of Washington campus where Velasco periodically took classes between 1927 and 1931, only a handful of the approximately one hundred Filipino students dated white women because of the hostility against interracial dating and, in the late 1920s, sororities ceased inviting Filipinos to their parties. It even became risky for an interracial couple to walk across campus.[13]

Filipinos had also become scapegoats for social problems. In April of 1929, there was a health scare when the Seattle City Council accused Filipinos of bringing spinal meningitis and other diseases to the city. Between 1928 and 1932, labor unions, such as the American Federation of Labor, repeatedly sought the expulsion of Filipinos from the United States, accused them of taking jobs away from deserving whites, and thereby gained the support of organizations such as the American Legion, the Native Sons of the Golden West, and the American Coalition. Another source of tension between whites and Filipinos in the 1930s lay in the Filipinos' patronage of taxi-dance halls where white, working-class women danced with Filipino men who purchased tickets. The halls represented some of the few places where Filipinos could gain admission, but to many whites, they were places of vice where Filipinos preyed upon white females.[14]

Nor was hostility against Filipinos in Seattle and in the Pacific Northwest during the time that Velasco sought the company of white women unique. Mob violence broke out in other places, particularly in California after a white policeman arrested a Filipino who accompanied his white fiancé in public. Shortly thereafter, the local chamber of commerce and a judge publicly announced that Filipinos were a menace to white people, and the incidents sparked four days of rioting in which whites attacked several targets, including a new dance hall that had catered to Filipinos. Hundreds of whites went on a rampage, attacking the Northern Monterey Filipino club, beating up dozens of Filipinos, and shooting one to death. In 1930, there were other incidents in California, including a threat to burn down an entire town if the local police chief did not rid it of Filipinos. In Reedley, whites threw a stick of dynamite into a group of sleeping Filipino laborers. In Imperial, whites wounded and killed several Filipinos with another bomb.[15]

Velasco and other Filipinos faced hostility from other quarters as well. While white mobs threatened them with violence, white politicians fought them with laws. An Oregon law prohibited interracial marriage, as did a California law, such as a statute that prohibited interracial marriage between white persons and "Negroes, Mongolians or mulattoes." Between 1930 and 1932, Filipinos, trying to establish their legal right to marry across racial lines, challenged the statute as being inapplicable to them, arguing that, because they were of the Malay race, the law did not apply to them. However, after a California court held that the statute did not prohibit marriage between whites and Filipinos, the state legislature amended it so that "Malayans" could not marry whites, and the law remained in effect until November of 1948, several years after the United States, in international tribunals, had participated in punishing German and Japanese for race-based policies abroad. If Velasco had found a white woman in California willing to marry him, he would have had to wait nearly two decades more before American laws made such marriages legal.[16]

Nor were states alone in seeking sanctions against Filipinos, as the United States Congress proved. In 1928, Representative Richard Welch of California sponsored two congressional bills to limit Filipino immigration. During the next several years, Representative Albert Johnson of Washington introduced various Filipino exclusion bills. In 1930, two senators proposed limiting Filipino immigration to students and government officials. In 1934, the Tydings-McDuffie Act slashed the number of Filipinos entering the United States to fifty per year. The next year, Congress enacted a law to ship back to the Philippines any Filipino who did not have steady employment.[17]

The fact that many Americans of the time faced hardships because of the Depression exacerbated racial hostility against Filipinos, including accusations that Filipinos brought down wages, lowered living standards, took jobs away from white people, preyed upon innocent white women, and lowered moral standards. That the Filipinos faced whites' increased hostility during the Depression was not necessarily surprising. Among other non-whites who felt the brunt of white prejudice during the period were Mexicans and Mexican-Americans. During the 1930s, white public officials throughout the Southwest sent over 400,000 Mexicans and Mexican-Americans to Mexico. Of this number, most were legal residents, and some were American citizens. Among them were those who had lived in the United States for three or four decades. The Filipinos, like the Mexicans, were the scapegoats of both race prejudice and white laborers' fears about loss of work.[18]

In spite of the threats of violence, legal sanctions, and the prejudices of the women themselves, Velasco persistently, albeit unsuccessfully, sought a romantic relationship with a white woman, possibly for several reasons. One was that he was trying to find someone to fill the void in his life as a result of Sixta Aquino leaving him. Even after the passage of four years since their breakup, he remained distraught about losing her; in April of 1928, for example, he recorded in his diary that he still loved her. The following spring, he again became disconsolate over the end of their relationship, and whenever he thought of her, he could not eat. As in the past, he had recurring dreams about her. Another possible reason that Velasco sought out white women was that, during the early 1930s, he and other Filipino men outnumbered Filipino women by 14 to 1. The demographic imbalance—any personal racial preferences aside—would have provided Velasco, as well as other Filipinos, with little choice in the matter. Another possible explanation, of course, was that finding a white American mate might have symbolized entry into the American mainstream.[19]

Velasco's efforts to start a relationship with a white woman between 1928 and 1931 occurred at a time when women like Multmueller were heirs to the increased political awareness of middle-class white women and the concurrent rise in hostility against Filipinos across the United States. Whatever the reasons for Velasco's romantic failures, they symbolically represented his failure to assimilate; the inability to find a mate among the ruling race represented his inability to enter fully into the world of white Americans. His efforts also highlighted the persistent tension between his effort to become a part of the American mainstream and the factors that prevented him from doing so.

## II. Poetry and Journalism

The tension arising from Velasco's effort to join the American mainstream was evident not only in his efforts at romance, but also in his other endeavors, including his literary ventures and the continuation of his ties to Filipino issues, friends and family. One indication of his efforts to become part of American culture through his talents as a writer appeared in his choice of themes. Although he wrote on a variety of topics, as in Bellingham several years previously, he conspicuously avoided Filipino and racial issues when he wrote for a white audience. While attending classes at Seattle Pacific College, he wrote term papers about Caucasian authors, such as Carl Sandburg and William Shakespeare, rather than Filipinos. Another theme was Alaska, which appeared in poems including "Alaska Night," describing Alaska's natural environment, and "My Prescription," portraying the state as a place to escape from city life. He wrote poems about women, including one that he dedicated to Clare Love, the young violinist whom he had met during one of his trips to Alaska. "Your Eyebrow," described a woman's face; "To a Nurse" was a poem dedicated to a nurse Velasco had met in Montana; and "The Dream" described the smiles of a lover. Other themes appeared in "A Golden Page," which was about the passage of time, and "Let Us make Friends," which was about building bonds among travel companions. He also wrote about the natural world. "Brown Birdie" described the flight of a bird, "The Tide" was about waves on the sea, and "My Ship" compared human lives to ships.[20]

By 1931, not only Velasco's choice of themes, but also his relations with an American publisher, indicated that he was making inroads into the American literary world. In November of 1931, Poets Guild Publishers contacted Velasco about publishing two of his poems, "Just Smiles" and "Alaska Night." The following month, the publisher confirmed that both poems would appear in the upcoming anthology, *Poets and Poetry of 1931*.[21]

In selecting themes about nature, women, and a variety of other topics, Velasco stayed away from addressing issues concerning Filipinos. The fact that a large American publisher included him among American poets in its anthology seemed to indicate that his entry into the American literary world had borne some fruit. In spite of his increasing success as a published writer, however, in personal relationships, he remained unable to shed his racial identity, and his achievements as a writer did not cross over into other realms.

Velasco nevertheless did not abandon ties to his racial and cultural heritage. To the contrary, he continued to express Filipino nationalistic themes when he wrote for a Filipino audience. An example was "A Filipino Serenade," which was ostensibly an imaginary work about the coming of evening. Implicitly, however, the image of the moon in the poem was a metaphor for the Philippines, and the poem's expression of longing for his home islands contrasted sharply with Velasco's choice of themes in writings he intended for a white audience.[22]

The distinction between the themes Velasco chose when writing for Filipinos and those he selected when addressing white Americans was important because it placed his work within a genre of works by other Filipino authors—a genre that reflected tensions between Filipino writers' identities and their efforts to assimilate into Euro-American culture. On the one hand, Velasco and other Filipinos tried to master the English language and gain fame as American writers. On the other, many had been aware—since the beginnings of the American occupation of the Philippines—that race separated them from their white counterparts.

The theme appeared in other literary venues as well. Among playwrights in the Philippines, Filipinos' initial awareness of the racial difference between themselves and their American colonizers had appeared in plays celebrating the Malay race and using indigenous dialects for decades, particularly because the use of indigenous languages was a form of rebellion against American imperialism. By the 1920s, however, many Filipinos felt less antipathy towards the United States and accepted the use of English to express indigenous themes. Among the consequences were that Filipino writers, including Bienvenido Santos, N.V.M. Gonzalez, and Jose Garcia Villa, wrote in English during their stay in America as well as after their return to the Philippines. By the 1930s, official sanction and recognition of English came with the Quezon government's awarding of prizes to literary works in Tagalog, Spanish, and English. Velasco's persistence in expressing nationalistic themes in works intended for a Filipino audience even as he, when writing for an American audience, expressed non-Filipino themes, was thus consistent with the bifurcated cultural and linguistic experiences of other Filipino writers of his time.[23]

Another aspect of Velasco's efforts to maintain ties with his racial and cultural heritage even as he ventured into the world of white Americans appeared in his journalistic work. Since at least the end of 1926, he had served as both editor and writer of the *Philippine Seattle Colonist*. While in Alaska during the summers between 1927 and 1931, he also wrote for and edited the *Sea Gull News,* which circulated among the state's Filipino cannery workers.[24] Furthermore, his avocation as a journalist linked him to other Filipinos who published newspapers catering to the cannery laborers. Sebastian Abella, an acquaintance of Velasco, a student at the University of Washington, and former editor of the *Philippine Seattle Colonist,* was founder of the *Sunny Point News*. Leo Galima and Emeterio Cruz edited the *Chomly Weekly*, and Antonio Velasco, Velasco's younger brother, and Joe Fernandez were co-editors of the *New Cuadra Gossips*. The two Velasco brothers and the other Filipino journalists worked in concert, moreover, by exchanging information. In February of 1929, for example, Velasco published in his own newspaper, the *Filipino Forum,* a story that he had received from a Filipino in Minneapolis about racial friction at the University of Minnesota.[25]

Velasco's continuing journalistic ties to Filipinos appeared in other ways, too. In 1929, Marco Aquino, secretary of the Filipino Progressive Association of Bremerton and a friend of Velasco, helped sell advertising space in the *Filipino Forum*, which Velasco had founded in 1928 in Seattle. Between January and December of 1929, he gave Velasco various news items concerning Bremerton Filipinos, helped sign up new subscribers, and invited Velasco to Filipino social events in Bremerton. In July of 1927, Crisanto Ticman of the Bureau of Audits of the Philippine government in Manila wrote to him asking for information about another Filipino. In 1928, Velasco corresponded with the University of the Philippines debate team, which was then touring the United States in tournaments against Americans. In 1930, he was involved with the Filipino Literary Society of Seattle. Velasco also exchanged correspondence with national Filipino organizations such as the Filipino Students' Christian Students, which was based in New York and, in 1931, his activities included collecting donations for a fund benefiting a Filipino boxer.[26]

In his work as a journalist, Velasco was heavily involved with Filipino issues, and this contrasted sharply with his efforts to downplay—if not actually hide—his racial identity among white Americans. It was not necessarily surprising, however, that Velasco was involved in seemingly contrary endeavors. Even as he sought acceptance among white Americans, he was becoming increasingly aware of the divisions between himself and them. By July of 1928, he was sensitive enough to the differences between races so that, even when recording his thoughts in his diary, he explicitly identified the race of at least one of the women whom he courted. That summer, even though he and other Filipinos spent part of July Fourth with their Caucasian comrades in celebrating the holiday, he recognized in a short speech the racial division between Filipinos and whites. By 1929, he had also become aware of whites' claims that Filipinos brought loathsome diseases into the United States. In November, he wrote to the *Seattle Post Intellingencer* in order to criticize Seattle police chief Louis J. Forbes' statement about the "chief evil" of Seattle dance halls being white women's mingling with Filipinos. In January of 1930, he wrote again to the *Post Intelligencer*, asserting that many white Americans were not "broad-minded and tolerant." Even as Velasco, in his relationships with women and in poetry intended for a white audience, ventured into the world of white Americans, he was increasingly aware of the racial divide and, moreover, willing to openly voice his awareness.[27]

## III. Intra Ethnic Tensions

Although Velasco was becoming increasingly cognizant of racial differences, he realized that even the world of Filipinos did not necessarily provide him with a safe haven. Even among members of his own race, there were divisions. In 1928, one predicament grew out of Velasco's efforts to publish the *Philippine Seattle Colonist*. Manuel Rustia, the previous publisher of the *Colonist*, had warned Velasco against becoming involved in the publication of another newspaper, the *Philippine Digest*. After reading an article in yet another Filipino newspaper, the *Philippine Republic,* which alleged that Velasco was involved with the *Digest*, Rustia became suspicious of Velasco's efforts to continue working with the *Colonist*. Rustia had begun to think that Velasco might, through his involvement with the *Digest,* solicit the advertisers of the *Colonist*. Another factor exacerbated the tension between Velasco and Rustia. Velasco was financially indebted to Rustia, and he was unable to pay him back. As a result, Rustia wrote a letter to the *Digest* describing Velasco as "an irresponsible person." In April of 1928, the ill feeling between Rustia and Velasco, who had formerly been colleagues on the *Colonist*, prompted Velasco to write a long letter to Rustia to correct Rustia's misunderstandings about his role with the *Digest*, reiterate his promise to repay the debt, and express hope that they could restore amicable relations.[28]

Other sources of tension among Filipino journalists were evident when one of them, who had published the *Chomly Spectator* with Velasco in Alaska, blamed its demise upon the ignorance of other Filipinos. He told Velasco that its end came as the result of "narrow-minded, idiotic and stupid . . . boys among us here" who attempted to turn it into a gossip tabloid. Velasco's effort to remain true to his ideals as a journalist caused additional tensions with Filipinos. In November of 1928, Velasco told a Filipino reader of his newly-established *Filipino Forum* that he intended the "exposing [of] attempted graft and rotten schemes" regardless of whether the perpetrators were "American" or "Filipino." It was an explicit statement of his willingness to act against members of his own ethnic group.[29]

Velasco also found that there were limits to what he could ask of his compatriots. In the spring of 1929, Benigno Sevidal objected after Velasco indicated in the *Forum* that Sevidal was a member of the *Forum*'s staff. Sevidal had given Velasco news items for publication in the *Forum,* but he did not wish to be under any formal obligation to it, nor did he wish Velasco to convey that impression. In the summer of 1929, Velasco asked another Filipino writer and journalist, Sebastian Abella, to help him edit the *Forum.* Abella also turned down Velasco's offer; he had already committed to studying full time at the University of Washington. In spite of his efforts to help Velasco in some ways, such as finding advertisers for the *Forum*, his friend and colleague Marco Aquino, too, did not always bring good tidings. In March of 1929, for example, he told Velasco that he had been unable to sell advertising space to businesses in Bremerton. The following month, he again reported to Velasco that he had experienced little success in selling advertising.[30]

It was not only limits upon other Filipinos' contributions that caused Velasco difficulties, for Velasco himself was the cause of some problems. For example, he did not consistently honor promises to Aquino. In March of 1929, Velasco failed to send him the twenty copies of the *Forum* he had promised. Several weeks later, he still had not honored his commitment; he sent only half of what he had originally pledged. The following month, he again failed to send Bremerton subscribers copies of the paper. Even after Aquino repeatedly reminded Velasco of the need to honor commitments, Velasco, a year later, was still not sending copies of the *Forum* to some subscribers, who then complained.[31]

In 1930 as in 1929, Velasco's participation in intra-ethnic activities again led to conflict. In late spring, Velasco became involved in a controversy surrounding the mishandling of a fund for Filipinos. The controversy pitted Velasco against Lorenzo Zamora, the publisher of the *Philippine Digest* and a member of the board of trustees of a community fund for Filipinos. There had been rumors about misappropriations from the fund and the culpability of the board. Around the same time, Zamora had asked Velasco to consider a merger between his paper, the *Digest*, and Velasco's paper, the *Filipino Forum*, but Velasco, because of his knowledge of Zamora's possible complicity in the scandal, declined the invitation.[32]

In 1931, Velasco's journalistic ideals caused a conflict with another Filipino writer, this time over an issue of plagiarism. Velasco discovered that Franco Manuel had plagiarized a poem, copyrighted it, and then published it under his own name in a nationally-circulating journal, the *Filipino Student*. Velasco informed the journal of the plagiarism and condemned the act as "literary piracy."[33]

Velasco experienced mixed results when dealing with Filipinos outside the journalistic world as well. In canneries during summers, Velasco enjoyed prestige among Filipinos. By the 1928 season, he was in charge of thirteen other Filipinos at Todd, Alaska. In 1929, Filipinos in different parts of the United States had heard enough about Velasco—possibly a labor contractor or foreman by then—to seek his help in finding employment. In February, several Filipinos in Vancouver, Washington asked him for assistance in securing cannery work. Filipinos in California, too, asked him for cannery jobs. In March, Velasco's brother Antonio also asked for work, both for himself and for another Filipino. In 1931, Velasco was again in a position to control job assignments.

The connection that some Filipinos made between his name and cannery work was a mixed blessing, however. Velasco and many Filipino cannery workers came from middle- and upper-class families in the Philippines and had attained educational levels unusual even for Caucasians. Whatever stature they enjoyed in the canneries, therefore, probably could not offset their awareness of having to toil as menial laborers, something that even the poorest, uneducated whites shunned as being degrading. The contrast between the Filipinos' qualifications and the reality of the limited employment opportunities due to race was particularly stark because many were destined for prominent positions in the future. Victorio Edades graduated from the University of Washington and became a painting instructor in a Philippine university. Marceline Bautista became a high school principal who served the Philippine government's Bureau of Education. Felix Espino graduated from Oregon State and became a chief chemist in a sugar mill in the Philippines. Juan Ruiz graduated from Columbia University and became a teacher at the University of the Philippines. Many other Filipinos who, like Velasco, worked as manual laborers in Alaska similarly had high qualifications. As a result, even though they had difficulty finding work in anything other than manual labor in the United States, the work to which they consigned themselves was consistent with neither their aspirations nor their qualifications.[34]

For Velasco, the prestige he enjoyed among Filipinos in cannery work was problematic also because it did not provide him with an adequate income. By the end of 1931, he had spent every summer working in salmon canneries but was still suffering financially. As a result, he had constantly to seek financial help from other sources. In June of 1929, he wrote to Linfield College in McMinnville Oregon, a benefactor of Filipino students, to ask for a loan to help pay educational expenses. In December of 1929, he sought a loan from the University of Washington Filipino Clubhouse Fund. In January of 1931, he asked a Filipino acquaintance, Jose Fernandez, for twenty dollars to help pay for his transportation from Dinuba, California, to Seattle. Even after returning from cannery work in the fall of 1931—which was supposed to support him for the rest of the coming year—he was so short of funds that he had to ask an uncle for a loan. His persistent need for financial help in the period between 1927 and 1931 was a harbinger of future financial predicaments. Several years later, he still expected summer work in canneries to provide him with only enough money to pay off his previous year's debts; he had no expectation that it would pay living expenses during winters.[35]

In other areas of his life, too, Velasco enjoyed only mixed results in interactions with other Filipinos. Between 1927 and 1931, he was often in touch with his brother Antonio. During the summer of 1928, they both worked in Alaskan canneries and, in 1929, Velasco attended his sibling's high school graduation in Bellingham. Later that year, the brothers maintained contact when the younger of the two moved to Pullman in eastern Washington. When Antonio went to Montana in the spring of 1930 to work on a railroad, the brothers corresponded. Velasco also stayed in contact with other family members and relatives, including his sister Leonor, a cousin, his aunt Teresa, and his uncle Fred. Although Velasco communicated regularly with family and relatives, his relationships with them were not always harmonious. Family members often seemed to have a mistaken impression about his finances, constantly asking him for gifts and money. In 1929, his sister Leonor wanted him to enlarge her photograph and return it to the Philippines, and she also asked for money. In the spring of 1931, she again told him that she had no money with which to continue her education and asked for help. Nor was she the only relative to request Velasco for things. In January of 1931, Velasco's cousin Corrado Legaspe asked him for a raincoat. Explaining that his own family was too poor to buy him one, he assumed that Velasco had the money to do so.[36]

Not only relatives abroad, but also those in the United States, wanted Velasco's assistance. In January of 1931, a relative in California asked Velaco to come down and drive him to Seattle because he was out of work and had no funds to pay his own way. When Velasco failed to reply to his letter, he repeated his request and, even after Velasco sent him money, he was not satisfied and wanted Velasco to help him get a summer job in Alaska. Another relative, Velasco's aunt Teresa, who had arrived in San Francisco in late 1931, also sought Velasco's help. She did not explicitly ask him for money, but she hinted that she needed assistance by telling him that she was too poor to buy even postage stamps. In the meantime, those outside the family also wanted things from him. In October of 1931, a Filipino acquaintance who was studying in Los Angeles wanted Velasco to help him pay his room and board. When he had not yet received money from Velasco by the beginning of November, he again asked for help.[37]

Velasco's family, relatives, and friends posed additional demands and challenges, such as asking him for information about other Filipinos who had come to the United States. In August of 1929, his sister Leonor requested information about their brothers. She and others in his family often reminded him of their aspirations, such as her quest to further her education, and of the difficulties they had in trying to reach them. In June of 1929, for example, Leonor told him that their sister Anuncion had to stop studying because of lack of funds.[38]

Another source of tension in Velasco's relations with his family lay in the fact that he was not always diligent in corresponding with them. When a relative wrote to him on 4 July 1927, it was to let Velasco know that he had been trying to locate him for years; the only reason he finally learned of Velasco's whereabouts was because he happened to stumble upon a newspaper that had published his photograph. Nor was he the only one who told Velasco of family expectations. In 1929, his sister Leonor reminded him that she, too, had not heard from him, and for at least the next two years, she often scolded him for not writing more frequently.[39]

Velasco's family also implored him to return to the Philippines. In the spring of 1931, Leonor told him that she would be glad if he returned and that their grandmother often cried when she spoke of him. At the end of 1931, when his aunt Teresa arrived in the United States she, too, reminded him that his grandmother wished for his quick return to the Philippines. As in other venues involving Filipinos, even among members of his family, Velasco's efforts to keep in touch with his own race and culture produced mixed results.[40]

Between 1927 and 1931, the disjuncture between Velasco's efforts to assimilate and his racial, cultural and personal ties to the Philippines was becoming increasingly difficult to ignore. Velasco himself was becoming more aware of the racial divide between himself and whites, and the widespread racial hostility against Filipinos only complicated his efforts to bridge the distance between himself and them.

One of the clearest indications of the limits to Velasco's ability to become a part of the American mainstream was his continuing failure in relationships with white women. In personal affairs he was able—perhaps through charm and other qualities—to make friends even in an era of extreme racial hostility. Yet, there was a line he was consistently unable to cross. He found repeatedly that the white women who accepted him as a friend were uncomfortable about having a Filipino man as a lover or a husband. At the same time, Velasco's involvement with members of his own race proved to be hardly trouble-free. Not only his activities as a writer and journalist, but also his ties to family and relatives, proved that all too clearly.

Between 1927 and 1931, what emerged was Velasco's increasing awareness of racial differences and a new willingness to take sides. In 1929, when Seattle Police Chief Forbes described Filipinos as a social evil, for example, Velasco did not stand by passively. Rather, he openly challenged the white man for his stupidity. Moreover, even though Velasco sought the company of white women, he was more willing to criticize them. While taking classes at Seattle Pacific College, he wrote an essay describing his humiliation when a young white woman refused to accompany him to a movie. The receptionist at his date's dormitory forced him, all dressed up, to stand by a window as she cast a "suspicious" sidelong glance at him and exchanged looks with another receptionist. After making him wait, his date finally came downstairs to meet him but refused to honor her earlier promise to accompany him to the show. Assuming a superior air, the young woman, erroneously assuming that she was better-qualified than he, told him that she was willing to help him with his lessons. Velasco's essay, highlighting the racism of the three young white women, indicated that it was not only white men, but also white women, whom he was willing to criticize for racist views. His description of the young woman's ignorant assumption that she was his superior—an attitude based not on objective merits but on the color of her skin—bordered on contempt. He had come a long way from simply straddling two worlds. He was now beginning to choose sides.[41]

# 5

# Transitions (1932 to 1938)

Between 1932 and 1938, Velasco's life reflected a continuation of his recent shift away from trying to become equally involved with Filipinos and whites. Moreover, his stance against white Americans hardened. Even as he continued to pursue a white woman for his mate and increasingly gained respect from American publishers as a writer, in other realms, he seemed intentionally to abstain from activities with Caucasians. As before, however, no less so than in other periods, his embrace of relationships with Filipinos was not trouble-free. He experienced not only interracial tensions with whites both in the public and private parts of his life but also intra-racial tensions with other Filipinos, a fact that was evident in his activities as a writer, as a laborer caught up in the unionization movement of the 1930s, and in his personal relationships with other Filipinos, including members of his own family.

## I. Delphine Brooks

In 1932, Velasco finally found a white woman who accepted him as her lover. She was Delphine Brooks of Wapato, Washington, whom Velasco had met at some point before February. Ironically, even though she eventually accepted him as a romantic partner, race affected both the beginning and the end of their relationship.[1]

Initially, Brooks controlled the relationship, and she was determined to keep even her friendship with a Filipino man secret. In November of 1933, for example, she informed him that she would be in Seattle for Thanksgiving and would send him a telegram upon her arrival, but she instructed him to reply with a note addressed to "Grace," a pseudonym to hide her real identity. She also told him to meet her in a hotel lobby instead of coming to where she would be staying. At other times, too, she was determined to hide their relationship. She instructed him not to let anyone see him put his letters to her in her mailbox at the Washington State Normal School in Ellensburg where they were both students. She also warned him against reading her letters in class and, on at least one occasion, she threatened never to speak to him again if he ever told anyone that they corresponded. Another time, she told him not to reveal their correspondence because "American men hate Fili. men." Even in late 1933, after they had known each other for about two years, she had qualms about their relationship becoming public, a fact that came through when she arranged for him to visit her in Wapato and she gave him terse, explicit instructions to contact her on a specific day at a specific address.[2]

She tried to keep him at a distance in other ways as well, such as making excuses not to see him. One time, she told him that she could not see him because of trouble with her hair. On other occasions, she hinted that she was incapable of fidelity, telling him that she had many boyfriends. She also tried to deflect his attention towards other women by telling him that she was not as pretty as they. She argued that other women, unlike herself, could cook, sew, and stay at home. She said that she was unprepared to give up her independence by marrying and that she was too young to be serious about anyone. She then proclaimed that she wished for nothing but studying drama and the stage. She also brought up race when she told him that Filipinas make better wives than white women and that he should go back to the Philippines. Like Eleanor Multmueller, she tried, at least initially, to prevent their relationship from becoming a romantic one. The tension between the genuine affection she had for him and her reluctance to have him as her lover came through in the way she addressed him—casually, as "happy heart," "dear you," "V.V.," "Dear Poet," and "V.A.V."[3]

Around the end of 1933, however, she gradually began to accept him as her boyfriend. One of the first signs of the change occurred in November when her engagement to an American—an ironic rebuttal to her earlier statement to Velasco that she was too young to be serious about anyone—ended. She then began showing fidelity to Velasco such as forgoing dances when he was not with her, telling him not to have affairs with other women, and addressing him as "sweetheart," "honey boy," "Darling Victorio," and "Dearest Victorio." In late 1935, she explicitly declared that she could accept being with him and, by the following year, she told him that she did not care what people thought of her because of her relationship with him—presumably an issue with others because of his race. Eventually, she considered marriage, told him that he was the only one she had ever loved, and expressed her elation at being his girlfriend and told him that she had to keep pinching herself as a reminder that their affair was not a dream.[4]

Ironically, even though Velasco had finally found a white woman willing to accept him as a lover, he continued flirting with other women. On 8 August 1934, after returning to Seattle from work in Alaska, he went out to dinner with another young woman. A week later, he developed a crush on a girl from Montana. On New Year's eve, 1934, he accompanied two women to a restaurant and then to a dance until 3 a.m. On New Year's day, he went horseback riding with them and, in the evening, went to a card party, where he became attracted to yet another young woman.[5]

Velasco's triumph over racial barriers was short-lived. The beginning of the end of his relationship with Brooks started less than a year after she had begun to accept him. Even before the end of 1935, Brooks had occasionally become uneasy. She began to complain about him being mean to her, and her worries about their relationship continued into the following year. In the fall of 1936, she expressed her disappointment at his behavior towards her during a recent visit. Several months later, a bitter tone entered their relationship. On 30 March 1937, Velasco told her to go to dances without him, yet, on 14 April, barely two weeks later, he expressed his surprise that she had actually gone to one. Then he told her—perhaps sarcastically—to enjoy herself at other dances as well and that she did not have to write if it was not convenient. By late 1936, his behavior towards her led to soul-searching and disillusionment, something that came across on 9 October 1936, when she told him that he had destroyed the idealized image she had held of him.[6]

Paradoxically, the fissures in the relationship appeared even as Velasco continued to surmount racial barriers by gaining the acceptance of Brooks's family. When he once sent a gift of fish to them, they returned the favor by sending him food. When Velasco wrote to Mrs. Brooks, he addressed her as "Mother," and he referred to her father as "Dad." Other acquaintances of Brooks's family also accepted him. On at least one occasion, Brooks read Velasco's poetry in church. Likewise, Velasco's Filipino friends accepted Brooks as his girlfriend, and she was welcome at a variety of their social events. Moreover, in spite of the widespread hostility against interracial couples appearing in public, they often went to dances and shows together. The fact that Wapato was in the Yakima Valley, at the center of anti-Filipino hostility during the period, made Brooks and her family's acceptance of Velasco particularly significant. Yet, in August of 1937, the relationship came to an end.[7]

Velasco's relationship with Brooks indicated how race shaped his life. Brooks's initial efforts to discourage his overtures revealed how uncomfortable she was about having a romantic relationship with a Filipino. Like Eleanor Multmueller, Brooks consistently reminded Velasco of the boundaries of their relationship. Yet Brooks, like some of the other white women whom he had courted and who had accepted him at varying levels of intimacy, was unusual, perhaps even extraordinary, in that she was unwilling to accept popular prejudices wholesale. Even before she met Velasco, she had Filipino friends, such as Sebastian Abella, who thought of Brooks as his "big sister" and was close enough to be her confidante. Velasco's relationship with Brooks for nearly seven years indicted several important things about him and his times. It showed Velasco's ability to cross racial boundaries, and it also indicated that some women, even those who had absorbed a lifetime of racially pejorative ideas, were able, in varying degrees, to cast some stereotypes and taboos aside and challenge established norms.[8]

Yet, even though both Velasco and the women were able, at least to some extent, to transcend racial boundaries, events outside the relationships indicated that race always remained in the background. The events were a constant reminder of Filipinos' degraded status in the United States regardless of any outward triumphs. Even as Brooks and Velasco began to surmount racial barriers in their own relationship, events in Washington, D.C. set the stage for national, race-based action against Filipinos. On 10 July 1935, President Roosevelt signed into law the Filipino Repatriation Act. The act's purpose, as the House Committee on Immigration and Naturalization unabashedly explained on 11 May 1933, was "to provide for the return to the Philippine Islands of unemployed Filipinos." In 1934, the same year that Brooks began accepting Velasco as her romantic partner, the United States Congress enacted the Tydings-McDuffie Act, whose exclusion provision limited Filipino immigration to fifty per year and indicated what Americans across the country really felt about them.[9]

As the Depression deepened during the early 1930s, Filipinos continued to feel the hostility of whites who blamed them for economic problems. Even Filipinos with an advanced education considered themselves lucky if they could find any kind of a job. Virgil Duyungan, a member of the upper social class in the Philippines, thought himself fortunate to work as a cook. Yet, the difficulties—not only economic but also emotional—took their toll, and some lapsed into mental illness, such as one in Seattle who, in September of 1933, awoke from his sleep in a rampage and stabbed two of his countrymen.[10]

Race shaped the relationship between Velasco and Brooks from beginning to end. At first Brooks, like other white women whom Velasco had courted, set clear boundaries to their relationship. Even though Brooks eventually accepted him, events in the broader context indicated the enduring problems of race.

## II. Poetry

Between 1932 and 1938, Velasco's poetry seemed to continue in the same vein as it had earlier. When he submitted his work for publication in the popular American press, he continued writing about themes that did not explicitly pertain to Filipinos. Poems like "To the Commonwealth of the Philippines," which explicitly expressed Filipino patriotism, were rare. However, there were some significant changes. Even when writing for a white audience, the underlying themes began to reflect Velasco's identity as a Filipino.[11]

On their surface, many of his poems did not explicitly pertain to Filipinos. "The Song of Spring," described seasonal changes. In "Question" compared material wealth to friendship. "Sunshine" was about nightfall. "Ideals" was a poem condemning greed. "Outlook" was about the ability of a wise person to look beyond the obvious, and "A Soul for Gold" was a poem he dedicated to the Lindberghs following the kidnapping of their baby. In "The Corner Newsboy," Velasco wrote about young men selling newspapers on street corners. Other topics included Alaska. "Silver Hours" was about evenings there, and "Outlook" described his voyage to an Alaskan port. As in earlier periods, he wrote a variety of poems about romance. In "To You," he compared rays of sunshine to the charms of a lover. "Sweetheart" was about seduction. In "There is the Moon Again," he wrote about lovers exchanging secrets in nighttime trysts. "Regret" was about separation, as was "Tears," which bemoaned the end of a romance. Velasco also wrote about individual women. "Ella Fetters," "To Helen," "To Ruby," "A Poem for Jean," "To a Girl with Sweet Smiles" were examples of the genre.[12]

Even though many of his themes seemed analogous to those in his earlier poetry, there were subtle changes. Between 1932 and 1938, at least some of the poems that ostensibly seemed to be on non-ethnic themes nevertheless described the racial separation between Filipinos and Caucasians. "The City" was one such poem, reflecting different levels of meaning. Explicitly, the poem was a commentary about the vices of city life. Velasco criticized the things he saw in cities, including noise, the greed of entrepreneurs, and urban poverty. However, the poem carried another message as well. The last line sarcastically asserted that cities represented "the acme of civilization." The words revealed that the poem was not just about urban vices; it was also a refutation of the notion that modernity represented the highest of human ideals, and it was a bitter social and political commentary on American cities. In "Ambition," Velasco again buried ethnic themes in a poem that seemed to be a commentary about unbridled ambitions. On its surface, the poem seemed only to offer a commonplace criticism of the desire for material wealth. On the other hand, its allusions to a home far from the place where he followed his ambitions suggested comparisons to a Filipino's emigration to the United States, dreams of material gain, and homesickness. As in "The City," Velasco had succeeded in writing about universal themes while, simultaneously, expressing the exilic experiences of Filipinos. Other works similarly reflected Velasco's experiences as a Filipino in the United States. "Camia" seemed to be nothing more than a description of a small, white flower. Yet, as Velasco implied in a note he later scribbled onto the poem, it was an expression of Filipino nationalism. The flower was native to the Philippines, and the poem compared its austere beauty to the ostentatious and artificial tastes of a foreign land, the United States. In "City Shadows," he described the intimidating appearance of tall concrete buildings. Implicitly, however, the poem deplored the insignificance of people in large, modern cities. Consequently, it may have been a commentary about his own sense of insignificance in the United States.[13]

There were other changes. One was that his poetry on romance and women began expressing equivocal feelings. In some works, he exaggerated the personal qualities of individual women; in others, he emphasized the sense of loss. Some poems such as "To Ruby," "Ella Fetters," and "A Poem for Jean" expressed unqualified admiration for individual women. In other works, however, the tone was less optimistic. Poems such as "Tears," "Regret," and "Resolution" expressed remorse and sadness. At other times, contrary themes appeared within a single work. In "To Helen," he described both the joy that comes with dreams about romance and the frustrations that come with the realization that they will never come true. In "A Voice," Velasco described jilted lover tossing memorabilia of an affair into a fire in order to forget his lost love only to find, after destroying them, that she remained embedded in his consciousness. Another poem, "The Rain," also expressed contradictory themes. He observed that, although rain brings rainbows, it also destroys them. The incongruities indicated that Velasco was finding a way to express the contradictions in his own life, and they may have reflected his effort to understand the lessons he had learned from his own relationships with women. Among them was his knowledge, by the beginning of the 1930s, that he could consistently find white women who would accept him as a friend yet refuse him as a lover.[14]

There was another change. In the past, he had employed objects from nature as symbols for human events. By 1935, Velasco had begun taking a different tack. Women had become not merely real-life personalities, but also symbols for social and political themes. In "Modernity," the heavy makeup and smoking habits of a young woman represented the shallowness of contemporary fashions. In "White Petals of Yester-Spring," the falling petals of a flower symbolized human shortsightedness.[15]

Ironically, even as Velasco's poetry increasingly reflected a new willingness to criticize the United States and articulate a nascent, albeit disguised form of Filipino nationalism, American publishers began to recognize his work. Although his stance on race was hardening behind a front of apolitical themes, the period was not only his most prolific, but also one of his most successful. In May of 1936, a New York publisher told him that it had tentatively accepted several poems for its *Contemporary American Men Poets*. In the spring of 1937, Avon House invited Velasco to submit two of his poems, "The Rain" and "City Shadows," for publication in its *Yearbook of Contemporary Poetry*. That same year, Beacon Publications published his work in *Christmas Lyrics of 1937*. Another New York publishing firm, the Paebar Company, informed Velasco of its intention to publish one of his poems. Poetry House, also of New York, informed him of its interest in publishing "Workers" in its *Poetry House Anthology*.[16]

The apparent paradox between Velasco's increasing fame among American publishers even as he was becoming more hardened where racial differences were concerned was not as inexplicable as it may at first have seemed. The two seemingly contrary trends appeared in the work of other Filipino writers of the time. By the 1920s and 1930s, many Filipino writers had begun emulating American aesthetics and celebrating Caucasian racial characteristics. Consequently, the apparent contradiction between Velasco's glorification of white women even as he criticized Americans generally may have been the result of his acculturation to American aesthetics rather than a reflection of his true feelings towards the United States. As such, he exhibited what some Filipino scholars have identified as the paradox of Filipino uncertainty about their own cultural and racial identity.[17]

## III. Work

In yet another venue, there were some changes, some of which were contrary to expectations. If Velasco had hoped that, in the world of Filipinos, he would not have to face the same difficulties that he faced among whites in other contexts, he was mistaken. For some of the most extensive work he did among his own compatriots, in labor activism, proved to be a setting not only for solidarity, but also for conflict. Although ethnic solidarity appeared in Filipinos' unionizing efforts in some instances—such as in those pitting Filipinos against Caucasians, Chinese, and Japanese—there were also conflicts within racial lines.

One source of inter-ethnic tension was race discrimination, which separated Filipinos and other Asians from whites. Whereas whites received decent accommodations aboard the ships that took them to the canneries, Filipinos oftentimes endured abhorrent conditions. Although whites could expect nutritious meals, Filipinos typically received nothing more than seaweed, tea, and boiled rice. At other times, meals consisted of bread without butter and potatoes and onions in broth. Once at the workplace, whites, while performing the same labor as Filipinos, received higher pay. Cannery management also segregated ethnic groups from each other in living quarters and attempted to prevent Filipinos from fraternizing with white women. Race-based distinctions between Filipinos and whites were blatant, and Filipinos were well aware of the racial separation between themselves and whites. The resulting race consciousness among Filipinos was apparent in at least one cannery newspaper, the *Sea Gull News.* In one instance, the *News* protested cannery management's prohibitions against Filipinos mingling with whites during dances and other social activities. In another instance, the newspaper published a cartoon of an Asian cannery worker reflecting whites' racial caricatures of Asian men. Like other Filipino cannery workers, Velasco was well aware of the inter-ethnic tension, as his essay, "Let Us Make Friends," which urged Filipinos and whites to coexist, indicated.[18]

Additional inter-racial conflicts pitted Filipinos against other Asians. Conflicts between Filipinos and the Chinese and the Japanese came from two main sources. One was Chinese and Japanese domination of job assignments in canneries. The other was the result of differences in lifestyle between Filipinos and Chinese. Since the 1880s, Chinese labor contractors had been making agreements with canneries to supply labor for Alaskan canneries. Between the 1880s and the 1920s, the majority of workers were Chinese and Japanese. When Filipinos began coming to the United States in greater numbers in the mid-1920s, they began to compete with both groups for cannery jobs. Moreover, because Chinese and Japanese labor contractors controlled the distribution of jobs, the Filipino newcomers were in an antagonistic position to both the Chinese and the Japanese labor contractors and workers. In 1933, the tension between Filipinos and the other Asian groups became particularly apparent during one of the New Deal's National Recovery Administration (NRA) hearings. When Virgil Duyungan, a Filipino labor leader, appeared before the NRA in San Francisco to support unionization, he implied that his proposed cannery workers' union would not include Chinese or Japanese.[19]

Cultural differences also led to friction. Chinese labor contractors, who were accustomed to a bland diet of broth and rice, provided the same food to the Filipino workers they hired. Meals, often consisting of fish heads, were nearly unpalatable to the Filipinos, leading them to complain about the food and prepare their own. However, they could do so only by buying food at exorbitant prices from the labor contractors, who were often Chinese and Japanese. Canned fruit and vegetables could cost between 35 and 60 cents per can, and the issues about food exacerbated tensions among the Filipinos, Chinese and Japanese.[20]

Although racial and cultural differences led to conflict, their absence did not preclude problems. Filipinos were often at each others' throats because of differences in their regional origins in the Philippines and other contentious issues, such as unionization. Some, including Pio De Cano and his followers, favored the contract labor system whereas others, such as Virgil Duyungan and his supporters, wanted a union.

Duyungan's arrival in Seattle in 1933 inaugurated both the beginnings of successful unionization efforts and some of the most devastating conflicts among Filipinos. On 19 June, Duyungan and others obtained a charter from the American Federation of Labor and established the Cannery Workers and Farm Laborers' Union (C.W.F.L.U.). In 1934, in part because of Duyungan and other Filipinos' efforts at exposing abuses of the contract system, the National Recovery Administration held hearings that ultimately contributed to the system's demise. Subsequently, in May, the C.W.F.L.U. held its first successful strike for wage increases.[21]

Yet, the Filipinos' unionization successes led to conflict. One of the first signs of dissension appeared when John Ayamo, a Filipino attorney who had initially supported Duyungan, accused him of establishing the union for personal economic and political motives. Then, anti-unionist Filipinos, under labor contractor Pio De Cano's leadership, argued that they wanted harmony with the canneries, not a union that would allegedly only exacerbate labor-management relations.[22]

A cooperative working relationship, though, was not the only motive of some Filipinos opposing unionization. According to historian Chris Friday, many of those favoring the contract system were Filipinos who had a stake in the old system. Some, such as Pio De Cano, were labor contractors themselves, who, with the end of the contract system, would suffer a diminution of their income as well as political power once they lost their positions as intermediaries between canneries and laborers. Velasco, who may have been a foreman or a contractor, had something to lose. On 5 January 1934, he wrote to one of the Alaska canneries, one owned by the New England Fish Company, to offer his services as a contractor. On 21 December 1935, he again represented himself as a contractor when he offered to recruit Filipinos for an Egegik, Alaska cannery. The fact that, for a number of years, many Filipinos had been asking Velasco for positions in canneries provided further, circumstantial evidence that he was a contractor. Because of the Chinese and Japanese hold on job assignments, Filipinos such as De Cano—and probably Velasco—who had managed to break into contracting may have jealously guarded their positions, so if Velasco was a contractor, he had an economic incentive for resisting unionization.[23]

Aside from the personal stake that Filipino labor contractors had in the contract labor system, there were additional factors leading some Filipinos to oppose unionization. According to Chris Friday, newly-arrived Filipinos who faced hostility among Americans had few opportunities for employment and felt indebted towards Filipino contractors who provided them with assistance and were often part of a network of acquaintances and family relations. Opposition to unionization, therefore, did not necessarily rest on ideological principles; rather, it meant not upsetting a network of personal and familial ties. For Velasco, opposition to unions was probably due to a variety of reasons, including his desire to stay in strongman De Cano's good graces and his wish to continue enjoying the prestige and political power that might have accrued from his status as a contractor.[24]

After May of 1935, the unionists and their opponents gradually resolved their differences, and the unionization effort gained momentum. In late 1936, however, the nadir of the intra-ethnic factionalism came when a gunman killed Virgil Duyungan, possibly at the instigation of cannery personnel who had mistakenly thought that his death would end the labor movement. Their underestimation of the resolve of the rank-and-file led to a backlash against canneries and labor contractors in favor of unionization, making a cannery workers' union a permanent fixture in the industry.[25]

Divisions among Filipinos grew, however, from more than ideological and political sources, including differences in places of origin in the Philippines. Cliques appeared in organizations like the Pangasinan Association, which limited its membership to those who came from an area in the southern part of the Philippines with its own dialect. An example of the significance of geographic and linguistic differences occurred during Duyungan's unionization efforts in 1933, when unionists tried to convince Filipinos from different parts of the islands to join in a united front against the salmon cannery industry. For Velasco, the regional differences were not merely academic; he himself was involved with the Pangasinan Association throughout much of his stay in the United States and made personal efforts to bridge the geographical loyalties among Filipinos.[26]

Such issues relating to regional origins explained why some unionists favored locals' control of union affairs and others advocated for the A.F.L. international's control. In 1933, Local 18257's first year, there was already a dispute between some A.F.L. locals and the international. The disagreements were over the international's effort to compel locals to follow leaders who lacked knowledge about their affairs. According to economist Gerald Gold, the issues included disputes over locals' control of matters such as taxation; the international allegedly required union members to pay taxes at a rate beyond the means of cannery and agricultural laborers. Another reason that workers wanted local control was because migratory labor involved the performance of different jobs across varied industries and locations and, consequently, eluded the international's efforts to standardize locals' obligations.[27]

For Velasco and other Filipinos, work was full of contentious issues. The arenas of conflict were legion, moreover, because they occurred at myriad levels. They involved inter-ethnic conflicts between Filipinos and whites, Filipinos and Chinese, and Filipinos and Japanese. They also involved controversies pitting Filipinos against other Filipinos for ideological, political, personal, geographical, and economic reasons. For Velasco, therefore, involvement in a venue where he found himself among other Filipinos was no guarantee that he could free his life of conflict any more than when he was among whites. Moreover, relationships with other Filipinos could be just as deadly, as Virgil Duyungan's assassination proved.

## IV. Journalism

Another venue in which Velasco experienced intra-ethnic tensions was in journalism. Between August of 1931 and April of 1932, Velasco had written for the Ellensburg State Normal School's *Campus Crier*, and he was probably the only Filipino among his white colleagues on the paper. Between 1932 and 1938, after leaving Ellensburg, however, his journalistic endeavors were limited to those involving only Filipinos. Like his involvement with other Filipinos in the unionization movement, though, these endeavors did not lead to peace in his life. [28]

One of the first indications of Velasco's increasing racial exclusivity appeared in his brief, intermittent studies at Washington State College in Pullman between the fall of 1931 and the end of 1933. During his stay, he never became involved with any of the college's literary activities. His abstention contrasted sharply with his frenetic work between 1926 and 1927 with white colleagues at the Washington State Normal School in Bellingham.[29]

At first glance, his aloofness from Caucasians in journalistic work in Pullman might seem puzzling. Not only were non-whites on campus, but many were involved in a variety of racially-integrated activities. The American Society of Civil Engineers had at least one Filipino, the varsity boxing team had a Filipino member, and there was a variety of ethnic organizations, including a Filipino Club, a local chapter of the interracial Cosmopolitan Club, and a Chinese Students Club. The Filipino Club, moreover, flourished under the leadership of Dr. Carl Brewster, an adviser who enjoyed widespread respect among Filipino students for decades.[30]

Yet, the presence and participation of non-whites in a variety of extracurricular activities did not mean that there were no limitations on their ability to participate. While Velasco was at Washington State, its student body was overwhelmingly white. There was also no indication that anyone other than Caucasians served in any of the college's literary organizations. Both the Eurodelphian Society and the Quill Club had only white members. The college newspaper, too, had an exclusively white staff. The racial homogeneity may not by itself, though, have explained Velasco's lack of participation; while he was in Bellingham in 1926-1927, he had not only been a member of all-white literary organizations, but had also been a prominent leader. One possibility for Velasco's absence from the literary organizations at the State College, therefore, was that they would not accept him. Another possibility was that Velasco voluntarily abstained from participation. If this was the case, it was consistent with his increasing tendency to limit his activities to those involving only Filipinos. One indication that his stay in Pullman coincided with the new trend appeared in talks about the Philippines that he gave in area churches. Even though his audiences were presumably white, his involvement with them nevertheless represented a departure from the past. In Bellingham, which lacked any significant number of Filipinos, he had rarely discussed the Philippines or his Filipino heritage. In Pullman, in contrast, he seemed to embrace his Filipino heritage and openly discussed cultural issues, among whites.[31]

After Velasco left Pullman and resumed journalistic activities among Filipinos, he found nevertheless that Filipino journalism was another venue in which he faced challenges and conflicts among members of his own race. He enjoyed a greater network of contacts than ever before, but he also found more difficulties. In 1934, he was the editor of a nationally-circulating journal for Filipinos, the *Filipino Student*, and, in 1935, he became editor of Pio De Cano's recently established newspaper, the *Philippine Advocate*, in Seattle. As De Cano's editor, Velasco maintained contacts with Filipinos, including Diosdado Yap, a correspondent based in Washington, D.C., Teddy De Nolasco, also in the District of Columbia, and other Filipinos across the United States. In December of 1937, Juan R. Quijano, an attorney in Washington, D.C., invited Velasco to become a member of the Filipino League for Social Justice, a new organization dedicated to helping Filipinos in the United States and Hawaii. Velasco also communicated with high-ranking Philippine government officials working in the United States. In May of 1935, Velasco's correspondents included Pedro Guevara, a Philippine official, from whom he requested a statement of the Philippine government's stance on Philippine independence. In November, Velasco corresponded with the Bureau of Insular Affairs. In March of 1936, he invited Quintin Paredes, Commissioner from the Philippines, to publish a message from the Philippine government to Filipinos living in the United States.[32]

However extensive Velasco's contacts with other Filipinos were, there were problems, and ironically, journalism, the activity in which Velasco developed many of his ties to Filipinos, was often a source of trouble. Although the *Philippine Advocate* solicited and published news items from Filipinos outside of Seattle, it provided no compensation to its reporters, and this became an issue in November of 1935 when Teddy De Nolasco unsuccessfully requested compensation for a story that he had submitted. Velasco not only refused De Nolasco's request, but completely expunged the item from the paper. He also adopted an overbearing attitude towards other Filipinos. When Diosdado Yap sent an article about the Philippine flag for the Flag Day celebrations of 1935, Velasco, like a teacher correcting errant pupils, told Yap that he had neglected to mention the history of the celebrations.[33]

Other incidents involved Trinidad Rojo, a prominent Filipino leader. In March, 1936, Velasco sarcastically responded to Rojo's criticism of Velasco's journalistic abilities. Velasco referred to Rojo's criticisms as "compliments." He then refused to publish Rojo's story about Vincente Navea, Velasco's colleague on the *Advocate*. Velasco responded to Rojo's criticisms with self-righteousness and suggested that Rojo was self-aggrandizing. Ostensibly taking the high road, Velasco told Rojo that he himself-presumably in contrast to Rojo -adhered to the highest traditions of journalistic impartiality and objectivity. On other occasions during his tenure on the *Philippine Advocate*, Velasco adopted a similarly sarcastic, self-righteous tone. In a letter he ultimately did not send, he responded caustically to a request to cancel a subscription by telling the individual that the newspaper "cannot impose upon unwilling readers the torture of having them read against their will."[34]

Velasco's prickly relationships with other Filipinos continued in January of 1937, when he accused the University of Washington Filipino Alumni Association of falsely claiming credit for the success of the 1936 Commonwealth Celebration honoring the first anniversary of the Manuel Quezon government. In a letter to the president of the association, Velasco claimed that one of its members had falsely told the university's student newspaper that the organization was solely responsible for the event's success. Without mincing words, Velasco asserted that any journalist worthy of respect—presumably himself—must correct "lies." As in his confrontation with Rojo, Velasco apparently felt no compunction about attacking other Filipinos.[35]

Somewhat inconsistently, his persistent references to journalistic integrity were not indicators of his own conduct. His contention that journalistic accuracy had motivated his confrontation with the Filipino Alumni Association, for example, may have been a pretext for a wounded ego. Velasco's own involvement with the 1936 Commonwealth Celebration had roots in the previous year's festivities. Shortly before the 1935 celebration, Velasco had personally invited Clarence Martin, the governor of Washington, to address the celebrants, and he may have enjoyed the prestige that came with personally inviting the state's highest official. In the following year, when he discovered that the Filipino Alumni Association was claiming sole credit for the celebration's success, he may have felt that their claim overshadowed not only the efforts of other Filipinos in the current year, but also his own, recent contributions. It was not necessarily journalistic integrity, therefore, that had compelled Velasco to act.[36]

There were additional reasons to question Velasco's pretensions to journalistic idealism. At some time point during the *Advocate*'s two-year existence, publisher Pio De Cano and Velasco made a deal. De Cano agreed to advance funds to him in exchange for Velasco taking sole responsibility for any liability that might arise from publication of the paper. Because Velasco was often short of funds, the deal probably helped him financially. But it also made him personally indebted to De Cano. Whatever the motives behind the agreement, it belied Velasco's repeated declarations about letting nothing influence his journalistic work except his commitment to public service.[37]

Velasco's willingness to appease De Cano appeared in another way. The occasion was De Cano's decision to cease publication of the paper in 1937. In his written response, Velasco addressed De Cano in a manner contrasting sharply with the scorn he directed towards other Filipinos. Whereas he was sarcastic towards Rojo, belittling towards Yap and De Nolasco, and contemptuous towards the University of Washington Filipino Alumni Association, he was deferential to De Cano. He emphasized that he was aware of the sacrifices De Cano had made to serve his community and implied that public service was the only motive behind De Cano's establishment of the *Advocate*.[38]

Such an assessment cast doubts upon Velasco's own integrity. According to Gerald Gold, De Cano's newspaper was one of the anti-unionists' political tools and was supposed to counteract Virgil Duyungan's efforts to establish a cannery workers union. De Cano and his political allies, who had a stake in the contract system and feared a decline in their influence if a union spoke on behalf of Filipino workers, battled unionization. One plan involved establishing organizations which supposedly were to work for laborers' interests but which, in fact, opposed the union. They were the Filipino Laborers Protective Association and the City Employees Association. Another part of De Cano's plan involved establishing a newspaper, which was where Velasco came in. In 1934, De Cano's founding of the *Philippine Advocate* in order to counter the establishment of a union led him to recruit Velasco as his editor and to use the paper as the means for disseminating anti-union propaganda. Moreover, he did so by appealing to Filipino nationalism. For example, he told Filipinos that subscribing to his newspaper was a patriotic act. In May of 1935, De Cano went a step further by enlisting the aid of Filipinos who controlled cannery job assignments. On the 28th, he told his Filipino foremen to do "anything" they could "toward promoting the circulation of the paper" and that he would consider their efforts "a personal favor."[39]

A further indication of Velasco's involvement with De Cano's anti-union schemes appeared in Velasco's association with the *Advocate*'s editorial staff. According to Gold, Vincente Navea, De Cano's business manager and Velasco's colleague on the *Advocate*, was a sales and collection representative of the Pacific Outfitting Company. Navea, like De Cano and Velasco, may thus have had a personal stake in the continuation of the contract labor system. The company sold clothing and other articles to Filipino cannery workers and perhaps participated in the contract system's abuses. Prior to the establishment of a cannery workers union in 1933, the company may have been one of the firms that required cannery job-seekers to purchase goods as a prerequisite to working. At the least, as De Cano's editor and Navea's ally, Velasco was part of a political machine favoring the status quo and opposing reforms.[40]

Velasco's involvement with De Cano and the unionization controversy was problematic in other ways as well. Although both unionists and anti-unionists claimed the high ground, it was apparent that neither had clean hands. In May of 1935, the president of the Maritime Federation held a hearing and concluded that Duyungan and his union supporters and De Cano and the Protective Association were all exploiting cannery workers. As editor of the *Advocate*, Velasco apparently had no qualms about serving as one of De Cano's minions.[41]

There was, however, another side to Velasco's involvement with De Cano and the *Philippine Advocate*. Even if Velasco was one of De Cano's political cronies, he may have been so at least partly out of sincere motives. It was not only those who challenged Velasco, but also De Cano himself, who received an earful of Velasco's pedantic statements about upholding journalistic ideals. In April of 1937, Velasco told De Cano that he edited "a clean newspaper, living up to the highest standard of journalism, namely, presenting the news without bias and telling the truth." He stated further that, "when a newspaper becomes an organ of an individual or a group, it cannot render the fullest service that the community demands." His statements may have struck De Cano as being either disingenuous or completely naive, for De Cano's 28 May 1935 letter to his foremen, indicating that he expected them to use their influence over the rank-and-file to get them to subscribe to the paper and, presumably, heed its anti-union messages, clearly indicated the power De Cano wielded and his intention of using the paper as a political tool for his anti-union agenda. Yet, even if Velasco's statement contradicted the realities, he may have been useful to De Cano. If Velasco was indeed naive enough to believe that the paper represented nothing more than an altruistic effort to serve Filipino readers, then De Cano may have found his pretensions to idealism useful for masking the newspaper's political purposes. In all probability, Velasco's motives for his alliance with De Cano represented a mixture of idealism—which had been apparent in other times in his life as well—and political ambition.[42]

Velasco's involvement with De Cano hinted at the existence of tensions that were present among Filipinos in other ways, too. Velasco confided in his long-time colleague and friend Marco Aquino about their colleague, Trinidad Rojo, exchanging snide comments behind his back. In an exchange of letters about Rojo in July of 1936, for example, Aquino referred to Rojo as an "old fool" who was a "nut and out of his head." On 4 November, Llamas Rosario of the New York-based Filipino Students Christian Movement in America invited Velasco to manage the inaugural issue of a new, nationally-circulating journal for Filipinos. Rosario's offer to Velasco was not without a catch, however: Velasco was to finance publication of the first volume. Velasco apparently never accepted Rosario's offer or in any other way maintained contact with him. Even Velasco's friendship with Marco Aquino posed challenges because, like other Filipino friends and acquaintances in the past, Aquino made requests that may have been difficult for Velasco to honor. On 18 August 1937, for example, Aquino asked Velasco for a personal loan. Because Velasco, like other Filipinos, depended largely on a small income from manual labor, making loans to others was probably a practical impossibility. Thus, Velasco's relationships with other Filipinos in a variety of settings, including cannery work, journalism, and personal relations, were no more free of contentious issues than were his relations with whites.[43]

## V. Family

Insofar as Velasco sought relief from the rigors of public life through family relationships, he was again disappointed. In this venue, as in others, relations among Filipinos provided no trouble-free haven but additional difficulties. In some respects, contact with his family in the Philippines provided Velasco with solace. During the thirties, his primary contact was his sister Leonor, who apprised him of things such as the health of his grandmother and reminded him that his family welcomed news about him. She also kept him apprised of the sisters' efforts to pursue education, such as their sister Anuncion's efforts to begin a pre-law course at the Philippines' Far Eastern University and, early in the spring of 1937, of her own plans to graduate with an Associate's degree later that year. She described the sisters' other activities, such as their Christmas celebrations and plans for the Eucharist. She kept him informed of her contact with other family members in the United States, including their brother Antonio and their uncle Frederico, and when she received copies of the *Philippine Advocate* from him, she was elated. She also assured Velasco that his friends, such as Marco Aquino, would be welcome at their home in the Philippines. When she learned of Velasco's affair with Delphine Brooks, she told him that the family would welcome her as another member of the household. Velasco's contact with his family also meant that he received holiday greetings and gifts. In late 1935, for example, his sister told him that she was going to send him a Christmas card and, a few months later, she sent him a photograph of herself and their sister Anuncion. Velasco, in turn, reciprocated his sister's efforts by telling her of his activities.[44]

Yet, whatever comfort contact with family brought, it also meant involvement with their problems. At times, Leonor scolded him for not writing more often. In May of 1936, she reminded him of his family's expectations of hearing from him on a regular basis. In June, she criticized him for not replying to the letter she had sent to him several days earlier. In December, she accused him of forgetting her. In other ways, too, she imposed on him. When she had difficulty reaching other members of his family in the United States, she depended on him for information. In December of 1935, as in other instances, she asked him for information about Antonio. Even though she expressed her appreciation to Velasco for receiving copies of the *Philippine Advocate*, she simultaneously reminded him that she wanted him to send copies to her more often. Between 1935 and 1937, she often reminded him of their grandmother's poor health. She also expected him to send gifts—a sweater, for example. Moreover, when she described the efforts she and her sisters were making to further their education, it was not always good news that she conveyed. On 21 June 1936, when she told him that Anuncion was thinking of a career in the legal profession and that their sister Mercedes was nearly finished with high school, she reminded him that their future was nevertheless uncertain because they had little money. Nearly two years later, she was again reminding him of the family's financial hardships by telling him that Anuncion and Mercedes had decided to stay home until she could finish her education.[45]

Between 1932 and 1938, Velasco's retreat from the world of whites continued the trend he had begun over the previous several years. By the beginning of 1932, he had begun limiting his involvement with whites to a narrow realm, including primarily his involvement with Delphine Brooks and the poetry he published in several anthologies. Yet, in contrast to his years in Bellingham, in which he seemed to keep a strict demarcation between his involvement with whites and that with Filipinos, by 1932, he was moving more into the Filipino world, and racial and cultural themes often characterized his work. The hardening of his racial views did not provide him with peace, however. If he had expected that retreat into a world comprised only of Filipinos would shield him from conflict, he learned that this was not always the case.

# 6

# World War Two (1939 to 1947)

In some ways, the war years reflected continuities from Velasco's previous experience in the United States. There were few significant changes in his private life, including his relationships with whites generally and with his family. In his public life, however, there were notable changes, especially in his new willingness to engage in *realpolitik*.

## I. Continuities

During the war years, there were continuities in Velasco's personal life. They were apparent in his sincere appreciation of Euro-American culture, his persisting ambivalence towards whites in other respects, and in his relationships with friends and family.

One indication of Velasco's sincere appreciation for American culture appeared in his continuing patronage of Euro-American cultural events. He attended a wide range of events, including musical performances, operas, and ballets. Such patronage was nothing new. During his first years in Seattle, he frequently went to American movies and, during the 1930s, enjoyed Euro-American entertainment even when racial hostility against Filipinos was so strong that public establishments sometimes denied them admission. Moreover, Velasco was not unique among Filipinos in his taste for American entertainment. Many Filipinos appreciated American culture at least partly because they had internalized what one scholar has referred to as "white aesthetics," which, among other things, presumed that European and American things were superior to those of Filipino origin. One example was manufactured products. There was an assumption that Filipino products were inferior to "stateside" products, American-made goods. The appreciation for European and American things even led to the idea that praising Filipino things was "anti-American."[1]

Velasco's continuing attraction towards Euro-American culture also appeared in his social contact with white women, as in the spring of 1942, when his dinner companions included two white females. Several months later, white women again accompanied him to a dinner and a lecture. At other times that year, he socialized with white women in a pattern of behavior that he had followed since he had first arrived in Seattle in 1924.[2]

Ironically, Velasco's appreciation for Americans and their culture came with another legacy from his earlier years: the generally mixed feelings he harbored towards both. There was no evidence, for instance, even when Filipinos and whites were supposed to be allies in a war against tyranny, that he ever had a white male as a friend. Except for white women, Velasco's companions remained those of his own race. Among his most frequent friends and associates were Filipinos, including Ray Anchetta, Felix Zamora, and Zoilo Paragas. When he went to dances, it was often with members of Filipino groups, such as the Bataan and Corregidor Bowling Association. The places he went also indicated that he limited his social circle to Filipinos. When he headed to events such as press club meetings and dances, they were often at the Rizal Club, a venue whose namesake was the martyred Filipino hero, Jose Rizal. Other places, such as the Golden Pheasant, were in Seattle's Chinatown, and he seldom ventured outside of the area except for the University of Washington, which he did possibly in part because prejudice against Filipinos abated during the Second World War due to joint American-Filipino efforts against the Japanese in the Pacific War.[3]

After the war, again with the exception of white women, Velasco continued to limit his social circle to Filipinos. His engagement books were filled with plans to attend social events, including birthday celebrations, christenings, anniversaries, and dances with other Filipinos. One short period not long after the end of the war provided an example. In early September of 1946, he went to the Puyallup Fair with Felix Zamora. About two weeks later, he attended a friend's birthday celebration. The following day, he planned to go to another birthday party. Several days later, he went to a christening and, the next day, a wedding anniversary. The following week was equally busy. For the remainder of the year, his calendar was filled with similar social engagements with Filipinos.[4]

The legacy of mixed feelings Velasco had towards whites was also evident in his continuing participation in Filipino nationalistic events and his circle of professional contacts. Among the events and organizations he patronized were the Commonwealth Banquet in honor of the Philippines and the University of Washington Filipino Alumni Association's meetings, dances, and social gatherings, and his professional contacts were limited to Filipinos, including various representatives of the Philippine government[5]

Another continuity from the past lay in his relationships with friends and family. His associations with them, such as with his brother Tonieng, brought him some comfort. Tonieng, who was farming in California, corresponded with him about various subjects such as mutual acquaintances Zoilo Paragas and Mike Padua, work in Alaska, Velasco's efforts to pursue his education, the draft, and Tonieng's agreement to give Velasco financial help. Velasco also kept in touch with his brothers Pete and Joe.[6]

As in the past, however, contact with friends and others close to him also brought stress. Even though Tonieng offered to help Velasco, he also asked for favors. For one three-month long period in 1944, he repeatedly asked Velasco to send him some personal belongings that he had left behind in Seattle. As in the past, Velasco felt obliged to provide information about his siblings to family in the Philippines, and he had to listen to Tonieng's complaints about work on his farm, lost profits, and losing workers to the war effort. Velasco's brother Pete, too, called upon him for favors, such as helping him in his presidential election campaign in the Pangasinan Association. However, Pete did not respond in kind, as when Velasco asked him, then a member of another Filipino benevolent society, the Asingan Association, for financial aid from its treasury. Pete refused the request, saying that the organization could not help Velasco because he was not a member.[7]

Velasco's patronage of Euro-American cultural events, his relationships with white women, and his continuing, sometimes tension-filled relationships with friends and family represented continuities. As in the past, Velasco engaged in conduct that originated in the pre-World War II period but which persisted throughout the war years.

## II. Milestones

In his public life, in contrast to his private life, there were major changes. It was here that a new willingness to engage in shady deals and underhanded conduct marked a turning point from his previous experience in the United States. Whereas in his private life, inconsistencies were typically the result of genuine ambivalence, in his public life, they were often due to his conscious willingness to use various means to accomplish ulterior goals, particularly in his roles as a cannery labor activist and as a journalist.

It was in his relationship to the salmon canning industry that Velasco publicly expressed one set of goals while he sought to achieve ulterior ones. During the war years, he responded to the industry's pleas for help in retaining Filipino laborers by appealing to widespread, pro-war sentiments. Yet, his words, ostensibly advocating for the Americans, were, in reality, expressing support for the United States primarily in order to maneuver himself and his union, Local 7 of the C.W.F.L.U., into positions of influence vis a vis the cannery industry and rank-and-file laborers.

Velasco and the local had an unprecedented opportunity to gain influence with the cannery industry because it was facing labor shortages, a fact that led it to court Local 7, its erstwhile adversary, for help in retaining Filipino workers. On 31 October 1942, a representative of the Astoria & Puget Sound Canning Company asked Velasco for help in convincing Filipino laborers to stay at cannery work rather than join the armed forces or the war industry. He told Velasco that "government officials" preferred that Filipinos work in the canneries rather than serve in the army or navy and that the company would help draftees secure deferments. Velasco responded to the industry's pleas by publishing items in his newspaper, the *Filipino Forum*, to encourage Filipinos to stay at their cannery jobs. A winter, 1942 article, for example, told readers how to request draft deferments so that they could work in cannery jobs during the 1943 canning season.[8]

Velasco's response to the industry's pleas was not due to any real desire to help, however. It was probably due, rather, to the practical benefits that Local 7 could gain. The war years created an opportunity for cannery workers to gain the industry's respect. After the United States declared war in December of 1941, the salmon canneries became highly dependent upon leaders like Velasco who had influence among Filipino laborers because they had lost large numbers of their workers. By the end of the war in 1945, almost sixteen million men, including thousands of Filipinos, had joined the armed forces, and the impact upon the labor pool for cannery work was dramatic. In the first summer after the United States entered the war, Local 7 lost between five and six hundred laborers. By 1943, the pool of approximately 3,000 men who had worked in canneries prior to the 1942 season had decreased 20 percent, and those with experience had fallen by about 50 percent. Moreover, not only the armed services, but also the defense industry, claimed many Filipinos, who sought better jobs in shipyards and aviation plants. By 1945, the canneries' labor shortage was so severe that the industry recruited laborers from California farms and other parts of the country, even paying their transportation costs to Alaska for summer work. Still, in spite of all the efforts that both the union and the industry made, filling all of the canneries' labor needs was a near impossibility.[9]

Velasco helped the industry because, by maneuvering himself and the union into a position as the liaison between it and Filipino laborers, he increased both the union's and his own prestige and influence. Cannery owners and management badly needed workers, and the union and its leaders—including Velasco—were in a position to supply them. Because of ubiquitous Filipino support for the American war effort, Velasco was able to appeal to patriotic ideals in order to gain the trust of the rank-and-file and convince laborers to stay at their cannery jobs. The results spoke for themselves. On 15 December 1942, Local 7 members raised $48,050 for war bonds. By the end of the war, the union had raised $185,000. The effort, as Velasco had probably foreseen, was successful at least partly because many Filipinos may have wanted to gain whites' acceptance, and supporting the American war effort, unifying against the Japanese, and repeating racist slogans such as "beat the Japs" provided them with the opportunity to demonstrate their loyalty. By tapping into and manipulating his fellow Filipinos' longing for acceptance, Velasco was able to use the wartime labor shortage to raise the union's prestige and influence with both the cannery industry and the rank and file laborers.[10]

Velasco's motives, possibly to tap into wartime sentiments to increase the standing of the union—and of himself as well—among Filipinos marked a milestone in his experience in the United States. His manipulation of patriotic rhetoric and his rapprochement with the cannery industry represented mainly practical efforts to put Local 7 into a stronger bargaining position with management and owners. He was beginning to learn how to say one thing while pursuing alternative goals.

His use of the war as an opportunity to pursue hidden agendas also began to appear in his work as a journalist. In his own newspaper, the *Filipino Forum,* he asserted that supporting the Americans required action, that focusing on private matters in a time of war was hypocritical, and that whites and Filipinos needed to fight a common enemy, the Japanese, in a joint effort to protect world freedom against tyranny. He also argued that whites were dying alongside Filipinos because both groups suffered terribly under the Japanese occupation. He wrote about a Filipino soldier who martyred himself rather than lower the Philippine flag under Japanese orders. He described the heroic resistance of other Filipinos. He also publicized events, such as the Washington state supreme court chief justice's attendance at a Rizal Day celebration as its guest of honor, to suggest that Filipinos and whites were casting aside the racial animosities of the past; "This is no time to cry over the proverbial spilt milk," he reprimanded his readers. He lauded General Douglas MacArthur's return to the Philippines, and, in a story about cooperation between the Philippines and the United States in resisting the Japanese, he made Filipinos and Americans seem like equal partners in the Pacific War. Velasco seemed to have become one of the many Filipinos who saw the war as an opportunity to show off his patriotism to the United States.[11]

Yet, like the aid he gave to the salmon canning industry, Velasco's support for the United States was due to a mixture of sincere motives and practical considerations. He was sincere to the extent that, like most Filipinos, he felt animosity towards the Japanese because of their invasion and occupation of the Philippines. Supporting any country, including the United States, which opposed the Japanese, was tantamount to patriotism towards the Filipino people. The logic that Velasco may have followed appeared in a leaflet in which the author—who may have been Velasco himself—juxtaposed the lyrics of two national anthems: "God Bless America" and "Philippines My Philippines," suggesting that helping the one meant loyalty to the other. Additionally, Velasco's praise for the United States against the Japanese may have been partly the result of a history of contentious relationships between Filipinos and Japanese because of their competition for jobs in Alaskan canneries, a fact that persisted until the eve of war.[12]

However, devotion to the United States was probably not the impetus behind Velasco's expression of support for the Americans. His real loyalties lay with the Philippines, not with the United States. His exhortations on behalf of the United States were probably the result of his knowledge that American victory would end Japanese rule. He certainly was not unique in this respect. Even exiled Philippine President Manuel Quezon engaged in it when he asked Pio De Cano to encourage his compatriots to purchase war bonds and contribute to the American war effort because, he publicly announced, "in the victory of the United States and the United Nations lies the only hope of our beloved country." Quezon urged Filipinos to support the United States not necessarily because of a personal desire to aid the Americans in the Pacific War, but because of his belief that American victory could lead to his real goals: ouster of the Japanese and the establishment of an independent Philippines. Trinidad Rojo also appreciated the connection between supporting Americans and gaining benefits for Filipinos both in the Philippines and in the United States. On 16 August 1944, Rojo, who was then president of Local 7, encouraged Filipinos to purchase American war bonds because, he argued, if the United States could retake the Philippines by early 1945, Filipino men could return to work in Alaskan canneries for the summer canning season. Presumably, from Rojo's perspective, supporting America could lead to specific benefits for Filipinos: freeing the Philippines from Japanese rule; helping Filipinos in the United States gain jobs in Alaskan canneries; increasing the number of Filipino workers in the C.W.F.L.U., and, consequently, raising the union's bargaining position in negotiations with the cannery industry; and, by augmenting the number and influence of Filipinos in the union, squeezing out the influence of other ethnic groups, such as the Chinese, Koreans, Mexicans, and native Alaskans, who had competed for jobs in the past.[13]

If Velasco saw aiding the United States as an opportunity to pursue other goals, he was thus not the only one to do so. Nor was World War II unique in providing Filipinos with the chance to pursue dual agendas, one of which—Filipino nationalism—may have even been contrary to stated goals. In the late 1890s, for example, Emilio Aguinaldo had initially cooperated with the United States against the Spanish because of his belief that the Americans would oust Spain from the Philippines. Then, as during the Second World War, Filipino patriots' sought mainly an independent Philippines.[14]

That Velasco used pro-American rhetoric to help Filipinos was evident also in the mixed messages he sent out. His 24 December 1942 *Filipino Forum* article about the Rizal Day celebrations bringing whites and Filipinos together was one such example. Dr. Jose Rizal, whom the Spanish executed in 1898, remained a symbol of resistance not only against Spanish hegemony, but also against colonialism generally, including that of the Americans. The mere fact that Velasco continued his participation in Rizal Day events with all their anti-colonial, anti-American overtones, therefore, cast doubt upon the fervor of his pro-American rhetoric.[15]

Another factor raising doubts about Velasco's sincerity when he called for friendship between Filipinos and Americans lay in the fact that he rarely, if ever, included whites among his newspaper's audience. He published stories of interest only to Filipinos; he assumed that his readers, even during a time supposedly representing unity between Filipinos and whites, did not include whites. Among the items he published were those about Filipino social events such as birthday celebrations, children's parties, activities of the University of Washington Filipino Alumni Association, wedding anniversaries, private social gatherings, happenings in the Philippines, a union meeting, changes in employment among Filipinos, Filipino efforts to organize an agricultural union, Filipino resistance to the Japanese in the Pacific, and the heroism of Filipina nurses. Velasco seemed to take it for granted that the people to whom he spoke and the ones who listened were not white.[16]

A final reason why Velasco's appeals to help the United States were probably not evidence of sincere affection was his continuing awareness of American racism. He could not see whites in an idealized light nor ignore their racism, which was painfully evident in spite of the notion that Americans were guardians of world freedom. In the summer of 1943 in Los Angeles's "zoot suit riots," white United States Navy personnel rioted and beat up Mexican males, and white policemen arrested the Mexican victims, instead of the perpetrators, even as 300,000 Mexican Americans served in American uniform around the world. Throughout the war, many white tavern and restaurant owners refused to serve black enlisted men even though owners typically provided full service to Axis prisoners of war. Even as Americans denounced Hitler's racial pogroms, 120,000 men, women, and children of Japanese descent remained under armed guard in desolate concentration camps scattered across the American West after losing most or all of their worldly belongings—as Jews had done in Nazi Germany. Race riots in Harlem and Detroit took the lives of American blacks and, in Seattle, white landlords routinely refused to give African Americans places to live and bus drivers called them "niggers." In 1943 in Detroit, half the white female workers at the US. Rubber Company walked off the job in a "hate strike" when African American women began operating machinery in their plant.[17]

Velasco was well aware, moreover, of racism affecting his own life as well as those close to him. On 22 October 1942, one of the most poignant indications of his knowledge of persistent American bigotry appeared when his brother Tonieng told him, "This country is not fair at all any way to dark people." Racism was a familiar topic to Velasco, and he and his most intimate confidants could neither avoid nor forget it. On 12 September 1943, in a speech about race relations that Velasco gave before the Bahai Society of Seattle, he described racism in the United States as "a visible lack of tolerance" that was "all around us." Not stopping there, he asserted, "in this very country, so fittingly called the melting pot of the races, incidents of race prejudice are not uncommon, and by their very familiarity and commonness to the average reader . . . [have] . . . lost a portion of its significance." His awareness may have led even to exploring new choices about the women with whom he socialized. At the beginning of 1944, for the first time since he had broken up with Sixta Aquino eighteen years previously, Velasco reversed a two-decades long trend by seeking the company of a Filipina.[18]

The inconsistency between ideals about American freedoms and the persistent realities of American racism even found its way into Velasco's newspaper, although possibly unintentionally. The 9 April 1943 issue of the *Filipino Forum*, which described Filipinos' ability to purchase real property in spite of a 1920 alien land law, implicitly reminded its readers that whites used American courts to discriminate against non-whites. Even stories supposedly indicating equality between Filipinos and whites clumsily revealed the racism that divided the two groups. The February, 1945 issue of the *Filipino Forum* revealed the persistence of segregation in a story about Filipinas selling United States war bonds. Velasco told his readers that the Women's Division of the King County War Finance Committee had acknowledged that the Filipino women of Seattle were among the most successful Filipinas selling war bonds. Although the story indicated how successful the Filipino women were, it also implicitly showed that their efforts were segregated from those of white women. Another story, describing the formation of the Philippine Relief Club, exposed a similar irony.

Stories that highlighted racial egalitarianism revealed instead a country where even patriotic acts were based on white supremacy.[19]

Velasco's exhortations to Filipinos to support the Americans reflected sophisticated efforts to tap into popular, pro-American sentiments that were widespread among Filipinos and thereby manipulate patriotic rhetoric to advance Filipino nationalism. Although he genuinely wanted the Americans to beat the Japanese, his desire, like that of other Filipinos, was less an expression of patriotism to the United States than a wish for Philippine independence and freedom from American control.

It was perhaps Velasco's growing knowledge that he could say one thing while doing something else that led him further down the path towards the uses of *realpolitik*. Whereas his manipulation of wartime rhetoric may have been largely the result of a desire to help Filipinos, in union activities, his pursuit of ulterior goals carried more sordid implications and marked a turning point in his experiences in the United States. It was in this context that he began to transition from one who had nearly always—at least in public life if not necessarily in private—acted on behalf of his kinsmen to one who became willing to act against them; he began to place his own interests ahead of others in a conscious effort to gain personal influence and power.

One example of the transition appeared in Velasco's seemingly altruistic efforts on behalf of other Filipinos. On 8 May 1943, he asked the Resident Commissioner of the Philippines to help secure a middle-aged Filipino's release from military service by explaining that he, a man in his late 30s, was of "an advanced age" and in ill health. Velasco's words indicated that he was trying to help a fellow Filipino in need. However, another part of the same letter suggested a less flattering motive. Velasco stated, "If he is released, we could use him in the Alaska salmon industry." It was thus not simply Villalobos's welfare that was at stake, but also the fact that his release from military service might give Local 7 another foreman. For Velasco personally, the intervention may also have held other, benefits, such as gaining Villalobos as a political ally. Villalobos's service in the union could be helpful, too, because, as Velasco explained, "we [Local 7] have a contractual agreement [with the cannery industry] to supply the necessary labor." Because the salmon cannery industry had lost two thirds of its work force between 1941 and 1943, laborers, in particular experienced ones like Villalobos, were valuable commodities to both the industry and to Local 7: to the industry, he represented much-needed but all-too-scarce, experienced labor; to Local 7, he could be an important bargaining chip in its negotiations with the industry.[20]

Another of Velasco's seemingly altruistic efforts may have similarly been the result of ulterior motives. On 21 August 1946, Velasco, then treasurer of Local 7, asked Narciso Ramos of the Philippine Embassy in Washington, D.C. to send application forms for documenting the citizenship status of Local 7 members to guarantee individual Filipinos the privileges and protections of the Philippine government. Even though Velasco's willingness to obtain and distribute the forms to Filipino laborers seemed to be a public service, it might have been a political ploy. In his letter, Velasco specifically requested that Ramos send the forms directly to him at Local 7. The fact that Velasco wanted the forms indicated that simply making them available to all Filipinos in Seattle was not necessarily his intent. Probably, it would have been easier if he had arranged for the Filipino Community of Seattle, rather than Local 7, to distribute them, since it was the umbrella organization for a host of Filipino associations and reached significantly more Filipinos than did a single union local. The fact that Velasco was adamant about Local 7 distributing them, rather than other groups like the Filipino Community, suggested that effective distribution may not have been his goal. His wish that the forms come directly to him rather than to anyone else in Local 7 suggested, moreover, that he wanted to use them as a means of augmenting his own influence not only within the Filipino community at-large, but also possibly within the union.[21]

There were other indications that Velasco's purpose was something other than simply providing a service to Seattle's Filipino residents. Velasco implied to Ramos that no one besides himself could adequately serve as the conduit between the Philippine government and individual Filipinos for distribution of the forms. He explained, "I am constantly in contact with these questions and requests for assistance." Velasco justified his request that Ramos send the forms directly to the Local 7 office by stating, "Matters would be greatly expedited if we had these forms in our office." Further evidence that Velasco had a hidden political agenda appeared in a 19 September 1946 letter from the Philippine Embassy in which Jose F. Imperial, Acting Consul General, replied to Velasco's request for the forms, indicating that the embassy was reluctant about delegating distribution of the forms to a single private, non-governmental organization because doing so was the responsibility of the Philippine Consular Office in San Francisco. Not satisfied with the Consul General's denial of his request, Velasco made another effort but, instead of contacting Imperial, the official who had denied his original request, he approached Narciso Ramos, who served in the same office as Imperial. In a tone reflecting his frustration, however specious or disingenuous it may have been, over not having received the forms, Velasco asked Ramos to "immediately forward" the forms "to this office." He explained the urgent tone of his letter by stating, "[t]his delay is costing many of our members their means of livelihood."[22]

The manner in which Velasco handled the affair with the forms indicated the extent to which he had become versed in *realpolitik*, even at the expense of other Filipinos. His actions showed that he was not forthright in his dealings with the Philippine Embassy and that he had pursued the matter for reasons in addition to—or other than—the best interests of the Local 7 membership. One indication was the apparent inconsistency between Velasco's awareness of the procedures to follow in obtaining the forms and the motives that led him to contravene them. It was unclear, for example, why Velasco did not address his second request to J.C. Dionisio, the Philippine government official to whom Imperial had specifically referred Velasco for any future communication. Presumably, Velasco had received Imperial's denial of 19 September by the time he wrote the second request to Ramos a week later. The fact that Velasco made the second request after receiving Ramos's denial and that he did so to someone other than the person to whom Ramos specifically referred him indicated one of two things: the unlikely possibility that he was not yet aware of Imperial's denial; or a conscious, purposeful circumvention of a process which Velasco believed would lead to another denial. Possibly, Velasco was willing to deceive members of his own government in order to gain political leverage for Local 7. Whatever his motives, he learned that circumvention of established processes could lead to success. On 2 October, J.C. Dionisio—ironically, the man to whom Imperial had first referred Velasco and whom Velasco had tried to avoid —informed him that he was sending one hundred copies.[23]

The controversy did not cease even after Dionisio had sent Velasco the forms. On 8 October, Velasco asked Dionisio for more. Again, he expressed indignation, and again the circumstances suggested that he may have feigned his frustration. "Our Filipino citizens here have been rather disappointed with the slowness of official action," he stated, and he complained that he "had to make a long distance telephone call to your office to remind you of this request." As in his letters to Ramos, he was careful to explain the urgency of his requests by asserting that Local 7 was providing the service as "a voluntary job of helping our countrymen fill out these forms." Circumstantial evidence also indicated that Velasco may have wanted to monopolize the distribution of the forms in order to keep both his allies and adversaries in check. Any Filipino who needed them would have to apply to Local 7 and Velasco, both of whom controlled access to the forms.[24]

There was another clue that Velasco's efforts to make Local 7 the liaison between the Philippine government and the mass of Filipinos were politically expedient and not simply altruistic: the potential income that the applications could generate. According to Dionisio's letter of 8 October 1944, there was a $2 fee for processing the applications and issuing identity cards. On 23 November, however, rather than contacting Dionisio again, Velasco sought someone different in the San Francisco Consulate General's office, Manuel Adeva, and disingenuously inquired whether the application fee was $5. Contrary to Dionisio's explicit words to Velasco in his 8 October letter, which identified the fee as $2, Velasco told Adeva, who served in the same office as Dionisio, that the "proper instructions [had not been] forwarded." Velasco had either forgotten Dionisio's explicit instructions about the amount or was trying to justify collecting a higher fee by feigning ignorance about the lower figure and by contacting someone other than Dionisio, who had specified the amount as being $2. The reply Velasco received confirmed the earlier instructions. On 2 December, Roberto Regala, Consul General in San Francisco, sent Velasco a telegram stating unequivocally that the fee was $2. As if anticipating suspicions about collecting excess money for a windfall, Velasco stated in his letter of 23 November to Adeva that he had been collecting $2. Ironically, Velasco's letter indicated knowledge of the $2 fee even as he asked what it was. His query, asserting that he had been collecting $2, implicitly revealed that he had probably been aware of Dionisio's instructions all along.[25]

If Velasco had succeeded in becoming the conduit through which the Philippine government distributed the citizenship identification applications and forms and charging $5, he may have been the one who collected the excess fees. Moreover, if he had collected monies exceeding the official fee by $3 for each form he distributed and collected, he would have realized a windfall of several hundred dollars between the time he received the first batch of one hundred forms in early October and the time he received Regala's telegram on 2 December, and he would have done so from rank-and-file members who had put him into the treasurer's office to represent their interests. Sordid motives may have been behind Velasco's efforts because of the ruthless politics of the time. As the unionization movement of the 1930s and the elections of the early 1940s had made clear, there was bitter factionalism among Filipinos within Local 7 based on a seemingly endless array of reasons. Gaining control over vital processes, therefore, would have been an effective weapon in the bitter political battles that Velasco and other Filipinos waged against each other.[26]

It was, however, in union election campaigns that Velasco's use of *realpolitik* was particularly apparent. The 1941 campaign, for example, showed Velasco's capacity for ruthless politics against his own people. In Zoilo Paragas's pursuit of the presidency of Local 7 against Vincente Navea, Velasco sided with Paragas. In doing so, Velasco broke away from Navea, who had formerly been his ally while fighting the unionization movement of 1935-1937. Nor was it enough for Velasco simply to betray his former friend and ally. He may have even become actively involved in an effort to smear Navea when Paragas's supporters contacted Velasco to have him distribute defamatory campaign materials. In a note signed only as "Never Mind Who We Are," the authors told Velasco, "Be sure to lambaste Navea" because the "boys must know the dirty crook right now." Moreover, an "open letter" the Paragas faction distributed to "All Cannery Workers" attacked Navea's character. The letter, addressed to rank-and-file members of Local 7, began by stating, "Stop the farce . . . Get rid of Navea and other 'honorary stooges' who are preying on your wages. And elect Zoilo C. Paragas for your next president." The leaflet also resorted to red-baiting by repeatedly referring to Navea as "Comrade Navea" and comparing him to Joseph Stalin. "Navea is as bad as Stalin," it asserted, "for he maneuvers placement of all vacant foremen." As a "dictator," he supposedly resembled Adolph Hitler as well. The leaflet also accused him of exploiting laborers with increased union dues, and it asserted that it was his misuse of union funds for chop suey dinners that had "made his stomach so big."[27]

Paragas's campaign, with which Velasco was involved, also denigrated incumbent president Trinidad Rojo by publishing defamatory and inaccurate information. For example, it suggested that Rojo disregarded the seniority system in cannery job assignments to Alaska. The accusation was at least partially untrue, for Rojo had actually refused the request of at least two of his own cousins for jobs because of their lack of seniority. Paragas's supporters also attacked

Rojo by stating that "he is nothing but a rubber stamp of . . . Navea." Yet, ironically, it was Rojo himself who had tried to mend the factionalism that had arisen over the dues controversy the previous year.[28]

Velasco's involvement in intra-ethnic factionalism continued into another election campaign two years later. In 1944, Velasco, who had been Local 7's Chief Clerk since 26 January, ran against two other Filipinos for the treasurer's office, and his unsavory methods appeared in comments he shared with a political ally, Prudencio Mori. Velasco's campaign, like Paragas's run for the presidency in 1941, employed smear tactics in which he cast aspersions upon his rivals both in private and in public. On 31 July 1944, Velasco described Cardona to Mori as someone lacking courage, Navea as holding a "dumb-like silence in the face of . . . important issues," and his other rival, Johnny Lucero, as having an "inferiority complex" and a "tendency to yield almost blindly to the dictates of Communist-like dictators." Nor did Velasco limit his disparagement of his two political opponents to private confidences. His campaign leaflet described Cardona as a "non-entity" and Lucero as an "incompetent . . . flop . . . who should be expelled" from Local 7. Furthermore, the leaflet asserted, Lucero was a "blind follower" of others above whose influence he "cannot rise."[29]

Even his rivals' positive attributes became deficits as far as Velasco was concerned. On 31 July 1944, he had admitted to Mori that both Lucero and Cardona were "honest." In his campaign leaflet, however, Velasco stated that "honesty . . . is not enough." "Character . . . integrity, and traits of leadership," he asserted, were the most important traits of the treasurer. He explained further that the treasurer must not be a "man who submits blindly to the dictates of people who are subversive and un-American in their activities." On 31 July, he described the undesirable candidate to Mori as a "yes-man," "a man who has no respect for scholarship," "a man without a conviction of his own," and one who "cannot appreciate the services of research." Predictably, Velasco extolled his own qualifications. His leaflet described him as an "outstanding journalist," "among the best contemporary writers," having "training in . . . research," and "not afraid to express his firm conviction."[30]

Velasco's tactics were devious, but they were not anomalies in union politics. Even Trinidad Rojo, one of the most respected union leaders, who enjoyed a relatively good reputation, engaged in shady activities in his 1944 campaign for the presidency of Local 7 when he ran against Prudencio Mori. Wishing to get rid of Mori as a rival, he offered to turn over the president's office to him halfway through the 1944-1945 term if Mori agreed to run for the office of vice president rather than president; Rojo proposed that he would leave the presidency after completing only half of his term, in January of 1945, even if the membership elected him, if it was the only way he could eliminate Mori as a rival. Rojo's tactics, however, almost backfired because, rather than gaining Mori as an ally, he gained a critic; Mori treated Rojo's offer as an "affront" to his "personal integrity."[31]

For Velasco, the war years represented a disturbing milestone because not all Filipinos acted with the same disregard for ethics. The gradual waning of nepotism in Local 7, for example, provided one indication that Velasco's questionable practices sometimes went against the general trend towards reform. Under the contract system, Filipinos had often depended on kinship ties to gain work advantage over other Filipinos in the Alaskan salmon canneries. As Gerald Gold has posited, this had been a common practice. Velasco himself was no stranger to it, as the constant requests family and friends made to him during the latter part of the 1920s and the early 1930s confirmed. Yet, at least some of the corruption of the contract system had begun to wane with time. Consequently, those who expected jobs other than through merit after Local 7's origins in 1937 and especially after Trinidad Rojo became its president, were disappointed. Notwithstanding the questionable deal that Rojo offered to Mori in the 1944 elections, overall he was one leader who tried to make the union less corrupt. As early as 1940, Rojo's attention to meritocracy rather than nepotism appeared in a letter he wrote on behalf of another member of Local 7. On April 1, he recommended Martin Benito on grounds that Benito had worked in Alaska during the previous year and, consequently, had seniority rights. Gerald Gold, who interviewed Rojo's contemporaries, confirmed that Rojo was one of the leaders who, in spite of personal idiosyncrasies, enjoyed the respect of many members of Local 7 largely because of his relatively neutral stance towards competing factions; contemporary documents, even those disparaging Rojo for supposed personality flaws, seem generally to confirm Gold's assessment.[32]

Velasco's bitter factional fighting, therefore, was thus not consistent with the conduct of all Filipinos within the union or with the efforts at reform. Moreover, by the end of the war years, Velasco was fast becoming one of the most heavy—handed in union politics—a trend that was apparent not only in union political battles, but in other instances, such as in his description of a *faux pas* at a social event involving several prominent Filipinos. He disparaged in bitter and scornful terms a Filipina community leader, Maxine Gonong, whom he described as "a woman who has all the earmarks of a conceited, selfish hypocrite . . . a publicity-seeker, and egotist whose lust for power is beyond all her innate and acquired capacities and capabilities . . . who has neither the support of her female contemporaries nor the respect of the intellegentsia of the community." The seemingly unforgivable sin that Gonong had committed was allowing another Filipino to introduce clumsily the famed Filipino general Carlos Romulo. The scorn that Velasco directed at Gonong seemed hardly consistent with the gravity of the harm she had apparently committed and revealed more about his character than it did about that of his intended target.[33]

There were various explanations for Velasco's involvement in questionable conduct. One was the existence of factions. In the summer, 1940 alliance between Velasco and Zoilo Paragas in their poltical battle against Vincente Navea, Navea's supporters, according to Paragas, tried to blame him for a proposed increase in union dues. Local 7 owed money to the CIO international, under whose aegis the C.W.F.L.U. operated, and president Trinidad Rojo created a committee to find a way to pay the debt with union dues. Among members of the seven-member committee were Navea and Paragas. Paragas told Velasco, however, that Navea prevented the committee from presenting possible solutions to the Local 7 rank-and-file members for their approval until after those who might oppose them, including Velasco, had left Alaska. According to Paragas, it was only after Velasco and others who opposed raising the dues had departed that Navea agreed to let the committee present its proposals to the membership. However, Paragas told Velasco, the rank-and-file thwarted Navea's delaying tactics by rejecting the dues increase. Rojo then reportedly intervened by appointing yet another committee to come up with a solution. Among those whom Rojo appointed was Paragas himself. The second committee proposed amortizing the debt over a period of two or three years in order to forestall the imposition of sharply increased dues. Navea, however, again intervened. This time, according to Paragas, it was by opposing the amortization plan and then blaming Paragas for the ensuing deadlock. Paragas attributed Navea's recalcitrance to bribes that he and others who opposed the amortization plan had received. The political antagonisms in 1940 indicated that the subsequent wartime tensions were nothing new. To the contrary, pre-war political alliances solidified as the war continued.[34]

Moreover, pre-war regional divisions contributed to tensions in union politics. In 1939, according to C.B. Mislang, vice president of the Pangasinan Association of the Pacific Northwest, some of the non-Pangasinane union members had shown an "unfriendly attitude" towards members of the association because they felt that Pangasinanes controlled the union. Regional differences giving rise to tensions within the union, however, were hardly surprising. Filipinos, at least through the pre-war period, identified with their geographical origins rather than with a single nation because, prior to the Spanish-American War, the Spaniards had encouraged divisions as a means of controlling the colonized population. During the pre-war years, regional differences had thus become one more factor contributing to union factionalism.[35]

During the war years, Velasco's public life included some notable departures from his pre-war experiences. Although some things, such as his appreciation for Euro-American culture and his involvement in Filipino issues, represented continuities from the past, others, in particular his tactics in union politics, demonstrated significant changes. The biggest change was that, even as he worked on behalf of Filipinos, he became increasingly involved in factional fighting.

There were different ways to explain the changes in Velasco's outlook and conduct, in particular as a union leader and journalist. One was that he had become more of a relativist. Ideological inconsistency between beliefs and actions was no longer an obstacle to his conduct so long as he was able to work towards and attain specific personal goals, especially in public life. In journalism, for example, he learned that he could most effectively muster support for his real agenda, Filipino nationalism and independence, by disguising it in the language of patriotism. He had also learned that skillful use of rhetoric could provide an effective and palatable means of disguising concepts—such as anti-colonialism and racial conflicts—that, if expressed directly in a time of national crisis, could be distasteful, even to Filipinos, at least some of whom felt genuine loyalty to the United States. The truth, then, was that Velasco probably had never lost his wariness about whites but had become well enough versed in *realpolitik* to know that he could appeal to broadly held sentiments in order to pursue hidden objectives, even when they were contrary to his public pronouncements. If lauding the United States as the symbol of democracy and freedom was an effective tool for attaining his actual goal—contributing to Philippine independence and the welfare of loved ones still there—then he was willing to swallow his pride and reservations about whites and do what he felt was necessary.

Velasco's acceptance of *realpolitik* had not emerged spontaneously during the war years. The process that led him to his new political consciousness was gradual. In 1926-1927, while he was at the Bellingham Normal School, he had become accustomed to admonishing his readers about upholding ideals in both journalism and in personal conduct, but between 1927 and 1933, he had begun to fall short in upholding his own ideals as he repeatedly failed to honor obligations to subscribers of the *Filipino Forum*. Increasingly, though, as he fell short of his own standards, he did not seem to mind it so much. Thereafter, it was only a short step to accepting the notion that inconsistencies between stated goals and his motives need not be the result of happenstance; to the contrary, he could manipulate his public persona in order to mask his true purposes.

Additional factors leading to Velasco's increasingly relativistic outlook may have been events in his personal life. His memories about losing Sixta Aquino made him physically ill at least as late as 1929, four years after she had left him. His breakup with Delphine Brooks in 1937, too, was a devastating experience. Between 1932 and 1937, he had first enjoyed, then lost the love of a woman he had been seeking for years: a white woman who would accept him as her companion, friend, lover, and mate and thus symbolize his entrance into mainstream America. As he wrote in his diary when they broke up, the day was one that he would "never forget." Another great disappointment, possibly contributing to disillusionment and the shedding of his ideals, may have been his repeated failure to find a way to return to his homeland. On several occasions during the 1920s, he had seriously contemplated going back to the Philippines because of bouts with homesickness only to learn that, in the United States, however demeaning his position, he could at least pursue his education and have some income—even if he had to perform manual labor. Another reason that going back to the Philippines was not a viable option, especially after 1934, when the Tydings-McDuffie Act limited the number of Filipinos who could enter American borders to 50 annually. If Velasco had gone back even on a short visit and then tried to reenter the United States, he perhaps could not have done so because of racial quotas.[36]

Losing Aquino, facing the realization that white women were uncomfortable about being with him, and then losing forever the opportunity to see loved ones in the Philippines may have battered his ideals and shaped an increasingly relativistic outlook. Moreover, the combination of personal disappointments and the inability to find meaningful solutions may have not only destroyed his youthful ideals, but also awakened him to a cynical awareness that those very ideals could help him achieve ulterior objectives.

Then, between 1935 and 1937, he became involved with various conflicts among Filipinos themselves. This was particularly true when, in his quest to become a journalist, he found himself the political tool of Pio De Cano, arguably the most powerful Filipino in the United States at the time. It was during his tenure as editor of De Cano's *Philippine Advocate* that Velasco met Vincente Navea, another big player in the corrupt contract system, and became his ally, colleague, and then enemy, in Local 7. Perhaps it was from men like De Cano and Navea that Velasco learned firsthand the skills and uses of political manipulation.

Still, disillusionment and a sense of loss were not the only possible sources of Velasco's education in *realpolitik*. As historian Michael Kazin has argued in his study of American populism, once leaders identify the core concepts driving mass movements, they learn to further other agendas, even at the cost of articulated ideals. So it may have been with Velasco. At some point, he had apparently learned that he could use American patriotic language to suit his own purposes: Philippine nationalism; Philippine independence; and, most importantly, political gain for himself. Thus, not only personal experiences, but also a new understanding of and appreciation for political realities and tools may have led him to the milestone he reached by the end of the war years.[37]

Velasco's political education, therefore, was notable not only for the inconsistency between pronouncements and goals, but also for his enhanced understanding that he could manipulate the needs of others in order to further his own, oftentimes hidden, agenda. In his rapprochement with the cannery industry, for example, he appealed to widespread Filipino dreams about fighting with white Americans against a common enemy in order to give voice to their hope for racial equality. Such political calculations inevitably led to ideological inconsistencies and unpredictable results. The greatest irony was that, by 1944, Velasco's facility in *realpolitik* set him against many of the very people he had sought to fight for in the first place. By the end of the war, he was fighting not just against whites; he was bitterly fighting against other Filipinos.

# Epilogue

Before he died in 1968, Velasco went through two other momentous series of events. Between the late 1940s and late 1950s, the most dominant events in his life were those involving union politics and one last, wild romantic fling.

In the summer of 1947, Velasco, who was serving as treasurer of Local 7, and two other disgruntled officers of Local 7 absconded from their positions, diverted $5,000 from the union treasury to form a new union, the Seafood Workers' Union (SWU), and tried to take the rank-and-file of Local 7 with them. Along the way, they sought to become the collective bargaining agent representing Alaskan cannery workers in negotiations with the salmon canning industry and publicly accused remaining Local 7 leaders of dishonesty, fraud, and communist sympathies, going so far as to refer to them as "puppets of the Communist International." Indeed, red-baiting was a major political tool. Martin Rendon, a vice president of the new union, accused Local 7 of being a front for an international communist conspiracy, and Cornelio Briones, its president, described Local 7 as being "backed up by Russia" whose "only concern is the welfare of the Kremlin." The organizers of the Seafood Workers' Union thus anticipated by several years the federal government's investigations and purge of suspected communists from labor unions between 1949 and 1955.[1]

Nor did they stop at simply breaking away; they attempted to destroy their erstwhile union. In the summer of 1947, Briones and others—including possibly Velasco—circulated a letter among Local 7 members, asking for a vote to revoke the union's charter. Among the consequences were not only the exacerbation of tensions that had already existed in union politics, but also the forestalling of the formation of a new contract between laborers and the salmon industry during the 1947 summer season. In a scenario reminiscent of other instances of betrayals and changing alliances, Velasco found himself bitterly opposing former colleagues in Local 7, including Trinidad Rojo.[2]

Ultimately, the leap of faith Velasco and his co-conspirators took ended unsuccessfully, largely because the National Labor Relations Board refused to certify the Seafood Workers' Union due to the involvement of its foremen in soliciting union membership. In 1948, moreover, the A.F.L. made a contract with the salmon industry independently of the Seafood Workers' Union and thereby weakened the SWU's bargaining position. Following the failure of the attempt to destroy Local 7, the latter reorganized as Local 37, which Velasco eventually rejoined, becoming a foreman.[3]

Velasco's last, long-term romantic fling, no less than betrayal of his own union, provided additional grist for a contentious decade during the 1950s. For the first time since his affair with Sixta Aquino some three decades earlier, Velasco had a lengthy affair with a Filipina. Yet, it was a sad denouement to his decades of effort to find a woman—of any race—who would love him, and few other events in his life reduced him to a pawn, helplessly carried along by events out of his control, than his affair with her. On 1 January 1952, in Seattle, he met Maria Louisa Dominguez in Seattle, who had been on her way to Los Angeles from New York while promoting her book about her famous father, a hero of the resistance against the Americans following the end of the Spanish-American War. She immediately became his constant companion and, shortly after their meeting, his lover. During the first four months of their relationship, they often saw each other in trysts in different parks and social events in the Seattle area, and they also had sexual relations.[4]

Within a year, however, Velasco lost control over the affair and the directions into which it took him. On 9 January 1953, witnesses discovered him in a bedroom in Dominguez's husband's house. Shortly before meeting Velasco, when she was in her mid-thirties, she had married Mariano Barrinuevo, in his late sixties. The discovery of Velasco's affair with her sparked a divorce trial in which the judge scolded her for preying upon an elderly man's affections. The scandal besmirched Dominguez's name. The trial also may have served as a catalyst for a Filipino newspaper in Wapato, Washington to accuse her of having been a spy for the Japanese during the Second World War. Over the next several years, in a series of court appeals from the divorce trial verdict and a separate lawsuit in which she brought a defamation case against the newspaper, Velasco found himself fighting alongside Dominguez, purchasing equipment for her, preparing legal documents, borrowing money on her behalf, chauffering her to different appointments in Bremerton and Seattle, and even facing angry attorneys on the stand as a witness, contradicting his own testimony and exposing himself to perjury. By the time the seedy events were over, he had lost Dominguez and had nothing left but unpaid bills, a heartache, and memories of only about four months of actual romance to make up for a seven-year nightmare.

Although the remainder of Velasco's life was never free of troubles, after the early 1960s, he never again became involved with controversies on the same scale as in the previous two decades. Instead, the most notable characteristic of his last few years was involvement in a broad range of activities both among Filipinos and Caucasians. He participated in public service efforts, such as a typhoon relief campaign in the winter of 1962, to solicit funds for the victims of a storm in Guam. He continued to publish the *Filipino Forum*, eventually expanding the list of recipients and subscribers to the Seattle mayor's office, the Seattle police chief, the Seattle Public Library, and various Filipino organizations in San Francisco, Sacramento, Salinas, and New York; maintained ties with Caucasians who were involved with the affairs of racial minorities in Seattle; and kept in contact with Filipinos in other parts of the United States who were promoting Filipino culture. During summers, he worked in Alaskan salmon canneries, much as he had done in the past. In his personal life, at about the time that the affair with Dominguez was ending, he met Josefina Querebin, whom he wed and who proved to be a compatible marital partner for the remaining years of his life.[5]

To some extent, he had come full circle between his arrival in Seattle in 1924 and his death in 1968. In both instances, he was extensively involved with both Filipinos and Caucasians, and during the years in-between, his life was full of controversies reflecting the myriad racial, gender, economic, and political themes of his times.

Victorio Velasco's life contrasts sharply with generalized implications in the extant literature that Asian Americans' experiences are nothing more than those of anonymous hordes swept up helplessly with neither a will of their own nor the ability to shape the world in which they live. To the contrary, Velasco's relationships with both whites and Filipinos showed the complex interplay of alliances, as well as enmities, both across and within racial lines, and the extent to which not only historical circumstances, but also individual choices and personalities, affected his life.

This study of Velasco, therefore, has a purpose beyond simply attempting to fill a gap in the scholarly literature on Asian Americans. It has a political purpose as well: countering the persistent racial stereotypes about Asians so ubiquitous in our own times and affecting the perceptions not only of adults, but also of youngsters who imbibe demeaning racial notions from early childhood and are thereby destined to make the United States of the twenty-first century one that continues inaccurate representations of Asian peoples. Whereas the worst consequence of the absence of monographs on Asian Americans in the scholarly literature is lack of information and possible simplification of their lives, in the world outside of the academy, the results are considerably more negative.

The absence of works treating Asians as individuals contributes to the widespread acceptance and perpetuation of racial stereotypes and race-based incidents today. Representations of Asian men as buffoons, math whizzes, spies, and screaming kung fu experts abound in today's mass media. Movies such as *Kung Pow* and *Police Academy*, television commercials that almost invariably depict Asian men as anemic-looking, slack-jawed, and sporting thick, black, horn-rimmed glasses and acting like clowns, and children's films like *Pocket Ninjas*, in which all the heroes are athletic-looking whites and all the villains are little, pot-bellied Southeast Asians with dark, shiny skin and rolling eyes, are pervasive. As the editors of *Aiiieeee!* suggested nearly three decades ago, stereotypes shape perceptions. They continue to do so at the beginning of the twenty-first century, echoing earlier racist representations of Asians, including the characters of Fu Manchu and Charlie Chan.[6]

Widespread acceptance of stereotypes, moreover, have led to more than simple misunderstanding. On a regular basis, hostile acts affect the lives of Asians in the United States. On 4 February 2003, for example, Howard Coble, a member of the United States House of Representatives, publicly referred to

American citizens of Japanese ancestry as an "endangered species" whose incarceration in American concentration camps during the Second World War because of their race was proper. His remarks came only weeks after basketball superstar Shaquille O'Neal, in a nationally-broadcast interview on the Fox network, referred to Chinese basketball player Yao Ming as "ching-chong-yang-wah-ah-so" and threatened to put an elbow in the Chinese man's face, a threat that, under some circumstances, amounts to an assault under both civil and criminal laws but which, in this case, seems to have elicited not the attention of law enforcement authorities, but the boisterous laughter of thousands of Americans across the United States. Nor was the interview an isolated incident. On 28 June, 2002, O'Neal had spoken in a "mock Chinese accent" and performed kung fu moves when discussing Yao on another Fox Television program. His caricatures of Yao inspired other acts. On 16 and 17 December, 2002, Fox Sports Radio's Tony Bruno invited his listeners to call in to his program and make racial jokes about Chinese. On 17 December, it was not only Bruno who indulged in repeating stereotypes about Asians, but also Americans across the country who took him up on his offer and, on a nationally-broadcast show, spent hours ridiculing Orientals. On Christmas day, 2002, the show apparently encouraged another well-known personality as well; ABC television's sports announcer Brent Musburger told a nationwide audience that "the hordes of China" might corrupt American basketball. Basketball fans and players may have taken the nationally-broadcast slurs against Chinese as free license to taunt Asians at will, as one Gonzaga University basketball player did on 19 January, 2003. On that day, Tyler Amaya, a member of the Gonzaga team, came across Chinese American Kenneth Lee and his wife, who were exiting a theater in Los Angeles, and taunted them with racial slurs of "ching-chong." It was an incident that elicited laughter from other members of the team who were witnesses and silence from the university's administration.[7]

The toleration of such incidents is reminiscent of the widespread acceptance of ideas about Uncle Toms, Sambos, and Aunt Jeminas in an earlier era, and they pervade public forums, family living rooms, and song lyrics. Today, T-shirts caricaturing Asians as hunchbacks with large buck teeth and bright, yellow skin are popular items at trendy, twenty-something stores like Abercrombie and Fitch, and the nationally-broadcast sport shows of today disparaging Yao recall the blackface comedians of the nineteenth century.

Although Velasco was hardly an angel, one indisputable fact emerges: no number of cardboard character, racial stereotypes about Asians so common in the United States today comes close to matching the complexity of his experiences and life. Consequently, this dissertation's goal has been not only to fill a gap in the scholarly literature on Asian Americans, but also to counter the widespread and commonly-accepted stereotypes about Asians that appear across the country today on a daily basis. Velasco hardly fit the image of the buck-toothed buffoon or kung fu expert who today invades American movie cinemas, the radio airwaves, and living rooms. He was a complex human being who defied racial stereotypes and, instead, was full of contradictions and inconsistencies.

Just as the biographies of civil rights leaders such as Dr. Martin Luther King have countered racist representations of African Americans appearing in minstrel shows and the like, this dissertation seeks to put to rest at least a small piece of today's Asian equivalents of the "tar baby" and Aunt Jemima.[8]

# Endnotes

## Introduction

1. The precise date of Velasco's matriculation into the public school in the Philippines is unclear. However, as he completed the four years of primary school education on 3 April 1914, eight months prior to his twelfth birthday on 6 December, he was probably seven at the time. Velasco, "Looking Back Over the Years"; Government of the Philippine Islands, "Primary Certificate," 3 April 1914; College Record, University of Washington, 10 October 1928; Box 12, "College Credentials"; Frank Bolima, Sr., "An Outstanding Publisher of the Pacific Northwest," 1, Box 1, Folder 1; *Inventory*, Victorio Acosta Velasco Collection, Accession No. 1435-003, Manuscripts and Archives, Suzzallo and Allen Libraries, University of Washington, Seattle, Washington [hereafter VVC].

2. It is not clear from materials that I have examined in the Velasco Collection at the University of Washington whether Velasco met Brooks at the University of Washington or at Central Washington State University in her home town in the Yakima Valley. However, her periodic allusions to visits with him Velasco in Seattle, as well as her references to transferring to the University of Washington, seem to suggest that they may have first met at Central Washington University.

3. Frank Chin, Jeffery Paul Chan, Lawson Fusao Inada, and Shawn Wong, *Aiiieeeee!: An Anthology of Asian American Writers* (New York: Penguin Books, 1991), 12-13; John Okada, *No No Boy* (Seattle: Combined Asian American Resources Project, 1976). Among the few existing autobiographies of Filipinos' lives is Norman Reyes' *Child of Two Worlds: An Autobiography of a Filipino American, or Vice Versa* (Colorado Springs: Three Continents Press, 1995). The best know work about the life of a Filipino is Carlos Bulosan's *America is in the Heart* (Seattle: University of Washington Press, 1946). However, this work is not so much an autobiography as much as a novelistic account of a Filipino's life.

4. Alice Y. Chai, "A Picture Bride from Korea: The Life History of a Korean American Woman in Hawaii," paper presented at the 6th Annual Conference on Ethnic and Minority Studies, La Crosse, Wisconsin, 19-22 April, 1978, cited in Mary L. Doi, Chien Lin, and Indu Vohra-Sahn, *Pacific/Asian American Research: An Annotated Bibliography, No. 1, Bibliography Series* (Chicago: Pacific/Asian American Mental Health Center, 1981), 34. Among the few extant book-length biographical works on Asians in the United States is John Little's *Bruce Lee: The Celebrated Life of the Golden Dragon*. However, it does not provide lengthy analyses of his subjects within the historical context. John Lee, ed., *Bruce Lee: The Celebrated Life of the Golden Dragon* (Boston: Tuttle, 2000). See also Lowell Chun-Hom, "Jade Snow Wong and the Fate of Chinese-American Identity," in *Amerasia Journal*, vol. 1, no. 1, 52-63, cited in Doi et al, 45. Among the few academic journals specializing in Asian American issues are the University of California, Los Angeles's Asian American Studies Center's *Amerasia Journal* and Johns Hopkins University's *Journal of Asian American Studies*.

5. Ronald Takaki, *Strangers from a Different Shore* (Boston: Little, Brown, 1989), 318-321, 329, 334, 337-354; Sucheng Chan, *Asian Americans: An Interpretive History* (Boston: Twayne, 1991), 76-77, 87. For one of the few book-length studies of Filipinos, see Susan Evangelista, *Carlos Bulosan and His Poetry: A Biography and Anthology* (Seattle: University of Washington Press, 1985).

6. Ye Le Espiritu, *Filipino American Lives* (Philadelphia: Temple University Press, 1995). For a bibliography of materials on Filipinos available at the Library of Congress, see Mary L. Doi, Chien Lin, Indu Vohra-Sahn, *Pacific/Asian American Research: An Annotated Bibliography, No. 3, Bibliography Series* (Chicago: Pacific/Asian American mental health Center, 1981), 160-168.

7. "Looking Back Over the Years: An Autobiography," undated, Box 12, "College Credentials," VVC.

## Chapter One

1. Government of the Philippine Islands, Department of Public Instruction, Bureau of Education, Division of Pangasinan, "Intermediate Certificate," 31 March 1917, Box 12, "College Credentials"; Victorio Velasco, "Looking Back over the Years," undated, Box 12, "College Credentials," VVC.

2. History Association Institute, City Y.M.C.A., Monthly Report Card, School Year 1919-1920; Bureau of Education, "Student's Permanent Record Card," 17 February 1920, Box 12, "College Credentials," VVC.

3. Victorio Acosta Velasco, *Lingyen and Other Poems* (Manila: Mission Press, 1924), 2-11.

4. Velasco, "Looking Back over the Years." For additional information and accompanying references, see Chapter Three.

5. National University, Manila, Philippine Islands, 12 October 1925, Box 12, "College Credentials," VVC; Washington State Normal School, Ellensburg, Washington, "Transcript of Record"; University of Washington, Seattle, Washington, "Grade Report," undated; State College of Washington, Pullman, Washington, "Transcript of the Record of Victorio Acosta Velasco," 16 December, 1933; Bolima, 2.

6. Velasco, *Lingyen and Other Poems*, 10.

7. Alexander A. Calata, "The Role of Education in Americanizing Filipinos," in Mina Roces, *Women, Power, and Kinship Politics*, 90. See also Bonificio S. Salamanca, *The Filipino Reaction to American Rule, 1901-1913* (Shoe String Press, Inc., 1968), 89-91; Agoncillo, *History of the Filipino People*, 8th ed. (Quezon City: Garotech Publishing, 1990), 372-373.

8. David Joel Steinberg, *The Philippines: A Singular and a Plural Place*, 2nd ed. (Boulder: Westview Press, 1990), 46-48; Maria Serena Diokno, "Benevolent Assimilation and Filipino Responses," in Roces, 77; Calata, in ibid., 94-95.

9. "Transcript of the Record of Victorio Acosta Velasco"; Washington State Normal School, Ellensburg, Washington, "Transcript of Record," University of Washington, Seattle, Washington, "Grade Report," undated; Bolima, 1, VVC. The names and positions of the individuals may be questionable since Frank Bolima, in his obituary of Velasco, may have based his information on contemporary sources rather than on period ones. The caveat applies also to other information from the Bolima manuscript. Velasco to President, National University, 15 September 1937, Box 1, Folder 1, VVC.

10. Princess Orig, "Kayumanggi Versus Maputi: 100 Years of America's White Aesthetics in Philippine Literature," in Roces, 106-110.

11. Agoncillo, 166, 379.

12. Ibid., 5, 77, 79, 105-108, 119-120, 122-126, 129-131, 145.

13. Doug Chin, *Seattle's International District: The Making of a Pan-Asian Community* (Seattle: International Examiner Press, 2001), 45-48.

14. Agoncillo, 342, 374-375.

15. Ibid., 308, 348-349.

16. Ibid., 374, 376-377.

17. Ibid., 328-333, 340-341.

18. Ibid., 312-319, 333, 379; Sharon Delmendo, "The American Factor in Jose Rizal's Nationalism," *Amerasia Journal* 24, no. 2 (1998): 54.

19. Agoncillo, 302, 379.

20. Aquino to Velasco, 12, 25 January; 25 October 1922; Appointment as Teacher in the Division of Davao, 14 August 1922, VVC; Aquino to Velasco, 18 December 1922, VVC.

21. Aquino to Velasco, 13, 25 January; 12 August; 20 September 1922, VVC.

22. Ibid., 13 January; 20 September; 24 November; 18 December 1922; 11 April 1923; c. July 1924, VVC.

23. Ibid., c. January; 13, 25 January; 12 August; 20, 22 September; 25 October; 24 November; 18 December 1922; Aquino to Velasco, c. July, 1924, VVC. The last time Velasco saw Aquino was at the outset of his journey from the Philippines on Thursday, 10 April 1924. Diary, 6-11, 17, 18, 21, 23, 25, 27, 29, 30 April 1924; 3 May; 6, 14-17, 21, 30 July; 14, 22 August; 15, 26 September; 13, 29 October; 7, 10, 21, 23, 24 November; 17, 26 December 1924; 19 February; 10, 12 March; 14, 15 May; 12, 24 June; 21, 23 July 1925, VVC.

24. Steinberg, 4; Roces, "Women in Philippine Politics and Society," in Roces, 159-160, 162-163; Agoncillo, 36.

25. Roces, 168-169, 175. For a book-length study of new opportunities for Filipina nurses, see Catherine Ceniza Choy, *Empire of Care* (Durham: Duke University Press, 2003), 15-19. For information about a particular nurse's experiences, see Mrs. Maria Abastilla Beltran, interview by Carolina Koslosky, television interview [transcribed], 5 May 1975, FIL-KING-75-9CK, Washington State Archives, Tape No. 14, Filipino American National Historical Society, Seattle, Washington [hereafter FANHS]; Sixta Aquino, "Appointment as Teacher of Davao," 18 November 1922, VVC.

## Chapter Two

1. Diary, 6-11, 18, 20, 21, 23, 25, 27, 29, 30 April; 3 May 1924, VVC.

2. Doug Chin, *Seattle's International District: The Making of a Pan-Asian American Community* (Seattle: International Examiner Press, 2001), 45, 55.

3. The home in which he found work on 1 December was the residence of a Mrs. Preston. Diary, 1, 4 December 1924, VVC; Trinidad Rojo, interview by Carolina Koslosky, 18 and 19 February, 1975, Tape A [transcribed], [FANHS]; Nancy Ordna Koslosky, "Filipino Immigrants Seek Jobs," *International Examiner*, November 1978, p. 8; Vicki Woo, "Seeking the American Dream: Housing Activist Al Masigat," *International Examiner*, November 1978, 1.

4. The second home in which Velasco found work was the Gaffney residence. He referred to the factory in which he worked as "Mr. Deller's Factory." Diary, 10-14, 17, 20-22, 25-27 December 1924; 11, 15, 18, 25 January 1925, VVC. He may have worked at the saw mill through at least the week of 20 May, when he began planning to go to Alaska for the summer canning season. Ibid., 30 January; 14 March; 20, 22 May; 1 June 1925, VVC. Under the contract system, individual contractors made agreements with

canneries to recruit labor. After the contractors recruited workers, the latter went to the canneries for the duration of the salmon canning season, which typically ran from May through August. In Seattle, when Velasco first arrived in Seattle, the principal contracting firms were those of Goon Dip, a Chinese man, and later, Pio De Cano, a Filipino. Both obtained laborers by contracting with the L.V.M. Trading Company, which also operated the hotel in which Velasco often lived between 1924 and 1926. Velasco was later associated with De Cano in a number of capacities, including editing the mouthpiece for his anti-union stance, *The Philippine Advocate*. Velasco to Carlos P. Romulo, 22 October 1951, Box 1, Folder 1, VVC; Gerald Gold, "The Development of Local Number 7 of the Food, Tobacco, Agricultural and Allied Workers of America-C.I.O." (M.A. thesis, University of Washington, 1949), 11, 47-48; Sid White and S.E. Solberg, *Peoples of Washington: Perspectives on Cultural Diversity* (Pullman: Washington State University Press, 1989), 123, 139; Chin, 57. Gold provides an example of forced purchases in his description of an instance in which the San Francisco-based contracting firm of Young and Mayer compelled 526 laborers at the beginning of the season to purchase suits. Of this number, 131 never received a suit even though the store deducted the price from their wages. The total deductions for all 526 men amounted to $24,969. However, because the suits were made of the cheapest quality materials, their actual market value was only $6,730. Gold, 18-19.

5. Ibid., 21-23.

6. Gold refers to the foremen's stockpiles of food as "slop chests" and gives prices for the 1933 season. A can of fruit or vegetables cost thirty-five to sixty cents a can, an egg cost ten cents, and synthetic whiskey was five dollars a pint. Ibid., 12-13, 23-25.

7. Diary, 14-16, 19, 27-29 July; 29 August 1924, VVC; Gold, 30-31.

8. Velasco to Garrott, 28 May 1926, Box 35, Folder 15, Cannery Workers' and Farm Laborers' Union Local No. 7 Collection, Accession No. 3927-1, Manuscripts and University Archives, Suzzallo and Allen Libraries, University of Washington, Seattle, Washington [hereafter CWFLUC].

9. In a letter Velasco wrote to Garrot, he said, "Does not distance, then, lend charm to the view, and absence heighten our love and appreciation, Mother [Mrs. Garrott], I must confess that I have learned to pay my tribute to whom it is due just now, when I found that the 'well is dry,' and distance has helped me to recognize the beauty and splendor of the place I once belonged to, in which, then, I saw nothing but the ordinary coarse matters of common things." Ibid.

10. On 25 January, Velasco quit his job at the Gaffney residence for unknown reasons. Paradoxically, in several instances he had recorded in his diary that his new employers were very pleasant. On Christmas day of 1924, Mrs. Gaffney gave Velasco a silk handkerchief, a silk necktie, a pair of gloves and a bag of candies. On 11 January 1924, upon her return from a trip to Portland, Oregon, she brought Velasco more candy. Some clues about why he left, however, lay in the attention Velasco gave to the cook, Godwin Thompson, who began to absent herself from the household in the days prior to Velasco quitting his job. From his first day at work on 12 December, he had taken notice of her and described her as "beautiful and young and single yet." On 18 December, he wrote in his diary that she "had been very kind to me" and, on 20 December, he invited three of his friends—probably Filipino men—to the Gaffney house to see her. The possible connection between the attention he gave her and the end of his employment was faintly reminiscent of his dismissal from the Preston residence on 4 December, where, the day before he lost his job, he may have given some attention to a young woman of the household who was a student at Broadway High School. In his job at "Mr. Deller's Factory," he may again have shown unwelcome attention to young women. On 21 January, when he began to notice Thompson's absence from the Gaffney household, he described the

young women at the Deller factory as "Beautiful girls [who] are the daughters of my boss . . . ." If he had lavished attention on the women at the factory, it would have been consistent with the attention he gave to young women in the other jobs and also to the female friends with whom he tried to develop romantic relationships. Unsurprisingly, perhaps, he seemed to have lost his new position at the factory; by 30 December, he was again looking for work. Diary, 4, 6, 14, 16, 19, 23, 27-29 July; 2-4, 11, 15, 19 August 1924; 3, 12, 18, 20, 25 December; 11, 15, 18, 21, 30 January 1925, VVC.

11. The perpetually-sleepy co-worker was Benigno Sevidal. The "heroic" co-worker was Felipe Blando. The machine may have been one for recycling flawed salmon tins. Velasco wrote, "To Emeterio Cruz is entrusted the responsibility of looking over the rolling cans as they hurry from their birthplace, passing thru their 'Jordan' where they have been baptized on their way to the bottom machine where they are prepared for the purpose that they are made, and finally into their temporary repose. Jose Carballo sees that there is no overcrowding, and mad rushing of the cans, but that they must line up before they step into the machine." Describing Sevidal's singing, he told Garrott, "No sooner has Benigno filled the air with his dulcet breath than we remember a Tagalog song by an American singer. These jazz pieces only make us yearn for a finer, nobler sonata . . . ." Velasco to Garrott, 28 May 1926, Box 35, Folder 15, CWFLUC.

12. Diary, 4, 18, 19, 29, 31 July; 1, 13, 16, 17, 18, 20, 29 and 30; August; 2 September 1924; 15, 29 January; 20, 27 February; 6 March; 30 June 1925, VVC.

13. Among the first theaters he went to were the Princess and the Jackson. Diary, 4, 6-8, 10, 13, 15 September 1924, VVC. One of his first poetic efforts in the United States was "A Lesson from Autumn," which he wrote on 3 December 1924. Diary, 3 December 1924, VVC. Velasco was a correspondent for the *Philippine Republic* between 1924 and 1927. For additional information about his journalistic activities, see: Velasco to President, National University, Manila, 15 September 1937, VVC; Velasco to Garrott, 28 May 1926, Box 35, Folder 15, CWFLUC; Diary, 30 June 1925; 9, 15, 29 January; 20, 26 and 27 February; 6 March 1926, VVC. The writing contest was one which the *Nation*, a nationally-circulating news and political journal, sponsored. Velasco to Garrott, 28 May 1926, Box 35, Folder 15, CWFLUC; Garrott to Velasco, 30 March, 13 May, 28 June, 3 August 1926, Box 1, Folder 13, VVC. Garrott's friendship with Velasco appeared in the sense of humor that came across in her letter; she said to him, "I will not call them masterpieces, for you yourself would hardly claim that distinction for them . . . . " Garrott to Velasco, 19 January 1927, Box 1, Folder 13, VVC. Velasco's whereabouts during the spring quarter of 1925 are not entirely clear. On 24 May 1926, he dropped out of classes at the University of Washington, so presumably, he had registered for the spring quarter and had committed to remaining in Seattle between late March or early April of 1925. Yet, his correspondence with Garrott, in which she apparently wrote to him from Seattle, indicated that he may not have been in Seattle during the entire winter or spring quarter. Ibid.

14. For Filipinos who had seen intermarriage between the Spanish and Filipinos during the Spanish occupation, romantic relationships with whites in the United States may have seemed logical. Yet, for many Americans, who had been accustomed to legal and social strictures against miscegenation since the mid-1600s, such liaisons opened up a "hornet's nest." Lan Cao and Himilce Novas, *Everything You Need to Know about Asian American History* (New York: Penguin Books, 1996), 168-170. See also Diary, 10, 17 and 18 October; 4, 6, 12 November; 8, 29 December 1924; 29 January; 6, 26 February; 15 June; 5 August, 1925, VVC.

15. Brown to Velasco, 14 February; 29 April 1925, Box 1, Folder 34; Velasco to President, National University, 15 September 1937, Box 1, Folder 1; Diary, 26 February; 22 May 1925, VVC.

16. The cannery might have been the one on Lummi Island in the San Juan Islands. The Lummi Island Packing Company, which later became the Carlisle Packing Company—where Marsh worked during part of the time she corresponded with Velasco—built a salmon cannery on the island in 1896. The Beach Packing Company—later called the Lummi Bay Packing Company—also operated a cannery at some point after 1910. In some of her correspondence, Marsh identifies her address as being "Beach." See also Beth Hudson, "A Very Brief History of Lummi Island and the Islanders," lummiislad.com, visited 20 July 2002. Yet one more possibility is the San Juan Island Salmon Cannery on Jackson Beach near Friday Harbor. Debra Sullivan, "Real Estate in the San Juan Islands,Washington State, San Juan Island Property, Offered," sanjuanproperty.com, visited 20 July 2002. A relic from Velasco's days which he himself may have used is the ferry boat MV Carlisle II, a sixty-foot diesel-powered boat built in 1917 on Lummi Island, originally serving as a lumber freighter and fish packer between the San Juan Islands and Bellingham and converted to a car ferry in 1923. "Horluck Foot Ferry," horluck.com, visited 20 July 2002; portorchard.com, visited 20 July 2002. Velasco had met several other women during the summer of 1925. He met someone called "Florence," one of Marsh's friends, and Anna Erickson, who also briefly corresponded with him. He maintained contact with Erickson by sending her photographs, which he had taken of her, and candy. There is no evidence of direct correspondence between Florence, whom Marsh mentions on several occasions, and Velasco. There is one letter from Erickson to Velasco. Anna Erickson to Velasco, 22 September 1925, Box 1, Folder 37, VVC. In one of his first letters to Marsh, he wrote, "All my life I have dreamed of the woman I could love, and I have kept my heart and molded my life for her. She would honor my honor and keep herself clean for me always. If she were sick I would nurse her; if she were weak I would be her strength; if she were paralyzed I would wheel her in the sun; if she were deaf I would be ears for her, lead her and read to her. And if she were insane I would be true to her until death, and I would love her . . . . " Velasco to Marsh, c. pre-28 September 1925; Marsh to Velasco, 11 November 1925, Box 1, Folder 55, VVC. It was debatable, of course, whether his words were as sincere as they seemed. Since at least as early as 1924, when he wrote about his experiences in Hong Kong, it had been clear that he had a penchant for using maudlin language even in his personal diary.

17. Marsh may have responded to Velasco's attentions because they had some things, such as a sense of humor, in common. On 16 November 1925, she was depressed about the rainy weather and told him an amusing story about how she was going to cheer herself up. She said, "Gee if it rains all the time here if it don't stop pretty soon I'm going to start wearing my bathing [suit]. Then I guess I will cause some excitement." Marsh to Velasco, 11 September; 10, 15 October; 9, 11, 16 November 1925; 18 December 1925; 6 January 1926, Box 1, Folder 16, VVC.

18. According to Velasco's college records at the University of Washington, he was enrolled in February of 1926, when he met Multmueller. "College Credentials," VVC. There were frequent references to Multmueller's visits to and overnight stays at the International House both in Velasco's diary and in the newsletter, *Mother's Bulletin,* which Jane Garrott, the housemother, sent out to the International House residents who were out of town. Diary, 6 March 1926; Jane Garrott, *Mother's Bulletin*, c. April, 2 June 1926 Box 3, Folder 29; Multmueller to Velasco, 30 April 1926, Box 1, Folder 18, VVC. During Velasco's own association with International House, it was located near the University of Washington. For at least part of the time, it was at 5014 15th Avenue N.E., just one block east of what is now University Way and within blocks of the main campus. At another point in 1926, it was four blocks east and ten blocks south of the 15th Avenue address at 4142 11th Avenue N.E. Garrott to Velasco, 13 May 1926; Garrott, *Mother's*

*Bulletin*, 7 July 1926, Box 3 Folder 29, VVC; Garrott, *Mother's Bulletin*, 14 July 1926, Box 35, Folder 23, CWFLUC; Garrott to Velasco, 30 March, 13 May, 28 June, 3 August 1926; 19 January 1927; c. 1926-1927, Box 1, Folder 13, VVC. The attorney who spoke at International House was W.D. Lane of Seattle, and the African American speaker was a Mr. Wells. The professor was Dr. Josef Hall, who gave his talk, "The End of the White Man's world," at Anderson Hall. Jane Garrott, International House, 7 July 1926, Box 35, Folder 23, CWFLUC.

19. Diary, 3, 4, 6, 7 February; 6, 14-19, 21, 30 July; 14, 22, 30 August; 2, 3 September 1924, VVC. Velasco's thoughts about Aquino also plagued him when he was awake. On 5 March 1926, he expressed his bereavement in his diary. No matter where he went or what he did, he wrote, he always came across something that reminded him of her, and even when he sought escape by sleeping, she appeared in his dreams. He wished that someday she would understand how much she continued to mean to him even though they were separated by seven thousand miles and she had forbidden him to contact her. Diary, 10, 11, 15, 18-20, 24, 27 February; 1, March 1926, VVC. Yet, Aquino was not the only Filipino woman he longed for. On 3 February 1926, he dreamt of visiting a woman, whom he referred to only as "Sayong," in the Philippines. Diary, 4 February 1926, VVC.

20. Ibid., 5 March 1926, VVC.

21. Ibid.

22. Marsh to Velasco, 10 October, 11 November 1925, Box 1, Folder 16, VVC.

23. Ibid., 15 October; 9 November 1925, Box 1, Folder 16, VVC.

24. Ibid., 10, 15, 16 October; 11, 16 November 1925, Box 1, Folder 16, VVC.

25. Ibid., 16 November, 18 December 1924, Box 1, Folder 16, VVC. In mid-November of 1925, there was an example of the amount of effort Marsh spent going to dances. She had a fight with her date and, as a result, did not have access to a car for the evening. She finally got hold of a car that belonged to her sister's boyfriend, but by that time, she no longer had a date. On another night, when she and her friend Florence—a mutual acquaintance of hers and Velasco—returned to Florence's home in the wee hours of the morning, the welcome turned sour when Florence's father came out and told Marsh to "get the hell out." Marsh to Velasco, 16 November 1925; 6 January 1926, Box 1, Folder 16, VVC.

26. On 30 April 1926, Multmueller returned from school at around 4 o'clock, which was an unusually early time for her. Multmueller to Velasco, 30 April 1925; 15 July 1926, Box 1, Folder 18; Garrott, *Mother's Bulletin*, c. April 1926, Box 3 Folder 29, VVC. Multmueller's formality both in her salutation ("Mr. Velasco") and signature ("sincerely"), however, might have been deceptive; formality with everyone except the most intimate of friends may have been no more than a reflection of her generally formal manners. For instance, when she referred to Jane Garrott, a friend, she always referred to her as "Mrs. Garrott." In one letter she wrote to Velasco in the summer of 1926, she excused cutting her letter short by stating that "prudence bids me cease"—she was trying to get to bed early. Multmueller to Velasco, 15 July 1926, VVC.

27. Although racial violence in Oregon and Washington did not occur on the same scale as in other places, it was nevertheless reminiscent of other acts of violence, including the 1885 mass murder of 28 Chinese in Wyoming. An exception was the Snake River massacre, in which white renegades murdered 31 Chinese and hacked their bodies to pieces with axes. David H. Stratton, "The Snake River Massacre of Chinese Miners, 1887," in Duane A. Smith, ed., *A Taste of the West: Essays in Honor of Robert G. Athearn* (Boulder: Pruett Publishing Company, 1983), 109-129. By 1910, 25 percent of Washington's population was of foreign ancestry, and only 20 percent were born in the state. Yet, for Euro-Americans and immigrants from western Europe, assimilation was a

relatively easy task. Jorgen Dahlie, "Old World Paths in the New: Scandinavians Find Familiar Home in Washington," *Pacific Northwest Quarterly* (April 1970): 66. Among the Europeans who were not always welcome were Communists and Russians. Timothy J. Sarbaugh, "Eamon de Valera and the Northwest," *Pacific Northwest Quarterly* 81, no. 4, 145-151; "Drive Russians Back to Canada," *Spokesman Review*, 28 April 1909, 11. For Asians, including the Japanese and the Chinese, assimilation was nearly impossible because of racial hostility. "Farmers Favor Curb on Aliens," *Spokesman Review*, 5 December 1919, 2, 8; *Countdown: A Demographic Profile of Asian and Pacific Islanders in Washington State* (Seattle: Washington State Commission on Asian American Affairs, 1982), 3-4; Roger Daniels, ed., *Anti-Chinese Violence in North America* (New York: Arno Press, 1978), 47-55, 103-129, 172-179, 204-212, 271-283; Lorraine Barker Hildebrand, *Straw Hats, Sandals and Steel* (Tacoma: Washington State American Revolution Bicentennial Commission, 1977); Frederick Rudolph, "Chinamen in Yankeedom: Anti-Unionism in Massachusetts in 1870," *American Historical Review* LIII, no. 1 (October 1947): 1-29; "The Chinese in the Frontier Northwest: A Sampler," *Pacific Northwest Forum* 6, no. 2 (1992), 60-79; "Unions Vote to Bar All Asiatics," *Spokesman Review*, 19 November 1913, 2-3; "The Chinese Can Not Come In," *Spokesman Review*, 29 June 1902, 1, 6; "Seize Japs: Walla Walla," *Spokesman Review*, 26 August 1910, 6. The hostility against Japanese and Chinese existed even though their numbers were small. In 1901, the entire Japanese population of Washington was 5,617, and the number of Chinese around 7,000. "Chinese are Scarce," *Spokesman Review*, 30 November 1901, 3-4. According to the Washington State Commission on Asian American Affairs, the population figure for Chinese in Washington Territory in 1870 was 234. In 1880, it was 3,186, and in 1900, 3,627. The number of Japanese who entered Washington Territory between 1902 and 1907 was 15,996. The Commission also provides population statistics for other Asian and Pacific Islander groups from the mid-19$^{th}$ century through 1980. The first large-scale increase in the Chinese population occurred following the completion of the transcontinental railroad in 1869. *Countdown*, 3-4.

28. Some Asian immigrants, unlike the majority of their counterparts, were successful. Chin Gee-hee, a Chinese labor contractor in Seattle at the turn of the century, earned the respect of both Chinese and whites. Willard G. Jue, "Chin Gee-hee, Chinese Pioneer Entrepreneur in Seattle and Toishan," in Douglas W. Lee, ed., *Annals of the Chinese Historical Society of the Pacific Northwest* (Seattle: Chinese Historical Society of the Pacific Northwest), 31-8. Takuji Yamashita spent the remainder of his life in Washington operating a small strawberry farm and running a hotel. Steven Goldsmith, "Takuji Yamashita," *Washington State Bar News* 55, no. 3 (March 2001): 22-23. Had Velasco been aware of Yamashita's experience, he may have never visited with a Mr. Franco, a "prospective law student," on 11 March 1925 and ordered books from one of the largest legal publishers in the country, West Publishing Company. Nor would he ever complete the law course he enrolled in nearly three decades later, in the fall of 1951, through La Salle Extension University. Diary, 11, 20 March 1925; Velasco to Romulo, 22 October 1951, Box 1, Folder 1; W-4 Extension Certificate, 7 September 1955; 1955 Job Assignment, 27 June 1955; W-4 Exemption Certificate, 29 August 1954, Box 7 Folder 7, VVC. Velasco's possible exploration of a legal education appears also in a diary entry not long after his arrival in Seattle. Diary, 16 January 1925, VVC (letter to a Mr. Cortes (?) of the Harvard University Law School). Ultimately, his inability to secure employment in anything other than manual labor led to him burning to death in a cannery bunkhouse in the fall of 1968 where he had been working as a foreman. *Inventory, Victorio Acosta Velasco Collection*, VVC.

29. Garrott to Velasco, 28 June 1926;19 January 1927, Box 1, Folder 13, VVC; Garrott, *Mother's Bulletin* (?), c. 1926, Box 35, Folder 15, CWFLUC.

30. Multmueller's words, in English, were: "But never more nor less" (author's translation). Multmueller to Velasco, 30 April 1926, Box 1, Folder 18, VVC.

31. Marsh to Velasco, 28 September; 10, 15 October 1925; 6 January 1926, Box 1, Folder 16, VVC. She told Velasco, "Don't come up to see me at New Years or any other time please, but we can be friends and write but thats all. I cant ever marry you and I am the loser." Marsh to Velasco, 18 December 1925, Box 1, Folder 16, VVC. Both Brown and Multmueller remained his friends and correspondents well into the following decade. See Chapters Four and Five and accompanying notes. Somewhat inconsistent with the grave tone of Marsh's words ending their relationship, however, was her excuse for why she was giving him only a curt explanation for not wanting to see him again. While she was writing her note to Velasco, she explained, there was a "dancing and petting party at the house," and she wanted to finish the letter quickly so that she could join the fun. Marsh to Velasco, 18 December 1925, Box 1, Folder 16, VVC.

32. John D'Emilio and Estelle B. Freedman, *Intimate Matters: A History of Sexuality in America* (New York: Harper & Row, 1988), 13-14; 34-38.

33. *In re. Estate of John T. Wilbur*, 44 P. 262 (Wash. 1896); "Refuse to Wed Jap and White," *Spokesman Review*, 3 August 1909, 6. On 12 January 1911, the legislator was Mr. Ghent. H.R. 34, 12th sess. (1911). Another was Mr. Wray. H.R. 50, 12th sess. (1911); H.R. 141, 12th sess. (1911). The committee that introduced the bill prohibiting a Caucasian from marrying a person of "negro, Chinese, Japanese or Mongolian blood" was the Committee on Miscellaneous in the Washington House of Representatives. On 24 January 1917, the legislator was a Mr. Jones, a member of the Washington House of Representatives. H.R. 87, 15th sess. (1917). The legislator who introduced the anti-miscegenation bill on 19 January 1921 was a Mr. Murphine. H.R. 40, 17th sess. (1921). One indication of the hypocritical reformist mindset of the state legislators appeared in their concerns about women's rights at the same time that they sought to prevent miscegenation. On November 16, 1925, a Mr. Westfall of the state Senate introduced a bill providing that married women may hold shares of stock in corporations independently of her husband. S. 63, Extraordinary sess. (1925). Also in the early 1920s, state legislators, like their counterparts in Congress, sought to protect women's right to independent citizenship. On January 26, 1921, a Mr. Cory of the Washington House of Representatives sponsored the *Joint Memorial of the House and the Senate*, affirming that American women have American citizenship independent of their husbands' nationality. One interesting point about the Joint Memorial, however, is that, unlike its congressional counterpart, the Cable Act of 1922, it provided that an American woman would not lose her citizenship if she married an "alien ineligible to citizenship." Theoretically, under the Joint Memorial, an American woman could marry a Japanese or Chinese without losing her citizenship. On the other hand, since the Cable Act was already in force, perhaps it was unnecessary to include the provision; the federal law would strip the woman of her citizenship even if the state law did not. *H. Joint Memorial No. 8*, 17th sess. (1921). The existence of the Cable Act, indeed, may have rendered moot the promulgation of any anti-miscegenation law at the state level. Even if there were no such state law, the federal law discouraged inter-racial marriages by imposing the drastic measure of stripping away an American woman's citizenship. Moreover, even if there were a state law, if it conflicted with the applicable federal law—here, the Cable Act—it would have been unconstitutional as a violation of the Supremacy Clause of the federal Constitution, which provides that any conflict between federal and state law results in the preemption of the analogous state provision. Other, federal constitutional provisions discouraging the enactment of such a law at the state level might have been the Equal Protection Clause and the Due Process Clause of the Fourteenth Amendment, both of which prohibit the states from enacting laws that conflict with federal constitutional provisions, including prohibi-

tions against discrimination based on race—an irony, since the Cable Act did precisely that. My position here differs markedly from the conclusions that Daniel Kwang Lee reaches in his Master's thesis at Washington State University in which he attributes the absence of an anti-miscegenation law in Washington to a less virulent form of racism than that in states which did have such laws. David Kwang Lee, "Why Washington State Did Not Have an Anti-Miscegenation Law" (M.A. thesis, Washington State University, 1998). The fact that there were murders and countless assaults against Filipinos and other Asians in Washington seem to belie Kwang's optimistic assessments.

## Chapter Three

1. "Many Students Seek Scribes Club," *Weekly Messenger*, 28 January 1927, 4; "Red Arrow Announces Contest"; "Literary Contest to be Sponsored by Scribes Club"; "Scribes Initiation Proves Dreadful to new members," *Weekly Messenger*, 21 January 1927, 1, 4; "Red Arrow Seeks Material for New Edition," *Weekly Messenger*, 29 April 1927, 4; "The Red Arrow"; "The Scribes Club," *Klipsun '27*, Special Collections, Western Washington University, Bellingham, Washington [hereafter WWUC], 56, 123; Diary, 5-7, 14 January 1927, VVC.

2. Velasco matriculated at the Washington State Normal School on 27 August 1926. *Western Washington College of Education Registration Up to 1957*, vol. 2,WWUC; "School Calendar," in *Annual Catalog 1926-1927*, WWUC; "Chinese Mob British at Hankow," *Bellingham Herald*, 3 January 1927, 1; "Seattle Oriental Killed in Lottery Ticket Fight," *Bellingham Herald*, 4 January 1927, 11; "Osaka, 'Venice of East,' Shaken by Quake," *Bellingham Herald*, 3 March 1927, 1; "100 Thought Drowned," *Bellingham Herald*, 18 March 1927, 2; "China's 'Joan of Arc,'" *Bellingham Herald*, 17 March 1927, 11.

3. "Estimate is Given"; "Haffner & Rathman's Final Clearance Sale"; Francis Beeding, "The Little White Hag," *Bellingham Herald*, 3 January 1927, 12; "Law Enforcement at Spokane Held 'Horrible'"; John B. Foster, "Risberg is Panned"; "Night School Open"; "Gardner is Cited"; "Washington-Made Toys Displayed at Seattle"; "Pacific Northwest Promised More Prosperity"; "Liquor Debate is Bitterly Waged"; "U.S. Girl Likened to Cedar Mop" (bobbing hair, according to the author, was a "criminal act" to some), *Bellingham Herald*, 4 January 1927, 1, 11; "Prize Dances Next"; "Physical Education Should Begin at the Home, Says Director," *Bellingham Herald*, 5 January 1927, 8; Edna Wallace Hopper, "Look at My Hair"; "Colorful Fan Important Part of Milady's Evening (illegible)"; "Social and Personal," *Bellingham Herald*, 6 January 1927, 8; "Sage Tea Turns Gray Hair Dark"; Lilian Campbell, "With the Woman of Today"; "Martin's First Winter Garment Clearance" (advertisement); "Use Sulphur if Skin Breaks Out"; *Bellingham Herald*, 26 January 1927, 8; "Fried Chicken and Country Gravy"; "Sausage as Roll Served Warm"; "Cone On Breakfast," *Bellingham Herald*, 18 March 1927, 7; *Annual Catalog 1926-1927*; *Annual Catalog 1927-1928*; *Western Washington College of Education Registration up to 1957*, WWUC.

4. "Y.W.C.A. Members Hear about India," *Weekly Messenger*, 6 August 1926, 1; "Herbert Gowen Tells Facts of Orientals," *Weekly Messenger*, 18 February 1927, 4; "Rules of the Road in Japan and Korea: Copy of Official Printed Rules," *Klipsun '27*, 8, 50, 65, 138. For additional information about the school, see: *Klipsun '26*; "Work on Library Building Starts within Four Weeks," *Weekly Messenger*, 7 January 1927, 1; *Annual Catalog, 1927*, 98; *Klipsun '27*; *Annual Catalog, 1926*, 6-10; *Annual Catalog*, 1927, 4-11; *Annual Catalog, 1926*, 86; "890 Students are Now in Normal," *Weekly Messenger*, 30 July 1926, WWUC, 1.

5. June Wetherell, "Song of a Science Class," in *The Red Arrow*, March 1927, Vol. I, No. 1, WWUC, 12.

6. Ibid., "A Bird's Dream of Heaven," *Weekly Messenger*, 7 January 1927, 2; Wetherell, "An Evening with Carl Sandburg," *The Red Arrow*, March 1927, Vol. I, No. 1, 5; Wetherell, untitled, *Weekly Messenger*, 21 January 1927, lines 3-4, 14-15, 24-25, WWUC.

7. Velasco, "June Wetherell, Winner of First Place in Literary Contest, Tells Intimate Secrets of Being a Poet," *Weekly Messenger*, 3 December 1926, 1. The newspaper in which Wetherell first published a poem was the Coupeville, Washington (?) paper. Wetherell went on to become a novelist with several titles to her credit. Among them were: *But that was Yesterday* (New York: E.P. Dutton & Co., Inc., 1943); *Close the Door Behind You* (New York: E.P. Dutton & Co., Inc., 1944); *Dead Center* (New York: E.P. Dutton & Co., Inc., 1946); *Run Sheep, Run* (New York: E.P. Dutton & Co., Inc., 1947); *The Glorious Three* (New York: Dutton, 1951).

8. Velasco to Wetherell, 12 March 1928, Box 8, Folder 40, VVC.

9. *The Red Arrow*, December 1927, Vol. I, No. 3, WWUC, inside cover. *Klipsun '28*, WWUC, 72. Wetherell continued with the journal through the winter of 1928. However, she was not an editor and, instead, served as a member of the advertising staff. In the spring of 1928, Wetherell continued her participation but only as a contributing writer. Sometime that spring, she left school altogether. Velasco's letter to her in March indicated that she had left school to accept a position with the *Seattle Daily Times*. Velasco to Wetherell, Seattle, 12 March 1928, VVC. For additional information about the Scribes Club and the *Red Arrow* after Velasco's departure, see: inside cover; Irene Schagel, "Rosary"; Jane L'Eveque, "One A-Fraidian Night," *The Red Arrow*, June 1928, Vol. II, No. 2, 11; inside cover; Irene Schagel, "Just a Day"; Jane L'Eveque, "A Bellingham Teacher Goes Original," *The Red Arrow*, June 1928, Vol. II, No. 3 (?), 5-6, inside cover, *Red Arrow*, December 1928, Vol. II, No. 4, inside cover, *The Red Arrow*, March 1929, Vol. II, No. 5; "Scribes Club," *Klipsun '28*, WWUC, 100.

10. Diary, 12, 15, 18-21, 24, 25, 28 January 1927; 2 February 1927, VVC; Velasco, "Poet Gives Advice to Young Authors"; "Literary Contest to be Sponsored by Scribes Club"; "'Red Arrow' Announces Contest," *Weekly Messenger*, 21 January 1927, 1, 4; "Many Students Seek Scribes Club," *Weekly Messenger*, 28 January 1927, 4; "Scribes Initiation Proves Dreadful to New members," *Weekly Messenger*, 4 February 1927, 4; *The Red Arrow*, March 1927, Vol. I, No. 1, 6; Washington State Normal School, Ellensburg, Washington, *Unofficial Copy Transcript of Record*, 5 October 1932, Box 12, "College Credentials," VVC (showing that Velasco qualified for 24 transfer credits from State Normal School in Bellingham); University of Washington, *Grade Report*, c. post-1937, Box 12, "College Credentials," VVC (showing that he received 118 (?) credits from the State Normal School in Bellingham and from the Washington State Normal School in Ellensburg); State Normal School, Bellingham, Washington, *Report of Student Grades Made on Intelligence and Achievement Tests*, c. 1926-1927, Box 12, "College Credentials," VVC (showing that Velasco received grades in five areas, although it is not clear for what quarter or whether a specific number of credits for each was involved); "World Politics Club," *Klipsun '27*. He may have accumulated as many as 24 transferable credits during two quarters of study. Washington State Normal School, *Unofficial Copy Transcript of Record*, 5 October 1932, Box 12, "College Credentials," VVC.

11. Velasco's tenure as a founder and first president of the Scribes Club and as editor of *The Red Arrow* was surprisingly short. After the first quarter of the journal's existence, he was no longer involved with either, and extant sources make no mention of him or of why he had left. His tenure as the leader of *The Red Arrow* came to an end with the publication of its first issue in March of 1927. A possible reason for his departure was the

end of his studies in Bellingham. Another possible reason may have been that, once Velasco, the only minority member of the journal, had established its credibility, other, incoming members had little reason to retain a Filipino as their leader. The next editor of *The Red Arrow* was Nelson Robinson. *The Red Arrow*, March 1927, Vol. I, No. 1, inside cover; "The Scribes Club"; "The Red Arrow," *Klipsun '27*, 56, 123; "The Red Arrow"; "Scribes Club," *Klipsun '28*, 71, 100; *The Red Arrow*, May 1927, Vol. I, No. 2, inside cover; "Red Arrow Seeks Material for New Edition," *Weekly Messenger*, 29 April 1927, 4; *The Red Arrow*, December 1927, Vol. I, No. 3, 6; *The Red Arrow*, June 1928, Vol. II, No. 2, inside cover; *The Red Arrow*, December 1928, Vol. II, No. 4, inside cover; *The Red Arrow*, March 1929, Vol. II, No. 5, WWUC, 3. For samples of other editors' and writers' statements and perspectives on the purpose of the journal, see: Edna Wise, "Editorial," in *The Red Arrow*, December 1927, Vol. I, No. 3, 6; inside cover; June Wetherell, "Futuristic," "Lew Sarett—*An Impression*," "Imagination," in *The Red Arrow*, May 1927, Vol. I, No. 2, inside cover, 10, 14, 17; "Red Arrow," *Klipsun '28*, WWUC, 71-72.

12. *Annual Catalog 1926*, 25-26. *Klipsun '28*, 85; "Science of Choosing Room-Mate is Ticklish Job, Says One Who is Well Versed on the Subject"; "Students Continue to Get Positions," *Weekly Messenger*, 13 August 1926, 1; "Many Men and Women at Normal Work to Meet School Expenses," *Weekly Messenger*, 11 February 1927, 1; "Opportunities for Work Investigated," *Weekly Messenger*, 30 July 1926, 1; "Faculty Members at W.E.A. Meeting," *Weekly Messenger*, 29 October 1926, WWUC, 1.

13. "Splendid Progress Made by Dancers," *Weekly Messenger*, 16 July 1926, 1; "College Club Dance on Sat. July 24," *Weekly Messenger*, 23 July 1926, 1; "Romeo and Juliet Plays Next Week"; "Calendar Indicates Busy Week Ahead," *Weekly Messenger*, 6 August 1926, 1, Calendar; Theodore Cederberg, "'Romeo and Juliet' Draws Capacity Audience on Two Consecutive Nights"; "Benedicts Cop Intra-mural Championship by Defeating Durr's Dummies," *Weekly Messenger*, 13 August 1926, 1, 2, Viking Sports Page; "'Dear Brutus' is Very Popular with Normal Playgoers," *Weekly Messenger*, 5 November 1926, 1; *Weekly Messenger*, 7 January 1927, Calendar; "Edens Hall Dames Hold Peppy Vote," *Weekly Messenger*, 21 January 1927, 1; "The Gondoliers' Show Here Tonight"; "Edens Hall Girls Stage Pajama Party," *Weekly Messenger*, 25 February 1927, 1, 4; *Klipsun '27*, 79; Velasco (?), "Heart Throbs," *Weekly Messenger*, 7 January 1927, WWUC, 4; Diary, 7 January 1927, VVC. For additional clues about Velasco's participation in social events, see: Velasco, "Here is Another Feature Exposing Everything about a Normal Girl," *Weekly Messenger*, 17 December 1926, 1, 4; Diary, 28 December 1926, 11 January 1927, VVC.

14. Diary, 7, 21, 24, 27, 28 January 1927, VVC; "World Politics Club," *Klipsun '27*, WWUC, 131.

15. Multmueller to Velasco, 6 November 1926; 10 February 1927; Leonor Velasco to Velasco, 30 March 1931, Box 1, Folder 31; Diary, 27 December 1926, VVC; "School Calendar, 1926-1927," *Annual Catalog, 1926-1927*, Washington State Normal School, WWUC.

16. Diary, 3-7 January 1927; "Filipino Representative Praises Women," *Varsity Filipino Weekly*, 21 December 1926, Box 4, Folder 11, VVC, 2; "The Scribes Club," *Klipsun '27*, WWUC, 123.

17. Velasco, "The Passing Week," in *Weekly Messenger*, 5 November 1926, 2; 28 January 1927, 2. See also analysis of his first collection of poetry, *Lingyen and Other Poems*, in Chapter One.

18. Velasco, "The Passing Week," in *Weekly Messenger*, 22 January 1926, 2; Velasco, "Facts and Theories," *Weekly Messenger*, 17 December 1926, WWUC, 2.

19. Velasco, "The Passing Week," *Weekly Messenger*, 11 November 1926, 2; 25 February 1927, WWUC, 2.

20. Velasco, "The Passing Week," *Weekly Messenger*, 3 December 1926, 2; 28 January 1927, WWUC, 2; Diary, 28 January 1928, VVC; Peter Novick, *That Noble Dream: The Objectivity Question and the American Historical Profession* (Cambridge: Cambridge University Press, 1988).

21. Velasco, "Ave Regina," in "Poet's Corner," *Philippine Seattle Colonist*, 7 January 1927, Box 14, Folder 1, lines 6-7, 12-13; Diary, 26, 28 December 1926; 27 January 1927; Victorio Edades, letter to the editor, reprinted in "Snappy Statements," *Philippine Seattle Colonist*, 7 January 1927, 8; "Good Spirit is Shown by Friends"; "Club Takes Part in Literary Contest," in *Varsity Filipino Weekly*, 21 December 1926, Box 4, Folder 11, 1; Velasco, "Her Malayan Majesty, Neny I and Court," *Philippine Seattle Colonist*, 7 January 1927, vol. IV, No. 1, Box 14, Folder 1, VVC, cover page; Princess Orig, "Kayumanggi Versus Maputi: 100 Years of America's White Aesthetics in Philippine Literature," in Roces, 100-114; Roces, "Women in Philippine Politics and Society," in ibid., 168.

22. Velasco, "Ave Regina"; "Review of 1926," *Philippine Seattle Colonist*, 7 January 1927, Box 14, Folder 1, 6, 13; Diary, 1, 9 January 1927, VVC.

23. Diary, 14 January 1927; "Dr. Starr to Talk on Japan and China"; "Colonist Aide Gets Promotion"; "Filipino Boxer Kayoes Two"; "1926 Rizal Day Biggest Ever"; "How Popularity Crown was Won," *Philippine Seattle Colonist*, 7 January 1927, Box 14, Folder 1, 1, 4, 6, 11; Vincent Navea, "Rizal, Hero and Martyr," *Philippine Seattle Colonist*, 7 January 1927, Box 14, Folder 1, VVC, 5, 10, 11; Velasco himself may have contributed an article describing the purpose of the *Colonist*. An anonymous article provided a sophisticated and critical analysis of American motives in the Philippines. There were many other expressions of Filipino nationalistic and anti-American sentiment in the *Philippine Seattle Colonist*: "Home Affairs"; David P. De Tagle, "Credit Deserved"; "Home Affairs"; "Snappy Statements"; "Colonist Information Service"; Madame Madeleine Sedgwick Richard, "America and the Movies"; "What Rizal Laid Out"; *Philippine Seattle Colonist*, 7 January 1927, VVC, 7-9, 12-14; "History Professor Condemns U.S. Policy in the Orient," *Varsity Filipino Weekly*, 21 November 1926, Box 4, Folder 11, VVC, 2.

24. Clarence Andrews, in Booker T. Washington, *Up from Slavery* (New York: Airmount Books, 1967), 11. See also, W.E.B. du Bois, *The Souls of Black Folk* (Chicago: A.C. McClurg & Co., 1903; reprint, New York: Bantam Books, 1983).

25. Multmueller to Velasco, 8 December 1926; 10 February 1927, VVC.

26. Ibid., 6 November 1926, VVC; Citizenship of American Women Married to Foreigners: Hearings on H.R. 4049 Before the Committee on Immigration and Naturalization, 65th Cong., 1st Sess. 5. See also Michael Serizawa Brown, "Race, Gender, and the Cable Act" (paper presented at the Joint Asian Pacific American American Law Faculty/Law Teachers of Color Conference, Seattle, Washington, 22 March, 2003).

27. Velasco to President, National University, Manila, 15 September 1937, VVC. HistoryLink.org gives the dates of his stint as the paper's publisher and editor as beginning in 1924. HistoryLink.org, visited 23 July 2002.

## Chapter Four

1. For specific events in which both Velasco and Multmueller both participated, see Chapter Two and notes. See also Multmueller to Velasco, 11 May 1927, VVC.

2. Ibid., 8 December 1926; 10 February, 11 May 1927, VVC.

3. Ibid., 6 November 1926; 11 May 1927, VVC.

4. The mayor Seattle women recalled in 1912 was Hiram Gill. They also campaigned for the eight-hour day for working women and, in 1913, for a minimum wage

law for women. John Putman, "'A Test of Chiffon Politics': Gender Politics in Seattle, 1897-1917," *Pacific Historical Review* 69, no. 4 (November 2000): 595-617. For information about female leaders in the Western states, see Karen J. Blair, ed., *Women in Pacific Northwest History: An Anthology* (Seattle: University of Washington Press, 1988); Gayle Gullett, "Constructing the Woman Citizen and Struggling for the Vote in California, 1896-1911," *Pacific Historical Review* 69, no. 4 (November 2000): 573-593. For additional information on political and reformist activities of Washington women, see Mildred Tanner Andrews, *Washington Women as Pathbreakers* (Dubuque: Kendall/Hunt Publishing Company, 1989), 3-28, 53-83. For a collection of writings about the history of women in the Pacific Northwest, see Elizabeth Jameson & Susan Armitage, *Writing of the Range: Race, Class, and Culture in the Women's West* (Norman: University of Oklahoma Press, 1997). For additional information on female political activism in Seattle during this period, see Sandra Haarsager, *Bertha Knight Landes of Seattle, Big City Mayor* (Norman: University of Oklahoma Press, 1994).

5. Multmueller to Velasco, 11 May, 24 December 1927; 20 April 1929; Diary, 23 March, 11 May 1929, VVC. See also Chapter Five and accompanying notes.

6. Annie Lincoln to Velasco, 8 June, 6, 27 December 1927; 4 December 1928; E.H. Lincoln to Velasco, 11 April 1929, VVC.

7. Lincoln to Velasco, 27 September; 6, 14, 16 December 1927; 4 December 1928; E.H. Lincoln to Velasco, 25 February, 15 March 1928, VVC.

8. Lincoln to Velasco, 24 January, 10 March, 5 May, 24 November 1929; E.H. Lincoln to Velasco, 23 March, 14 December, 1927; 25 February, 15 March, 14 April, 5 September, 6 November 1928; 3 January 1929; Diary, 27 November 1928; 24 January 1929, VVC.

9. E.H. Lincoln to Velasco, 25 February, 14 April, 5 September, 6 November 1928; 3 January, 11 April 1929, VVC.

10. Lincoln to Velasco, 5 May 1929, VVC; Diary, 6 May 1929, VVC.

11. Hope Tyler to Velasco, 29 June 1929, VVC.

12. Van Wechel to Velasco, 7 October, 13 November 1929, VVC. Velasco's address at the time he corresponded with Wechel is uncertain. The Washington State College student and faculty directory for 1929-1930 lists him as being a student during the 1929-1930 academic year, which presumably began in September of 1929. *Student and Faculty Directory, 1929-1930*, Washington State College, Manuscripts, Archives, and Special Collections, Washington State University, Pullman, Washington [hereafter WSUC]. Other records from the University of Washington indicate his presence at Washington State College in Pullman, although they do not give the date. See University of Washington, *Grade Report*, c. post-1942, Box 12, College Credentials, VVC. By October of 1929, Velasco may have already made several attempts to begin correspondence with Wechel; her reply to him in November indicates that she had received earlier correspondence from him. Her letter of 7 October 1929 indicates that Velasco possibly met her in the vicinity of Moxee, Washington during hop-picking season. Van Wechel to Velasco, 7, 10 October, 13 November 1929; 28 January, 10 March 1930; "Moxee Girls Grade Five Puts on Spurt to Defeat Ahtanum," [*Yakima Daily Herald*], newspaper clipping, c. January 1930, VVC; Dorothy Van Wechel to Velasco, 10 March 1930, VVC.

13. Diary, 21, 22 June 1928; 9 July 1928, VVC. The young lady was Clare Love. Diary, 25 June 1928, VVC. The poem Velasco dedicated to Love was "To a Violinist." Velasco, "To a Violinist," Box 3, Folder 3, VVC [published in *Poets on Parade* (Waterloo: Watchtower Books, 1937). See also Love to Velasco, 11 August 1931, Box 1, Folder 41, VVC; Diary, 24 June; 4, 7, 9 July; 4, 5, 20 December 1928; 23 January 1929, VVC; Evelyn Peterson to Velasco, 15 July 1930, VVC.

14. Ronald Takaki, *In the Heart of Filipino America* (New York: Chelsea House Publishers, 1994), 72; Takaki, *Stranger*, 326; Sucheng Chan, *Asian Americans: An Interpretive History* (Boston: Twayne Publishers, 1991), 53; Trinidad Rojo, interview by Carolina Koslosky; Margaret Mary Rae Duyungan, interview by Carolina Koslosky, 16 June 1975, Tape No. 13, FANHS.

15. Cordova, 118; David P. Tagle to Pedro Guevara, telegram, 16 April 1929, Box 1, Folder 46, VVC; Rhacel Salazar Parenas, "'White Trash' Meets the 'Little Brown Monkeys': The Taxi Dance Hall as a Site of Interracial and Gender Alliances Between White Working Class Women and Filipino Immigrant Men in the 1920s and 30s," *Amerasia Journal* 24, no. 2 (summer 1998): 115-134; Cordova, 211-215; Paul Cressey, *The Taxi Dance Hall: A Sociological Study in Commercialized Recreation and City Life* (Chicago: University of Chicago Press, 1932); Takaki, *In the Heart*, 66-68; Carlos Bulosan, letter dated 10 December 1937, quoted in E. San Juan, *On Becoming Filipino* (Philadelphia: Temple University Press, 1995), 192.

16. Takaki, *Strangers*, 326-328; Chan, *Asian Americans*, 53; Cordova, 116.

17. Cordova, 117.

18. Ibid., 119; Bill Ong Hing, *Making and Remaking Asian America Through Immigration Policy, 1850-1990* (Stanford: Stanford University Press, 1993), 63; Takaki, *In the Heart*, 64-65.

19. Cordova, 19, 125, 130; Julian Samora and Patricia Vandel Simon, *A History of the Mexican American People* (Notre Dame: University of Notre Dame Press, 1993), 136-137; Herbert B. Peterson, "Twentieth Century Search for Cibola: Post-World War I Mexican Labor Exploitation in Arizona," in Manuel P. Servin, ed., *An Awakened Minority: The Mexican Americans*, 2nd ed. (Beverly Hills: Glencoe Press, 1974), 113-132.

20. Diary, 5, 6, 28 April; 26-30 May; 16-18, 23, 30 June; 1, 2, 4, July 1928; 23 March 1929; 28 April 1929, VVC; Takaki, *In the Heart*, 69.

21. Velasco, "A Critical Study of Carl Sandburg's Poems," 26 January 1928; "Shakespeare's Heroes: A Critical Study," April 1930, Box 12; "Alas!" 16 December 1927 [published in *Seattle Pacific College News* on December 16, 1927); "Alaska Night," June 1928 [published in *Poets and Poetry of 1931* (Hollywood: Poets Guild Publishers, 1931)]; "My Prescription," June 1928; "To a Violinist," 22 June 1928 [published in *Poets on Parade* (Waterloo: Watchtower Books, 1937)]; "Your Eyebrow," c. 1928-1929; "A Golden Page," November 1927; "Brown Birdie," November 1929; "My Ship," 18 May 1931; "The Sea," 20 May 1931, Box 3, Folder 3; "To a Nurse," 16 September 1930; "The Dream," 10 November 1931; "Let Us Make Friends," 18 May 1931; "The Tide," 17 June 1931, Box 3, Folder 4, VVC.

22. Jenia Boudine to Velasco, 21 November, 2 December 1931, VVC. See also "Filipino Editor in American College—A Versatile Writer and Poet," *The Filipino Student*, June 1933, Box 3, Folder 25, 5; Velasco to Carlos P. Romulo, 22 October 1951; Velasco, "Published Poems," Box 3, Folder 4, 1937, VVC.

23. Velasco, "A Filipino Serenade," undated, Box 3, Folder 3, VVC.

24. Princess Orig, in Roces, 102, 105-106, 109-115; Marya Svetlana T. Camacho, "Race and Culture in Spanish and American Colonial Politics," in ibid., 43-74. For additional commentaries on the development of Filipino identity in the Philippines and in the United States, see Maria P.P. Root, *Filipino Americans: Transformation and Identity* (Thousand Oaks: Sage Publications, 1997).

25. *Sea Gull News*, 23 June 1928, Vol. 3, No. 1, Box 4, Folder 8, VVC. See also "The Sea Gull News Now Three Years Old," *Sea Gull News*, Vol. 3, No. 4, 13 August 1928, Box 4, Folder 8, VVC. Velasco's "Alaska Night." appeared in the 23 June issue. "Alaska Prescription" appeared in the 8 July edition. *Sea Gull News*, 23 June 1928, Vol. 3, No. 1, Box 4, Folder 8, VVC.

26. "Growth of Filipino Publications in Alaska," *Sea Gull News*, Vol. 3, No. 4, 13 August 1928, Box 4, Folder 8, VVC, 3. Velasco's participation in Filipino publishing efforts is evident from various sources. See Marco Aquino to Velasco, 31 January 1929, Box 8, Folder 21; ibid.; "What's the Matter with the New Cuadra Gossips," *Sea Gull News*, Vol. 3, No. 4, 13 August 1928, Box 4, Folder 8, 3; "To Our Contemporaries," *Sea Gull News*, Vol. 3, No. 4, 13 August 1928, Box 4, Folder 8, VVC, 3; anonymous, "What About a Port Althorp Paper?" *Sea Gull News*, Vol. 3, No. 4, 13 August 1928, Box 4, Folder 8, VVC, 3; Sebastian Abella to Velasco, 5 June 1929, Box 1, Folder 51, VVC.

27. Aquino to Velasco, 28 February, 5 March, 6, 19, 27 April, 5 May, 5 June, 15 December 1929; 5 January 1930, Box 8, Folder 21; Marco Aquino, "Bremerton News," c. April 1929, Box 9, Folder 36; Tenorio, (?) to Velasco, 27 June 1929, Box 1, Folder 52, Crisanto Ticman to Velasco, 24 July 1927, Box 1, Folder 46; Teodoro Evangelista to Velasco, 7, 10, 12 April 1928, Box 1, Folder 37; Macario C. Ribados to Velasco, 8 February 1930, Box 1, Folder 44; Manuel A. Edena to Velasco, 11, 17 October 1932; 13 February 1933; Velasco to "Filipino Boxing Fans," 28 February 1931, Box 8, Folder 48, VVC.

28. Diary, 4, 7, 9 July 1928, VVC. For excerpts from Velasco's speech, see *Sea Gull News*, 8 July 1928, Vol. 3, No. 2, Box 4, Folder 8, VVC. See also *Sea Gull News*, 23 June 1928, Vol. 3, No. 1, Box 4, Folder 8; David Tagle to Pedro Guevara, telegram, 16 April 1929, Box 1, Folder 46; Tenorio to Velasco, 27 June 1929, Box 1, Folder 52; Velasco to editor, *Seattle Post Intelligencer*, 27 November 1929 and 27 January 1930, Box 8, Folder 40, VVC.

29. Velasco to Manuel S. Rustia, 9 April 1928, Box 1, Folder 53, VVC; Velasco to Rustia, 19 August 1928, Box 1, Folder 53, VVC. Velasco may have incurred the debt to Rustia in early 1928; Velasco to Rustia, 14 January 1928, Box 8, Folder 40, VVC.

30. ________ to Velasco, 3 September 1928, Box 1, Folder 52; Velasco to Jose A. Reyes, 21 November 1928, Box 8, Folder 40; Benigno Sevidal to Velasco, 8 November 1928, Box 1, Folder 28, VVC.

31. Sevidal to Velasco, 24 February 1929; Sebastian Abella to Velasco, 5 June 1929, Box 1, Folder 51; Aquino to Velasco, Seattle, 5 March 1929; Aquino to Velasco, 27 April 1929, Box 8, Folder 21, VVC.

32. Aquino to Velasco, 5, 30 March; 19 April 1929; 20 January 1930, Box 8, Folder 21, VVC.

33. Aquino to Velasco, c. March 1930; Velasco to Lorenzo Zamora, 4 April 1930, Box 8, Folder 40, VVC.

34. Velasco to Abella, 28 November 1931; Velasco to editor, *The Filipino Student*, New York, 12 December 1931, Box 8, Folder 40, VVC. The work Manuel allegedly plagiarized was "Reverie: Zahir-u-Din" by Laurence Hope. Laurence Hope, *India's Love Lyrics* (New York: Dodd, Mead and Company, 1928), 127. The work which Manuel wrote, copyrighted, and published in *The Filipino Student* was "A Reverie." Victorio Velasco, untitled, c. 12 December 1931, Box 8, Folder 40, VVC. See also Abella to Velasco, 22 February 1931, Box 1, Folder 51, VVC.

35. Edena to Velasco, 11 October 1932, Box 1; Velasco, "On Board the [S.S.] Alameda," *Sea Gull News*, 23 June 1928, Vol. 3, No. 1; *Sea Gull News*, 8 July 1928, Vol. 3, No. 2, VVC. Velasco's unofficial title was "warehouse boss." "Second Season to Start on September the Seventh," *Sea Gull News*, Vol. 3, No. 4, 13 August 1928, Box 4, Folder 8, VVC; "Six White Boys Engaged," *Sea Gull News*, Vol. 3, No. 4, 13 August 1928, Box 4, Folder 8; Rufino M. Tandoc to Velasco, 12 February 1929; Leon Toquero and Apolonia Penor to Velasco, 22 February 1929; Tandoc to Velasco, 12 February 1929, Box 1, Folder 46; Antonio Velasco to Velasco, 17, 27 March 1930, Box 1, Folder 47; Antoniolenus [Antonio?] Velasco to Velasco ["Toriong"], 30 March 1931, Box 1 Folder 50,

VVC; Margaret Mary Rae Duyungan, interview by Carolina Koslosky; Velasco, "The Call of the 'Silver Horde,'" *Filipino Student* XII, no. 8 (June) , Box 3, Folder 25, VVC: 5.

36. Leonard W. Riley to Velasco 2 August 1929, Box 1, Folder 44; Velasco to Board of Trustees, U.W. Filipino Clubhouse Fund, 17 December 1929; Fred ["Frederick"] Velasco to Velasco, 31 October 1931, Box 1, Folder 47; Velasco to Jose Fernandez, 22 January 1931, Box 1, Folder 53; Velasco to Crisanto Ticman, 29 June 1933, Box 8, Folder 40, VVC.

37. *Sea Gull News*, 23 June 1928, Vol. 3, No. 1, Box 4, Folder 8; 8 August 1928, Vol. 3, No. 3, Box 4, Folder 8; Diary, 24 January 1929; E.H. Lincoln to Velasco, 11 April 1929; "Two Members Kick Out," *The Informer*, Vol. I, No. 2, 24 December 1929, Box 3, Folder 26, 2; Antonio Velasco to Velasco, 17, 27 March 1930, Box 1, Folder 47; Dalmarco to Velasco ["Toriong"], 4 July 1927; Corrado Legaspe to Velasco, 11 January 1930, Box 1, Folder 52; Leonor Velasco to Velasco, 7 February, 11 June 1929, 30 March 1931, Box 1, Folder 31, VVC.

38. Antoniolenus [Antony] Velasco to Velasco ["Toriong"], 6 January, 30 March 1931, Box 1, Folder 50; Velasco to Jose Fernandez, 22 January 1931, Box 1, Folder 53; Antoniolenus Velasco,to Velasco, 17 February 1931, Box 1, Folder 47; Teresa Acosta to Velasco, 27 November 1931; Sianong (?) to Velasco, 8 October, 3 November 1931, Box 1, Folder 51, VVC.

39. Leonor Velasco referred to the two brothers as "Tio" and "Tonieng." Leonor Velasco to Velasco, 4 August, Box 1, Folder 31, VVC. See also Leonor Velasco to Velasco, 7 February, 24 June 1929, 30 March 1931, Box 1, Folder 31, VVC.

40. Dalmarco Velasco to Velasco, 4 July 1927, Box 1, Folder 52; Leonor Velasco to Velasco, 7 February 1929, 30 March 1931, Box 1, Folder 31, VVC.

41. Leonor Velasco to Velasco, 24 February 1929, 30 March 1931, Box 1, Folder 31; Teresa Acosta to Velasco, 27 November 1931, Box 1, Folder 51, VVC.

42. Velasco to Crisanto Ticman, 29 June 1933; Velasco to *Seattle Post Intelligencer*, 27 January 1930 (quoting Arthur Brisbane), Box 8, Folder 40, VVC. Abella to Velasco, 22 February 1931, Box 1, Folder 51, VVC.

## Chapter Five

1. Sebastian Abella to Velasco, 22 February 1931, VVC. For information about Carlos Bulosan's relationships with white women, see Takaki, *Strangers*, 343-354; E. San Juan, *On Becoming Filipino* (Philadelphia: Temple University Press, 1995), 185-189. For a short biography of Bulosan, see: Carey McWilliams, "Introduction," in Carlos Bulosan, *America is in the Heart* (Seattle: Harcourt, Brace, and Company, Inc., 1943), xv-xx.

2. Delphine Brooks to Velasco, 2, 10 February 1932; 28 November 1933; Velasco, "Doubt," Box 12; Murray ________ to Velasco, 12 January 1934, Box 12, "College Credentials"; "Transcript of Record, Washington State Normal School, Ellensburg," Box 12, Folder 19, VVC.

3. Brooks to Velasco, 10 February 1932, VVC.

4. Ibid., 14 November 1933; 20 December 1935; 10 December 1936, VVC.

5. Diary, 14, 15, 17 August 1934; 1 January, 17 May 1935, VVC.

6. Brooks to Velasco, 3 December 1935; 25 August, 9 October 1936; Velasco to Brooks, 30 March, 14 April 1937, VVC.

7. Diary, 11, 12, 15, 18, 19, 26, 29 January; 13, 17, 18, 22, 29 February; 3 March, 1935; 1 February, 1 March 1936; Brooks to Velasco, c. 1934-1935; Velasco to Brooks, 24 February, 15 March 1937, VVC.

8. Brooks to Velasco, 2 February 1932, VVC.

9. Congress, House, Committee on Immigration and Naturalization, *Return of Certain Filipinos to Philippine Islands, Report No. 127*, 73rd Congress, 1st Sess. [statement of Mr. Dickstein]; Cordova, 120; Takaki, *Strangers*, 333. The United States Commissioner of Immigration in San Francisco characterized the act as being one "of friendship and good will." Congress, Senate, Edward W. Cahill, United States Commissioner of Immigration, *Congressional Record*, 74th Congress, 2nd Sess., (3 March 1936).

10. Margaret Mary Rae Duyungan, interview by Carolina Koslosky; Takaki, *Strangers*, 330; "Filipino Exclusion," *Argus*, 13 February 1932, 2; "Amuck Filipino," *Argus*, 16 September 1933, 4.

11. Velasco, "City Shadows" [published in *Crown Anthology*, Avon House, 1938], Box 12; "To the Commonwealth of the Philippines," Box 3, Folder 4, VVC.

12. Velasco, "Darkening Hills," Box 3, Folder 3; "The Song of Spring"; "The Question"; "The Rain"; "To You"; "There is the Moon Again" [published in *Modern American Poetry, 1937*]; "Regret," Box 3, Folder 4; "Sunshine"; "Ideals"; "Outlook"; "Workers" [published in *Contemporary American Men Poets—1937*]; "Ella Fetters"; "To Helen"; Velasco, "To Ruby," Box 3, Folder 5; "Outlook"; "A Soul for Gold"; "The Corner Newsboy" [published in *Christmas Hymns, 1937*]; "A Poem for Jean"; "To a Girl with Sweet Smiles" [published in *Modern American Poetry, 1933*]; "Silver Hours"; "Absence"; "Regret"; "Spring Thoughts"; "You"; "Fragrance"; "Inspiration"; "A Mother's Love"; "Spring"; "Sonnet"; "What is Beauty?"; "Doubt"; "Resolution"; "Sweetheart," Box 12, VVC; *Directory of Filipino Students in the United States, 1933-1934*, Folder #4048, Filipino Club Collection, Holland Library, Manuscripts and Special Collections, Washington State University, Pullman, Washington, 37 [hereafter WSUC].

13. Velasco, "The City"; "Camia," Box 12; Velasco, "Ambition"; Velasco, "To the Commonwealth of the Philippines," Box 3, Folder 4, VVC. See also Chapter Three and accompanying notes about Filipino exilic literature in the United States.

14. Velasco, "To Ruby"; "To Helen"; "Ella Fetters," Box 3, Folder 5; "A Poem for Jean"; "Regret"; "Resolution"; "A Voice"; "The Rain" [cited in Avon House's *Biographical Dictionary of Contemporary Poets*, c. 1937], Box 12, VVC.

15. Velasco, "Modernity," Box 3, Folder 4; "White Petals of Yester-Spring," [published in *Christmas Lyrics of 1937*], Box 12, VVC.

16. The poems were "Modernity," "City Shadows," and "Workers" [published in *Contemporary American Men Poets, 1937*]. See also: Velasco to Henry Harrison, New York, 16 May 1936, Box 8, Folder 40; David Gould to Velasco, 9 March, 1937, Box 1, Folder 9, VVC. Velasco responded to Gould's invitation by submitting the following poems: "There is the Moon Again," "The Rain," "A Voice," and "City Shadows." See Velasco's notation on Gould's second letter. In the spring of 1937, the editor of Avon House's *American Voices* anthology personally invited Velasco to submit work for the volume. Margaret Nelson to Velasco, 10 May 1937, VVC. Frank Bolima provides the following information about publishers who included Velasco's works or listed him among American writers: *Poets and Poetry of 1931* (Hollywood: Poets Guild Publishers, 1932); *Modern American Poetry—1933* (New York: Galleon Press, 1933); *Christmas Lyrics of 1937* (New York: Beacon Publications, 1937); *Paebar Anthology of Verse* (New York: The Paebar Company, Inc., 1937); *Contemporary American Men Poets* (New York: Henry Harrison Publishers, 1938); *The Crown Anthology of Verse* (New York: Crown Publications, 1938); *The Biographical Dictionary of Contemporary Poets* (New York: Avon House Publishers, 1938); *The Poetry House Anthology* (New York: Poetry

House, 1938); *Golden Gate Anthology* (New York: Tudor House, 1939). Velasco's poems also appeared in: *Philippine Free Press*; *Integridad*; *The Woman's Journal* [all in Manila]; *Philippine Republic*, *Bagumbayan*, *Philippine Mail*; *Philippine Advocate*; *Philippine Review*; *Philippine Monthly* [Filipino publications in the United States]. Bolima, 5-6; Leon V. Gordon to Velasco, 3 June 1937; Beacon Publications to Velasco, c. November 1937, Box 1, Folder 34; Praeger Co., Inc. to Velasco, 21 June 1937; Michael Everett to Velasco, 26 October 1937, Box 1, Folder 43, VVC. For additional information about Velasco's publishing efforts, see Chapter One and accompanying notes.

17. Princess Orig, in Roces, 101, 113.

18. Sucheng Chan, *Asian Americans: An Interpretive History* (Philadelphia: Temple University Press, 1991), 39; Friday, 113, 132-133; Cordova, 69.

19. Gold, 23; Friday, 66, 123-125, 129, 131, 137, 139-140.

20. Gold, 1, 23-24; Friday, 97; "Law & Order: 'Peaceful Picketing,'" *Argus*, 3 August 1935, 3.

21. Gold, 33-34, 40-43, 47; Friday, 142-145.

22. Gold, 46-48, citing *Philippine Advocate*, April 1935, 1.

23. New England Fish Company to Velasco, 9 January 1934, Box 35, Folder 16; Velasco to W.G. Warren, 21 December 1935, Box 8, Folder 40, VVC; Friday, 131, 139-140. See also Chapter Four and accompanying notes.

24. Friday, 138.

25. Ibid., 145-148; Gold, 29, 35, 43, 49-54. According to Gold, even though the N.R.A. hearings had nominally abolished the contract labor system following hearings in 1934, the system continued in practice. It was not until Filipinos resolved their differences among themselves and, following Duyungan's assassination, finally became convinced of the sincerity of his motives, that the union became an effective force uniting all cannery workers. Gold, 29-35, 43, 53-54. The Supreme Court's nullification of the National Recovery Act in 1935, according to Gold, further hampered efforts to correct abuses under the contract system. See also David Kennedy, *Freedom from Fear: The American People in Depression and War, 1929-1945* (New York: Oxford University Press, 1999), 328.

26. Velasco, vita, undated, Box 1, Folder 1, VVC; Friday, 139.

27. According to Gold, the reluctance of the A.F.L. international in responding to the concerns of agricultural workers contributed to the latter's formation, in July of 1937, of a new union, the United Cannery, Agricultural, Packing, and Allied workers of America, as a C.I.O. union. Gold, 56-57, 59.

28. "Filipino Editor in American College—A Versatile Writer and Poet," *Filipino Student*, June 1933, Box 3, Folder 25; Bolima, 3.

29. Washington Washington State Normal School, *Transcript of Record*, 5 October 1932; Murray ________ to Velasco, 12 January 1934; Frank T. Barnard to Velasco, 17 October 1934; State Normal School, *Transcript of the Record of Victorio Acosto Velasco*, 16 December 1933, Box 12, "College Credentials," VVC; *Faculty and Student Directory, Washington State College, 1929-1930*; *Chinook, 1932*, Index; "W.S.C. Filipino Club," *Chinook, 1933*, WSUC, 291.

30. "American Society of Civil Engineers," *Chinook, 1931*, 312; "Varsity Boxing and Wrestling," *Chinook, 1932*, 151; "W.S.C. Filipino Club," *Chinook, 1932*, 247; "W.S.C. Filipino Club"; "Chinese Students Club," *Chinook, 1933*, 291, WSUC. See also *Chinook, 1928*; *Chinook 1929*; *Chinook, 1930*, *Chinook, 1931*, *Chinook, 1933*, WSUC. For additional information about Filipinos at the State College, see: Denny to Carl Brewster, 5 July 1930; Felipe ________ to Brewster; Brewster to ________, 27 May 1943; "Program," 20 November 1937; Fortunato T. Basilio to Brewster, 26 February 1933; Jose Rizal, "My Last Farewell," Filipino Club Collection, Folder #4048, WSUC.

31. *Chinook, 1928*; *Chinook 1929*; *Chinook, 1930*; *Chinook, 1931*; *Chinook, 1932*; *Chinook, 1933*, WSUC. For additional information about the history of the Washington State College, see E.A. Bryan, *Historical Sketch of the State College of Washington, 1890-1925* (Spokane: Inland-American printing Co., 1928); William Landeen, *E.O. Holland and the State College of Washington, 1916-1944* (Pullman: State College of Washington, 1958); Burt Harrison, "An Index to E.A. Bryan's Historical Sketch of the State College of Washington, 1890-1925"; "Eurodelphian Literary Society," *Chinook, 1932*, 334; "American College Quill Club," *Chinook, 1932*, 340; "Eurodelphian," *Chinook, 1935*, 272; "The 1933 Chinook," *Chinook, 1933*, 76-77; "The Chinook Editorial Staff," *Chinook, 1933*, 78; "The Washington State Evergreen," *Chinook, 1933*, 80-81; "Evergreen Editorial Staff [First Semester]," *Chinook, 1933*, 82; "Evergreen Editorial Staff [Second Semester]," *Chinook, 1933*, 83; "Varsity Boxing and Wrestling," *Chinook, 1932*, WSUC, 151; Bolima, 3.

32. *Filipino Student*, XII, nos. 6 & 7 (April-May 1934): 1; Velasco, "The Call of the 'Silver Horde,'" *Filipino Student*, XII, no. 8 (June 1934), Box 3, Folder 25, VVC: 5. Velasco rejoined a host of other Filipinos engaged in publishing newspapers. At the time, Filipino newspapers like the *Filipino Citizen*, the *Cosmopolitan Courier*, and the *Philippine American Chronicle* were among other journals circulating among Filipinos, lib.washington.edu, visited 24 July; Bolima, 5; Juan R. Quijano to Velasco, Seattle, 22 December 1937, Box 1, Folder 44; Bureau of Indian Affairs to Velasco, 22 November 1935, Box 8, Folder 35; Velasco to Pedro Guevara, 1 May 1935; Velasco to Diosdado Yap, 11 October, 22 November 1935; Velasco to Teddy De Nolasco, 22 November 1935; Velasco to Quintin Paredes, 3 March 1936; Velasco to Lee Paul Sieg, 3 March 1936, Box 8, Folder 40, VVC. One bibliographic source on *The Advocate* indicates erroneously that it was Velasco's own paper. See lib.washington.edu, visited 28 May 2003.

33. Velasco to Yap, 11 October 1935; Velasco to De Nolasco, 22 November 1935, Box 8, Folder 40, VVC.

34. Velasco to Robert Flor, 22 November 1935; Velasco to Trinidad Rojo, 31 March 1936, Box 8, Folder 40, VVC.

35. Velasco to Melecio Toledo, 9 and 19 January 1937, Box 8, Folder 40, VVC.

36. Marco Aquino to Velasco, 1 July 1936, Box 8, Folder 21, VVC.

37. Velasco and Pio De Cano, "Agreement," c. 1934, Box 8, Folder 46, VVC.

38. Velasco to De Cano, 1 April 1937, Box 8, Folder 40, VVC.

39. De Cano to ________, 28 May 1935, Box 8, Folder 40, VVC; Marco Aquino to Velasco, 1 July 1936, Box 8, Folder 21, VVC.

40. Gold, 46-47.

41. Ibid., 46-49.

42. De Cano, 26 October 1935, Box 1, Folder 43, VVC; Velasco to De Cano, 1 April 1937, Box 8, Folder 40, VVC.

43. Marco Aquino to Velasco, 1 July 1936, Box 8, Folder 21; E. Llamas Rosario to Velasco, 4 November 1936, Box 1, Folder 44, VVC.

44. Leonor Velasco to Velasco, 25 December 1935; 23 May, 21 June, 2 December 1936; 5 February 1937; 24 February 1938, Box 1, Folder 31, VVC.

45. Ibid., c. 1933-1935; 25 December 1935; 23 May, 21 June, 2 December 1936; 5 February 1937; 24 February 1938, Box 1, Folder 31,VVC.

# Chapter Six

1. Artsci.washington.edu, bartleby.com, andros_dance.tripod.com, visited 28 September 2002; *Engagements, 1942*, 18, 19 February 1942; *Engagements, 1944*, 7, 17, 21 February; 1-5 March, 1 April, 1944; Box 2, Folder 14, VVC.

2. Velasco did not identify the race of the women. However, their names—Pratt, Brown, Wright, and Jones—indicate the likelihood that they were Euro-American. *Engagements, 1942,* 12, 13, 27 April, 6 May, 1 June 1942, Box 2, Folder 14, VVC. According to the 23 November 1942 entry, Brown's given name was "Dorothy." *Engagements, 1942,* 23 November 1942. "Dorothy" may also have been Dorothy Gates of Kent High School. *Engagements, 1942,* Memoranda. Another possibility was that she was Dorothy Loy, who may have been a student at the University of Washington and the daughter of a Mrs. Loy of Petersburg, Alaska. *Engagements, 1944*, 6 February 1944, Box 2, Folder 14, VVC. In 1942, one of his most frequent companions was "Lillian." It was she with whom Velasco spent much of his time during the New Year's holidays of 1942. However, he did not record her surname in his engagement book and, consequently, it is impossible to conjecture about her race or national origin. *Engagements, 1942*, 31 December 1942; 1, 2 January 1943. He may have met her at least as early as March, 1942 because his entry of 4 March 1942 mentions her. *Engagements, 1942*, 4 March 1942, Memoranda. See also *Engagements, 1944,* 1, 9, 21, 29 January; 6, 23 February; 26 November 1944.

3. *Engagements, 1942*, 12, 18 January; 2 February; 6, 16 March 1942, Box 2, Folder 14, VVC. Langoey's last name does not appear in the engagement book. Her full name appears, however, in an edition of the *Filipino Forum*. "Brevities," *Filipino Forum*, 24 December 1942, 2. Felix was probably Felix Zamora, Velasco's colleague in the Pangasinan Association of the Pacific Northwest. Zoilo Paragas was a member of Local 7 in 1939. C.B. Mislang to Zoilo Paragas, 1 July 1939, Box 6, Folder 23, VVC. "Ray" was possibly the same man who sent Velasco a card from San Francisco on 7 June 1948 and could have been Ray Anchetta, who appears in other documents in the Velasco Collection. Raymond Ancheta (?) to Velasco, 7 June 1948, Box 1, Folder 51, VVC. Although it was possible that Velasco met and socialized with those not appearing in his engagement calendars and that this might be one explanation for the absence of male Euro-American names, it was unlikely because, if he had any such significant relationships, he probably would have mentioned them, in particular because of his consistency in recording names, dates, and events throughout the four-decade span that his diaries and engagement calendars covered. For additional information on Velasco's social activities, see *Engagements, 1942*, 19 January, 22 February, 6, 20 April, 1 June, 31 December 1942; *Engagements, 1944,* 9, 30 January, 28 May, 7, 28 October, 16 November 1944, Box 2, Folder 14, VVC. For a firsthand account of the change in attitudes towards Filipinos during the Second World War, see Trinidad Rojo, interview by Carolina Koslosky.

4. *Engagements, 1946,* 8, 19-24, 26, 28, 29 September; 4-6, 11, 12, 17, 19, 26, 27 October; 6-8, 21, 22, 25, 31 December 1946, Box 2, Folder 14, VVC; Trinidad Rojo, interview by Carolina Koslosky.

5. Notable examples of those with whom Velasco had the most frequent contact were J.C. Dionisio of Stockton, California; officials of the Philippine government, such as Manuel A. Adeva, serving in the United States; and the President of the Philippines. *Engagements, 1944,* 26 March, 24 September,19 November, 3 December 1944, Box 2, Folder 14; Velasco to Dionisio, 28 December 1943, Velasco to Adeva, 24 January 1944; Velasco to Secretary, Department of Information & Public Relations, 22 February 1944; Velasco to President of the Philippines, 23 March 1944, Box 8, Folder 41, VVC.

6. Tonieng Velasco to Velasco, 25 June 1942, Box 1, Folder 31, VVC. The precise location of Tonieng Velasco's farm is not clear. However, on two occasions he refers to San Luis Obispo. Other mutual acquaintances may have included Vincente Navea. Tonieng Velasco to Velasco, 12 September 1942; Familia to Velasco, 22 October 1942, Box 1, Folder 47, VVC. Pete was in the United States and then with the American military in Europe. "Pete" was the Americanized nickname for "Petong." Pete Velasco to Velasco, 1 April 1940; 15 September 1944, Box 1, Folder 47, VVC. Joe was in Los Angeles after 11 October 1944, although his whereabouts thereafter are not clear from the correspondence. Familia to Velasco, 11 October 1944, Box 1, Folder 47, VVC.

7. Mutual obligations were part of a deeply-entrenched value system among Filipinos, and those who did not observe them gained a disfavorable reputation among their peers. Agoncillo, 9; Tonieng Velasco to Velasco, 25 June, 12 September 1942, Box 1, Folder 31; 10 October 1944, Box 1, Folder 47, VVC. Tonieng told Victorio that he was not happy with the fact that the only help he could hire for harvest were the wives of men who had left for service in the war and that, consequently, he was not making as much of a profit as he might have been able to otherwise. Pete Velasco to Velasco, 9 July 1940; 28 March 1941, Box 1, Folder 47, VVC.

8. Astorio & Puget Sound Canning Company to Velasco, 31 October 1942, Box 6, Folder 34, VVC. Among those who benefited from the armed services' willingness to grant deferments was none other than Trinidad Rojo, president of Local 7. Trinidad Rojo, interview by Carolina Koslosky.

9. Gail Nomura, "Washington's Asian/Pacific American Communities," in Sid White and S.E. Solberg, *Peoples of Washington: Perspectives on Cultural Diversity* (Pullman: Washington State University Press, 1989), 145; Cordova, 217-221; "Cannery Workers' Union Asks for Deferment of Experienced Cannery Men," *Filipino Forum*, 24 December 1942, 1; Tonieng Velasco to Velasco, 22 October 1942, Box 1, Folder 47, VVC; Gold, 98; Friday, 188-189.

10. Friday, 189.

11. Seattle Mayor William F. Devin was also scheduled to attend the Rizal Day celebration. "Chief Justice Simpson to be Guest of Honor at Program on Dec. 30"; Velasco, "On Coeval Life," *Filipino Forum*, 24 December 1942, 1, 2; "America Gave the Filipinos Something to Fight for Says Speaker," *Filipino Forum*, 15 February 1943, 1; Velasco, "On Coeval Life"; "Filipino Leader Says Liberation Sure to Come"; "California Filipinos Can Now Buy Real Property," *Filipino Forum*, 9 April 1943, 1, 4; "We Shall Keep Faith with America, Says Sec. Of Finance Hernandez"; "Food and Clothing Great Needs of Philippine People Today"; "Seattle Filipinos Fete MacArthur's Victory"; "Osmena Confers with Roosevelt," *Filipino Forum*, February 1945, 1; Friday, 189.

12. Maria Rosa Henson, *Comfort Woman: A Filipina's Story of Prostitution and Slavery Under the Japanese Military* (New York: Rowman & Littlefield Publishers, Inc. 1999) (describing the Japanese military's sexual enslavement of Filipino women); Agoncillo, 404-406, 423 (describing the Japanese military's mass murders of Filipinos); Peter Bacho, *Cebu* (Seattle: University of Washington Press, 1991), 47-58 (a novelistic account describing Filipino and Japanese atrocities against each other). For a general description of the Japanese occupation of the Philippines during the Second World War, see Agoncillo, 387-426. See also manuscript (no author), undated, Box 1, Folder 52; "Official 1941 Election Results," 1 October 1941, Box 6, Folder 25; Martha Okuda to Trinidad Rojo, 31 July 1940, Box 6, Folder 23, VVC. See also Chapter Five and accompanying notes.

13. Manuel Quezon to Pio De Cano, 18 September c. 1942-1943, Box 1, Folder 44; Rojo, 16 August 1944, Box 6, Folder 25, VVC. See also Chapters Two and Four and accompanying notes.

14. Agoncillo, 176-183.

15. *Filipino Forum*, 24 December 1942, 1, VVC; David Wurfel, *Filipino Politics: Development of Democracy* (New York: Cornell University Press, 1988), 7; Walter LaFeber, *The American Age: United States Foreign Policy at Home and Abroad Since 1750* (New York: W.W. Norton & Company, 1989), 202. For information on specific battles during the resistance to American colonial rule, see Agoncillo, 248-257; "Chief Justice Simpson to be Guest of Honor at Program on Dec. 30"; "U.W. Filipino Alumni Ass'n to Give Traditional Dance," *Filipino Forum*, 24 December 1942, 1.

16. "Brevities," 24 December 1942, 2; "America Gave the Filipinos Something to Fight for Says Speaker"; "Filipino Farmers Organize"; "Nurse from Bataan Lauds Filipino Chivalry," *Filipino Forum*, 15 February 1943, 1, 4; "Filipino Alumni Association to Hold Inaugural Dance May 1"; "Filipino Leader Says Liberation Sure to Come," *Filipino Forum*, 9 April 1943, 1, 4.

17. Quintard Taylor, *The Forging of an African American Community: Seattle's Central District, from 1870 through the Civil Rights Era* (Seattle: University of Washington Press, 1994), 167.

18. Tonieng Velasco to Velasco, 22 October 1942, Box 1, Folder 47; "Chief Justice Simpson to be Guest of Honor at Program on Dec. 30," 1; Velasco, "On Coeval Life," *Filipino Forum,* 24 December 1942, 2; "America Gave the Filipinos Something to Fight for Says Speaker," 1; "Nurse from Bataan Lauds Filipino Chivalry," *Filipino Forum,* 15 February 1943, 1; Velasco, "On Coeval Life," *Filipino Forum,* 9 April 1943, 4; "We Shall Keep Faith with America, Says Sec. Of Finance Hernandez"; "Seattle Filipinos Fete MacArthur's Victory"; "Osmena Confers with Roosevelt," *Filipino Forum*, February 1945, 1; Velasco, "How May Race Unity be Achieved?" speech delivered at Bahai Society of Seattle, 12 September 1943, Box 9, Folder 34, VVC. "Mary Lou" was probably Maria Louisa Dominguez. It is not clear precisely when he met her. However, the 17 January 1944 entry was the first time that she appeared in the materials that the author has studied. *Engagements, 1944,* 17, 22 January 1944, Box 2, Folder 14, VVC.

19. *Filipino Forum,* 9 April 1943, 1; "Women's Society Ranks First in War Bond Sales"; "Filipino Wives Form Club for Island Relief," *Filipino Forum,* February 1945, 1.

20. Velasco to Adeva, 23 November 1946; Velasco to Resident Commissioner for the Philippines, 8 May 1943, Box 6, Folder 24, VVC.

21. Ramos to Velasco, 20 August 1946; Dionisio to Velasco, 2 October 1946, Box 6, Folder 23; Velasco to Ramos, 21 August 1946, Box 6, Folder 24; Velasco to Resident Commissioner for the Philippines, 4 April 1943, Box 6, Folder 24, VVC; Cordova, 179.

22. Velasco to Ramos, 21 August 1946; 27 September 1946, Box 6, Folder 24, VVC. The form was the Certificate of Identity and Registration. Jose Imperial to Velasco, 19 September 1946, Box 6, Folder 23, VVC.

23. Imperial to Velasco, 19 September 1946, Box 6, Folder 23; Dionisio to Velasco, 8 October 1946, Box 6, Folder 24, VVC.

24. Dionisio to Velasco, 8 October 1946, Box 6, Folder 24, VVC.

25. Ibid.; Velasco to Adeva, 23 November 1946, Box 6, Folder 24; Regala to Velasco, 2 December 1946, Box 6, Folder 23, VVC.

26. Among the factors affecting union politics were: origins in specific geographical regions in the Philippines; support for the international's control or for local autonomy; advocacy of high or low taxes, and amortization or immediate payment of Local 7's debts.

27. "Official 1941 Election Results," 1 October 1941, Box 6, Folder 25; Anonymous to Velasco, c. 1944, Box 6, Folder 23; B.O.S., "All Cannery Workers," c. October, 1941, Box 6, Folder 25; Mori to Velasco, 31 July 1940, Box 6, Folder 23, VVC; Agoncillo, 9-13.

28. Trinidad Rojo to "Mang Iddong" 27 March 1940; B.O.S., Box 6, Folder 25, VVC.

29. Velasco, "In the Choice of Candidates," c. 1944; Committee-Velasco for Treasurer, "Elect Victor A. Velasco for Treasurer,"c. 1944, Box 6, Folder 25; Mori to Velasco, 26 July 1944, Box 6, Folder 24, VVC. Prudencio Mori, also of Local 7, was Velasco's confidante who helped him distribute his campaign materials. Mori to Velasco, 10 August 1944; Velasco to Mori, 31 July 1944, Box 6, Folder 24; Committee-Velasco for Treasurer, "Elect Victor A. Velasco for Treasurer," c. 1944, Box 6, Folder 25, VVC.

30. Velasco to Mori, 31 July 1944, Box 6, Folder 24; Velasco, "In the Choice of Candidates," c. 1944, Box 6, Folder 25, VVC.

31. Mori to Velasco, 26 July 1944, Box 6, Folder 24, VVC. The 1941 Local 7 election results indicate that "C.A. Abella" was Casimiro A. Abella. "Official 1941 Election Results," 1 October 1941, Box 6, Folder 25, VVC.

32. Trinidad Rojo to "Mang Iddong," 27 March 1940; Trinidad Rojo to Whom it May Concern, 1 April 1940, Box 6, Folder 24, VVC. See also Chapter Three and accompanying notes.

33. Velasco to Mori, 31 July 1944, Box 6, Folder 24; Mori to Velasco, 10 August 1944, Box 6, Folder 24; "Seattleites Play Hosts to Women Leaders," *Filipino Clarion*, June 1948, Box 14, VVC.

34. The Budget Committee consisted of Ventura, Manzano, A. Ancheta, Valdez, Trinidad Rojo, Vincente Navea, and Zoilo Paragas. Paragas to Velasco, 31 July 1940, Box 6, Folder 23, VVC.

35. Agoncillo, 14.

36. Hing, 35; Takaki, *Strangers*, 331; Cordova, 19.

37. "We Shall Keep Faith with America, Says Sec. Of Finance Hernandez," 1; "Seattle Filipinos Fete MacArthur's Victory," February 1945; "America Gave the Filipinos Something to Fight for Says Speaker," *Filipino Forum*, 9 April 1943, 1.

## Epilogue

1. Velasco and the others did not rely solely upon the diverted funds to build up the treasury of the new union. They also solicited money from private individuals. ________ to Max Gonzalez (?), 7 January 1947, Box 6, Folder 37, VVC. For information about the upstarts' red-baiting tactics, see: Cornelio Briones, untitled, c. 1947; Martin "Buddy" Rendon, "Warning! Danger!" c. 1947, Box 35, Folder 28, CWFLUC. For references to the diversion of funds, see Prudencio P. Mori and Trinidad A. Rojo to "All Foremen, Delegates and Members," 12 July 1947, Box 6, Folder 25, VVC. The position each of the new union's leaders held appears in the letterhead of its stationary. Briones to "Brothers," c. 1947, Box 6, Folder 38, VVC (listing Velasco as Secretary; Alex Azurin as Treasurer; Martin Rendon and Salvador del Fierro as vice presidents; Max Gonzales as Business Agent; and Frank Bravo as Sergeant at Arms. The trustees were P.C. Ancheta, P.S. Cardona, and S.D. Eleccion). Ibid. For confirmation of Velasco and Briones' positions in the new union, see: "Membership Card" for Victorio Velasco, Box 35, Folder 28, CWFLUC. For documentation of the new union officials' attempt to become the collective bargaining agent, see: Velasco to Alaska Salmon Industry, Inc., 2 December 1947, Box 7, Folder 28, CWFLUC. For additional information about the structure of the new union, see: "Constitution and By-Laws of the Alaska Fish Cannery Workers' Union of the Pacific, Chartered by the Seafarer's International Union of North America, affiliated with the American Federation of Labor," c. 1947-1948, Box 6, Folder 46, VVC. For information about federal efforts to purge communists from labor organizations, see Arlene

De Vera, "Without Parallel: the Local 7 Deportation Cases, 1949-1955," *Amerasia Journal* 20, no. 2, 1-25; and Robert Zieger, *The C.I.O., 1935-1955* (Chapel Hill: University of North Carolina, 1995), 253-293.

2. "Memorandum re. Contract," 8 July 1947, Box 6, Folder 25, VVC. For reference to the attempt to revoke Local 7's charter, see Prudencio A. Mori to "Dear Sir and Brother," 17 July 1947, and "Notice to Members of Cannery Workers and Farm Laborer's Union, Local Seven, FTA-CIO," Box 6, Folder 25, VVC. Rojo and Velasco had, by the time of the controversy, probably been acquainted for about two decades in a sometimes friendly, sometimes antagonistic, personal and political relationship. In July of 1947, Rojo was Administrative Secretary for Local 7, Prudencio Mori was Administrative Chairman, and Ernesto Mangaoang, Administrative Business Agent. "Memorandum re. Contract," 8 July 1947, Box 6, Folder 25, VVC. To some extent, Velasco and the other leaders of the new union had reason for optimism. By early September of 1947, there were nearly a thousand members of Local 7 who voted to dissolve the union. Briones to Velasco, 1 September 1947, Box 35, Folder 28, CWFLUC. On 8 December 1947, the National Labor Relations Board informed the union that it had complied with the Taft-Hartley Act's provision concerning communist affiliations, and on 12 August 1948, the new union finalized its consolidation with the A.F.L. Martin "Buddy" Rendon, "Warning! Danger!" c. 1947; United States of America, National Labor Relations Board to Velasco, 8 December 1947; Marcelo Nillo and Cornelio Briones, 12 August 1948, Box 35, Folder 28, CWFLUC.

3. Cornelio Briones, "Consolidation of All Interests into Seafarers' International Union, Alaska Fish Cannery Workers' Union of the Pacific (A.F.L.), c. 1947-1948, Box 6, Folder 46, VVC; Velasco to Martin "Buddy" Rendon, 28 May 1948, Box 35, Folder 28, CWFLUC.

4. *Engagements, 1952*, 1 January 1952, Box 2, Folder 14, VVC. Maria Luisa Dominguez Fleetwood, "Errors of the Court During My Divorce Hearing, June 10, 1954," Box 2, Folder 11, VVC, 2. It was her cousin who introduced her to Velasco, who then interviewed her about her book project in an article in the *Filipino Forum* in February of 1952. Maria Luisa Dominguez Fleetwood, "Errors of the Court During My Divorce Hearing, June 10, 1954," Box 2, Folder 11, 2; *Engagements, 1952*, 1, 3, 13, 15, 21, 22, 27, January; 9, 14 and 15, 9, 28, 29 February; 3, 8, 10, 20, 21, 24 March 1952, Box 2, Folder 14, VVC.

5. "List of Donors for the Guam Relief of the Typhoon victims," 3 December 1962, Box 8, Folder 48; Velasco (?) to Frank Bolima (?), 14 July 1967; Velasco to Jaime Cruz, 24 June 1964; Velasco to Bernard ________, 25 January 1965, Box 8, Folder 45, VVC. In the summer of 1964, John Harrington, a professor of sociology at the University of Washington, invited Velasco to join in a panel discussion entitled, "Non-Negro Minorities in Seattle," scheduled for 7 July 1964. Velasco to John S. Harrington, 10 June 1964, Box 8, Folder 45, VVC. Cita Trinidad, Deputy Commissioner of Tourism for North America, Republic of the Philippines, had invited Velasco to attend the 300th anniversary celebration of the founding of the city of New York at the Sheraton East Hotel on 13 June 1964, which Velasco attended. Velasco to Trinidad Rojo, 22 June 1964; Velasco to Alfred R. "Fred" Agron, 11 March 1966; Velasco to Consolidated Press, 4 August 1967, Box 8, Folder 45, VVC. Ironically, the woman with whom Velasco finally enjoyed a long-term, harmonious relationship remains nearly completely absent in the materials the author has thus far studied in the Velasco Collection at the University of Washington. She helped him raise at least two daughters—although it is unclear whether they were the offspring of a prior marriage she may have had—helped him with the *Filipino Forum* during the remaining years of his life, tried to continue its publication for at least several

editions following his death, and was the one who contributed the vast majority of materials now in his collection. *Inventory*, VVC.

6. Frank Chin, Jeffrey Paul Chan, Lawson Fusao Inada, and Shawn Wong, *Aiiieeeee!: An Anthology of Asian American Writers* (New York: Penguin Books, 1991), xxx. In *Pocket Ninjas*, young Caucasian adults and children skillfully exercise martial arts moves while Southeast Asians, invariably pot-bellied, unkempt, and clumsy, fall all over each other as they roll their eyes and try to throw kicks and punches. *Pocket Ninjas* (Burbank: Cine Excel Entertainment, 2002), DVD. In *Kung Pow: Enter the Fist*, a Caucasian man made up to look like an Asian man with his hair dyed jet black and mimicking Bruce Lee's screams, battles a pregnant-looking cow to the rave reviews of the *New York Daily News* ("Silly, Perfect Fun!" quoted on the back cover in Oriental-looking lettering) and *Boxoffice Magazine* ("A Zany Parody!" quoted on the back cover in Oriental-looking lettering) *Kung Pow: Enter the Fist* (Hollywood: Twentieth Century Fox, 2002), DVD. In *Rambo: First Blood II*, Sylvester Stallone, with his shirt off to reveal his prominent musculature, slaughters hundreds of scrawny little Asian men who abuse women, torture white POWS, and run at the sight of him, with a single machine gun, a bow and arrow, and a knife. The film to which this was a sequel received an Oscar nomination from the American Academy of Motion Picture Arts and Sciences. *Rambo: First Blood Part II*, special edition (Santa Monica: Artisan Home Entertainment, 2002) (original edition, 1985), DVD. In *Kickboxer 4: The Aggressor*, a Caucasian male martial arts expert and a Caucasian female street fighter break into the compound of a Chinese villain by the name of Tong Po, whom a Caucasian actor, with his eyes pinched into slants, his mouth widened, and his face covered with heavy, yellowed-hued makeup, portrays. Among the various scenes are those in which Caucasian female sex slaves service the men of the compound; Tong Po's Asian-looking henchmen torture a white woman to death by stripping off her clothes, cutting open her belly, and leaving her hanging by her wrists from the rafters of a ceiling; and Tong Po shoots unarmed whites with a laugh but, when having to fight the Caucasian hero, scurries away on his hands and knees like a scared rabbit. In another scene, there is a close-up of Tong Po's face in which he broadens his mouth into a wide grin, his teeth showing, and his eyes pinched into slants in a manner reminiscent of Fu Manchu movies six or seven decades ago. *Kickboxer 4: The Aggressor* (Los Angeles: Live Home Entertainment, 1994), VHS. In *American Streetfighter*, Gary Daniels, a Caucasian actor, portrays the white hero who battles a network of dark-skinned Asians of unclear origin (it is unclear what nationalities they are, although their racial characteristics are without doubt) who ship drugs into the United States inside the cadavers of slain Caucasian and African American martial arts contestants. In the end, Daniels' character fights the main villain, Ogawa, and slays Ogawa with his own sword, although he had initially been unarmed against the Oriental. In *The Joy Luck Club*, Asian men appear as lecherous old men, licentious womanizers, impotents, and sexual perverts. The film received wide acclaim from the mainstream motion picture world (Siskel & Ebert; *Los Angeles Times*; *Chicago Tribune*; *Los Angeles Daily News*; *Sneak Previews*). Amy Tan, *The Joy Luck Club* (Hollywood: Oliver Stone Productions, 1994), VHS. In *Death Ride to Osaka*, an innocent young white woman finds herself among other blondes and redheads whom Japanese gangsters have lured into prostitution and sex slavery. *Death Ride to Osaka*, Hearst Entertainment re-issue (Hearst Entertainment, 2002) (original version made in mid-1980s), DVD. In *Rising Sun*, a ruthless businessman murders a white woman by asphyxiating her after ripping off her panties on a table reserved for Japanese corporate meetings; his Japanese business partners try to buy up properties in American cities; and, upon learning of the murder, in a manner familiar to many Americans through pervasive racial stereotypes, feign "typical Japanese" civility and politeness in order to cover up the murder of the white woman. During the course of the film, the

character whom Sean Connery portrays explains to his sidekick, whom Wesley Snipes plays, how duplicitous the Japanese race is. In another scene, an ugly Asian man with a heavily-pockmarked face leers at a naked young blonde woman, who tells him that he is sick. *Rising Sun* (Hollywood: Twentieth Century Fox, 1993), VHS. The manufacture of films in the late twentieth century and early twenty-first century for a wide range of audiences from adults to young children and featuring Caucasian actors in heavy makeup to look like Asians and reenacting Fu Manchu-type stereotypes for American audiences today is reminiscent of films like D.W. Griffith's *Birth of a Nation*, in which the dark-skinned characters represent evil and the whites, the good who valorously vanquish the former, albeit not before they have committed a series of unspeakable crimes against whites in general and white women in particular. Other examples of today's media's perpetuation of racially-demeaning stereotypes and pejorative portrayals of Asian men appeared in an episode of the critically-acclaimed television series "The Practice" airing on Sunday, 7 December 2003, in which one of the show's regulars, a white female attorney, referred to a Chinese American police officer as " . . . idiot Chan." On the previous night, on Saturday, 6 December, on the Spokane affiliate of the Fox Network, a Japanese or Japanese American wrestler on that night's broadcast of the World Wrestling Federation's "Smackdown" series reprised his role as the villain who blinded his white rival's Caucasian girlfriend with black-colored liquid, which he spat into her eyes. For a broad array of these and other racist depictions of Asians circulating in the American popular media today in television programs and advertisements, see the author's collection of video-recorded images covering the period from 1999 to the present. For an insightful and lengthy analysis of twentieth century American movies' exploitation and use of racial stereotypes to convey popular notions of good and evil, see generally Richard Slotkin, *Gunfighter Nation: The Myth of the Frontier in Twentieth Century America* (New York: Maxwell MacMillan International, 1992). The popular media, moreover, disseminate race-based stereotypes denigrating Asians even as they adopt a liberal persona putatively protesting against social ills and inhumanity. One example is FM 106.1 of Spokane, Washington, which broadcast a song criticizing materialism with lyrics declaiming, "The Japanese always have their light on. [They should] turn the light on their friends." Broadcast 2 November, 2003 in Pullman, Washington. The persistence of portrayals of Asian men as being emasculated and outside the realm of the male sex has inspired some, such as Darrell Y. Hamamoto, a professor at the University of California, Davis, to produce an erotic film highlighting Asian male sexuality. James Hou, review of "Masters of the Pillow," *Festival Program, Northwest Asian American Film Festival, International Examiner*, 25 October 2003: 7. Among the related topics are the effect prevalent stereotypes have upon the values people unconsciously absorb when they see others of a different race. Moon Lee, "Stereotypes of Teachers through Verbal and Nonverbal Cues," Author's collection.

7. Howard Coble, quoted in Nhien Nguyen, "Intend to Not Offend," *International Examiner*, 19 Feb.–4 March, 2003, 3; Tony Bruno, quoted in Irwin Tang, "Shaq's Ethnic Slurs Deeply Offend One Yao Fan," *International Examiner*, 15 Jan.–4 Feb. 2003, 5; Brent Musbuger, quoted in Irwin Tang, "Shaq's Ethnic Slurs Deeply Offend One Yao Fan," *International Examiner*, 15 Jan.–4 Feb., 2003, 5; Doug Chin, "Gonzaga University Should Take Responsibility for Racist Taunting," *International Examiner*, February 2003, 2. The *International Examiner* is a Seattle-based Asian American newspaper that reports race-based incidents against Asians which the mainstream press ignores or refuses to publish. According to Irwin Tang of *AsianWeek* and the *International Examiner*, the *Los Angeles Times*, *Sports Illustrated*, the Associated Press, and other news organizations declined to publish information about the incidents. Pervasive racial prejudice, of course, has led to more than racial taunts, as Detroit automobile workers' murder of Chinese

American Vincent Chin with baseball bats on the night he celebrated his upcoming wedding indicated (the fact that one defendant held Chin by his arms from behind while the other battered his head with the baseball bat did not convince the trial judge that either man should spend a day in jail. Explaining his refusal to impose a jail sentence, he commented about the two murderers, "These aren't the kind of men you send to jail . . ."). Nhien Nguyen, "Remembering Vincent Chin," *International Examiner*, 19 June–2 July 2002, 1, 10-11; "Rededication to Justice: Vincent Chin 20th Year Remembrance," umich.edu, visited 11 November 2003.

8. One of the best examples of popular songs in recent times disparaging Asians is the popular 1980s tune "I'm turning Japanese I Really Think So" by the British rock group the Vapors, which is still being broadcast on radio stations across the United States. Musicstack.com, visited 27 February 2003. For information about the T-shirts, see pubweb.northwestern.edu, visited 27 February 2003 ("Abercrombie & Fitch, Co.'s new T-shirts make a mockery of the injustices and prejudices Asian Americans experienced in the past and present, and are as offensive had there been an African American Sambo depicted on the shirts"); geocities.com, visited 27 February 2003 ("Los Angeles, April 23, 2002-Today's protest rally in front of the newest Abercrombie & Fitch store in Los Angeles forced the store to delay its Grand Opening. Over 50 protesters joined in the chants, calling for Abercrombie & Fitch to publicly apologize with full page ads in major papers for its latest line of T-Shirts, sporting racist images of Asian Americans . . . caricatures, some with slant-eyed, conical hat-wearing, mispronounced English . . ."). A search on the internet located a wide array of articles concerning Abercrombie and Fitch's sales campaign, which offended Asian Americans who saw the perpetuation of the racial stereotypes as being analogous to racist portrayals of African Americans. Among items in the author's popular collection is a recent punk rock album with a cover consisting of a yellow face on an all-yellow background with slanted eyes and jet black hair. Linea 77, *Too Much Happiness* (New York: Earache Records, 2000), CD.

# Bibliography


## PRIMARY SOURCES

## ARCHIVES AND MANUSCRIPT COLLECTIONS

### University Archives

Western Washington University Archives, Bellingham, Washington

*Weekly Messenger* (1926-1929)
*Klipsun* (1927-1929)
*Western Washington College of Education Registration Up to 1957*, vol. 2
*Annual Catalog* (1926-1927; 1927-1928)
*Bellingham Herald* (1927)
*Western Washington College of Education Registration up to 1957*, WWUC
*The Red Arrow* (1927-1929)

University of Washington Manuscripts and Archives, Seattle.

Cannery Workers and Farm Laborers Collection
Carlos Bulosan Papers
Higano Family Papers
JACL Papers, in James Sakamoto Collection
Japan America Association of North America
Japanese-American History Project materials
Joseph Koide Collection
S. Frank Miyamoto Collection
James Sakamoto Collection
Pacific Northwest Regional Newspaper and Periodicals
Edwin J. Brown scrapbooks
Pamphlet File
Japanese Immigration Centennial Committee and Seattle Chapter, JACL
Washington State University Manuscripts and Special Collections, Pullman.

**Public Collections, Libraries**

Bainbridge Island Public Library, Bainbridge Island
Seattle Public Library
Spokane Public Library, Northwest Room Archives, Spokane, Washington

**Private Collections**

Asian American Bar Association of Washington, Seattle
Asian American Legal Defense and Education Fund, New York
Asian Law Caucus, New York
Filipino American National Historical Society Archives, Seattle
Filipino civil Rights Advocates (FILCRA), New York
Interim Program, Chinatown/International District Office, Seattle
Japanese American Citizens League, Seattle
National Asian Pacific American Bar Association, Seattle Chapter
National Asian Pacific American Legal Consortium, Seattle Office
National Network of Immigrant and Refugee Rights, Oakland, CA
Northwest Labor and Employment Law Office, Seattle
Pacific American Labor Alliance, Seattle Office
Wing Luke Asian Art Museum Archives, Seattle
*Annals of the Chinese Historical Society of the Pacific Northwest* (c. 1984-)
Chang-Hwa Benevolent Association Papers (undated)
Densho Project (c. 1995)
John Litz Collection
Wing Luke Collection (c. 1930s)

**Miscellaneous Collections**

Seattle Chinatown International District Preservation and Development Authority, Seattle
Seattle Department of Neighborhoods Historic Preservation Program, City of Seattle
Washington State Commission on Asian American Affairs, Seattle Office.
Washington State Historical Museum, Olympia
Washington State Supreme Court Temple of Justice, Olympia

**Newsletters**

*CAPAA* (newsletter of Washington State Commission on Asian Pacific American Affairs, Olympia) (2000-present)
*Courier Citizen*, JACL Seattle Chapter, Newsletter (c. 1945-present)
*Minidoka Irrigator* (c. 1942-1945)

*NAPABA Lawyer* (1989-present)

**Newspapers**

*The Advocate*
*Asian Reporter*
*Bellingham Herald*
*Bullseye*
*CAPAA*
*Chomly Spectator*
*Cosmopolitan Courier*
*Filipino American Herald*
*Filipino Citizen*
*Filipino Clarion*
*Filipino Forum*
*Filipino Student*
*The Informer*
*Integridad*
*International Examiner*
*Minidoka Irrigator*
*Minnesota Daily*
*Mother's Bulletin*
*The Nation*
*Northwest Asian Weekly*
*Pacific Citizen*
*Philipinyana*
*Philippine Advocate*
*Philippine American Chronicle*
*Philippine Digest*
*Philippine Republic*
*Philippine Seattle Colonist*
*Red Arrow*
*Sea Gull News*
*Seattle Daily Times*
*Seattle Pacific College News*
*Seattle Post Intelligencer*
*Seattle Times*
*Spokesman Review*
*Varsity Filipino Weekly*
*Weekly Messenger*
*Yakima Daily Herald*

## SECONDARY SOURCES:

### Books

Teodoro Agoncillo, *History of the Filipino People*, 8th ed. Quezon City: Garotech Publishing, 1990.

Asian Students Association, ed. *HomeGrown: Asian American Experiences from the Pacific Northwest.* Seattle: University of Washington Press, 1980.

———*Homegrown 3: Asian American Experiences*. Seattle: University of Washington Press, 1990.

Burke, Edward, and Elizabeth Burke. *Seattle's Other History*. Seattle: Profanity Hill Press, 1979.

Chan, Sucheng. *Asian Americans: An Interpretive History*. Boston: Twayne Publishers, 1991.

Chin, Doug. *Seattle's International District: The Making of a Pan-Asian Community*. Seattle: International Examiner Press, 2001.

Chin, Frank, Jeffery Paul Chan, Lawson Fusao Inada, and Shawn Wong, eds. *Aiiieeeee!: An Anthology of Asian American Writers*. New York: Penguin Books, 1974.

Chinese Historical Society of America. *Chinese America: History and Perpectives*. Brisbane: Fong Brothers Printing, 1995.

Choy, Catherine. *Empire of Care*. Durham: Duke University Press, 2003.

Daniels, Roger, ed. *Anti-Chinese Violence in North America*. New York: Arno Press, 1978.

———*Asian America: Chinese and Japanese in the United States Since 1850*. Seattle: University of Washington Press, 1988.

D'Emilio, John. *Sexual Politics, Sexual Communities*. Chicago & London: The University of Chicago Press, 1983.

Del Rosario, Carina A. *A Different Battle: Stories of Asian Pacific American Veterans*. Seattle: University of Washington Press, 1999.

Mary L. Doi, Chien Lin, and Indu Vohra-Sahn, *Pacific/Asian American Research: An Annotated Bibliography, No. 1, Bibliography Series*. Chicago: Pacific/Asian American Mental Health Center, 1981.

Espiritu, Yen Le. *Filipino American Lives*. Philadelphia: Temple University Press, 1995.

———*Asian American Panethnicity*. Philadelphia: Temple University Press, 1992.

Evangelista, Susan. *Carlos Bulosan and His Poetry: A Biography and Anthology*. Seattle: University of Washington Press, 1985.

Evans, Sara. *Personal Politics*. New York: Alfred A. Knopf, Inc., 1979.

Grob, Gerald N., and George Athan Billias, eds. *Interpretations of American History: Patterns and Pespectives*, 6th ed. New York: Simon & Schuster, Inc., 1967.

Hing, Bill Ong. *Making and Remaking Asian America Through Immigration Policy, 1850-1990*. Stanford: Stanford University Press, 1993.

Hong, Maria, ed. *Growing Up Asian American*. New York: William Morrow & Company, Inc., 1993.

Kwong, Peter. *The New Chinatown*. New York: The Noonday Press, 1987.

LaFargue, Thomas E. *China's first Hundred*. Pullman: Washington State University Press, 1987.

LaFeber, Walter. *The American Age*. New York: W. W. Norton Company, 1989.

John Lee, ed., *Bruce Lee: The Celebrated Life of the Golden Dragon*. Boston: Tuttle, 2000.

Matsumoto, Valerie J. *Farming the Home Place*. Ithaca & London: Cornell University Press, 1993.

McWilliams, Carey, ed. *America is in the Heart*. New York: Harcourt, Brace and Company, 1943; Washington Paperback Edition, 1973.

Moraga, Cherrie, and Gloria Anzaldua. *This Bridge Called My Back: Writings by Radical Women of Color*. New York: Kitchen Table Press, 1981.

Okada, John. *No-No Boy*. Seattle: University of Washington Press, 1976.

Okihiro, Gary. *Margins and Mainstreams: Asians in American History and Culture*. Seattle & London: University of Washington Press, 1994.

———Marilyn Alquizola, Dorothy Fujita Rony, and K. Scott Wong, eds. *Privileging Positions*. Pullman: Washington State University Press, 1995.

Paterson, Thomas G., ed. *Major Problems in American Foreign Policy*, 3rd ed. Lexington & Toronto: D.C. Heath & Company, 1989.

Reyes, Norman, *Child of Two worlds: An Autobiography of a Filipino American, or Vice Versa* Colorado Springs: Three Continents Press, 1995.

Roces, Mina. *Women, Power, and Kinship Politics: Female Power in Post-War Philippines*. Westport: Praeger, 1998.

Salamanca, Bonifacio S. *The Filipino Reaction to American Rule, 1901-1913*. Shoe String Press, Inc., 1968.

San Juan, Jr., Epifanio, ed. *On Becoming Filipino*. Philadelphia: Temple University Press, 1995.

Silberman, Charles E. *Crisis in Black and White*. New York: Alfred A. Knopf, Inc., 1964.

Steinberg, David Joel. *The Philippines: A Singular and a Plural Place*, 2nd ed. Boulder: Westview Press, 1990.

Takaki, Ronald. *Strangers from a Different Shore*. New York: Little, Brown & Company: New York, 1989; Penguin Books, 1990.

Takami, David. *Divided Destiny: A History of Japanese Americans in Seattle*. Seattle & London: University of Washington Press, 1998.

———Executive Order 9066: 50 Years Before and 50 Years After. Seattle: Wing Luke Asian Art Museum, 1992.

Tsutakawa, Mayumi, and Alan Chong Lau. *Turning Shadows into Light.* Seattle: Young Pine Press, 1982.

Velasco, Victorio Acosta, *Lingyen and Other Poems.* Manila: Mission Press, 1924.

Wegars, Priscilla, ed. *Hidden Heritage: Historical Archaeology of the Overseas Chinese.* Amityville: Baywood Publishing Company, Inc., 1993.

Wei, William. *The Asian American Movement.* Asian American History and Culture, ed. Sucheng Chan. Philadelphia: Temple University Press, 1993.

White, Sid, and S.E. Solberg. *Peoples of Washington.* Pullman: Washington State University Press, 1989.

Williams, Patricia. *The Alchemy of Race and Rights.* Cambridge: Harvard University Press, 1991.

*National Directory of Asian Pacific American Organizations.* New York: Organization of Chinese Americans, 1998.

## Journals

### Academic Journals

Chun-Hom, Lowell, "Jade Snow Wong and the Fate of Chinese-American Identity," *Amerasia Journal* 1 (1974): 52-63.

Sharon Delmendo, "The American Factor in Jose Rizal's Nationalism," *Amerasia Journal* 24, no. 2 (1998): 54.

Edwards, Louise, review of *Staying Alive: Women, Ecology and Development*, by Vandana Shiva, *Dialogues in Paradise*, by Can Xue, and *Daughters of the Canton Delta: Marriage Patterns and Economic Strategies in South China, 1860-1930*, by Janice E. Stockard. *Bulletin of Concerned Asian Scholars* 24 (1992): 59-66.

Fung, Colleen, and Judy Yung. "In Search of the Right Spouse: Interracial Marriage among Chinese and Japanese Americans." *Amerasia Journal* 21, no. 3 (Winter 1995/1996): 77-97.

Hom, Alice Y. "Stories from the Homefront: Perspectives of Asian American Parents with Lesbian Daughters and Gay Sons." *Amerasia Journal* 20, no. 1 (1994): 19-32.

Hwang, David Henry. "Evolving a Multicultural Tradition." *Melus* 16, no. 3 (Fall 1989-1990): 16-20.

Lawrence, Charles R. "Beyond Redress: Reclaiming the Meaning of Affirmative Action." *Amerasia Journal* 19, no. 1 (1993): 1-6.

Leong, Russell C. "South Asian Movements in the United States." *Amerasia Journal* 25, no. 3 (1999/2000): v-vii.

Mangaoang, Gil. From the 1970s to the 1990s: Perspective of a Gay Filipino American Activist. *Amerasia Journal* 20, no. 1 (1994): 33-44.

Miyamoto, S. Frank. "Problems of Interpersonal Style among the Nisei." *Amerasia Journal* 13, no. 2 (1986/87): 29-45.

Parrenas, Rhacel Salazar. "'White Trash' Meets the 'Little Brown Monkeys': The Taxi Dance Hall as a Site of Interracial and Gender Alliances between White Working Class Women and Filipino Immigrant Men in the 1920s and 30s." *Amerasia Journal* 24, no. 2 (Summer 1998): 115-134.

Prashad, Vijay, and Biju Mathew. "*Satyagraha* in America: The Political Culture of South Asians in the U.S." *Amerasia Journal* 25, no. 3 1999/2000): ix-xv.

Santos, Bienvenido N. "Pilipino Old Timers: Fact and Fiction." *Amerasia Journal* 9, no. 2 (1982): 89-98.

Saxton, Alexander. "The Racial Trajectory of the Western Hero." *Amerasia Journal* 11, No. 2 (1984): 67-79.

Shukla, Sandhya. "New Immigrants, New Forms of Transnational Community: Post-1965 Indian Migrations." *Amerasia Journal* 25, no. 3 (1999/2000).

TuSmith, Bonnie. "The Cultural Translator: Toward an Ethnic Womanist Pedagogy." *Melus* 16, no. 2 (Summer 1989): 17-30.

Takagi, Dana. "Maiden Voyage: Excursion into Sexuality and Identity Politics in Asian America." *Amerasia Journal* 20, no. 1 (1994): 1-17.

Vaid, Urvashi. "Inclusion, Exclusion and Occlusion: The Queer Idea of Asian Pacific American-ness." *Amerasia Journal* 25, no. 3 (1999/2000): 1-18.

Yang, Eun Sik. "Korean Women of America: From Subordination to Partnership, 1903-1930." *Amerasia Journal* 11, no. 2 (1984): 1-28.

Zwick, Jim. "The Anti-Imperialist League and the Origins of Filipino American Oppositional Solidarity. *Amerasia Journal* 24, no. 2 (Summer 1998): 65-85.

## Popular Journals

*A Magazine* (c. 1990-)
*American West* (1982-)
*Northwest Magazine* (1902-)
*Oregon Benchmarks* (n.d.)
*Puget Sounder* (1936-)
*Town Crier* (1910-)
*Washington Magazine* (1906-)

## Bibliographies

Dewberry, Suzanne J., and Nancy Malan, eds. *Guide to Records in the National Archives-Pacific Southwest Region, Paper 86*. Washington. D.C.: National Archives and Records Administration, 1995.

Doi, Mary L., Chien Lin, Indu Vohra-Sahn. *Pacific/Asian American Research: An Annotated Bibliography, No. 1*, Bibliography Series. Chicago: Pacific/Asian American Mental Health Center, 1981.

Espiritu, Len Ye, Ellen Wu, and Stephen Lee, eds. *Amerasia Journal: 30th Anniversary Cumulative Index*. Los Angeles: UCLA Asian American Studies Center, 2002.

Greene, Bill, and Bob Glass. *A Preliminary Guide to Records of Asian Americans and Pacific Islanders at NARA's Pacific Region (San Francisco)*. San Bruno: National Archive and Records Administration-Pacific Region, 2003.

John Litz. *Comprehensive Guide to the Manuscripts Collection and the Personal Papers in the University Archives*. Seattle: Wing Luke Asian American Museum, c. 1990.

Lowell, Wavery B. *Chinese Immigration and Chinese in the United States: Records in the Regional Archives of the National Archives and Records Administration, Paper 99*. Washington, D.C.: National Archives and Records Administration, 1996.

Miller, Larisa K., and Nancy Malan. *Guide to Records in the National Archives-Pacific Sierra Region, Paper 88*. San Bruno: National Archives and Records Administration, 1995.

Yu, Elena S.H., Alice K. Murata, and Chien Lin, eds. *Bibliography of Pacific/Asian American Materials in the Library of Congress. No. 3, Bibliography Series*. Chicago: Asian/Pacific American Mental Health Research Center, 1982.

## Trade Journals/Miscellaneous

Goldsmith, Steven. "Takuji Yamashita," *Washington State Bar News* 55, no. 3 (March 2001): 22-23.

National Asian/Pacific American Bar Association. *NAPABA Lawyer* (1989-).

*National Directory of Asian Pacific American Organizations*. New York: Organization of Chinese Americans (c. 1998).

## Published Reports

*1998 Audit of Violence Against Asian Pacific Americans: 6th Annual Report*. Washington, D.C.: National Asian Pacific American Legal Consortium, 1998.

Asian American Studies Program. *Directory of Asian American Studies Programs*. New York: Cornell University Press, 1988.

*Asian Pacific Americans in Washington State*. Seattle: Washington State Commission on Asian American Affairs, 1988.

*Countdown: A Demographic Profile of Asian and Pacific Islanders in Washington State.* Seattle: State of Washington Commission on Asian Pacific American Affairs, 1982 and 1989.

Donnelly, Nancy D. *Seattle Schoolchildren Who Speak Asian Languages at Home Residence by Census Tract 1980, 1984, 1988.* Seattle: Southeast Asian Studies Department, University of Washington, 1989.

Murata, Alice K., and Juanita Salvador-Burris. *Issues in Community Research.* New York: Pacific/Asian American Mental Health Research Center, 1980.

*Report to the Governor on Discrimination Against Asians.* Seattle: Asian-American Advisory Council, 1973.

United States Department of Justice. *Redress Regulations: Questions and Answers* Washington, D.C.: U.S. Department of Justice, Civil Rights Division (undated).

## LEGAL DOCUMENTS

### Washington State Legislature

#### Bills

Washington State Legislature. House. *A Bill Making it Unlawful for White Persons to Intermarry with Negroes, Japanese, Chinese, Hindus, or Persons of the Mongolian Race, or to have Carnal Intercourse with Japanese, Chinese, Hindus or Persons of the Mongolian Race Prescribing the Penalty for a Violation Thereof and Declaring an Emergency.* 12th sess., 1911. H.R. 34.

Washington State Legislature. House. *A Bill Prohibiting Marriage Between White and Colored Races, Providing Punishment for Violations Thereof, and Declaring an Emergency.* 12th sess., 1911. H.R. 50.

Washington State Legislature. House. *A Bill Prohibiting Intermarriage Between White Persons and Negroes, Chinese and Japanese and Providing a Penalty for its Violation.* 5th sess., 1917. H.R. 87.

Washington State Legislature. House. *A Bill Providing that No Marriage License Shall be Issued Where One of the Parties is of the White or Caucasian Race and the Other of the Yellow or Mongolian Race.* 17th sess., 1921, H.R. 40.

#### Legal Cases

*Barrinuevo v. Barrinuevo*, 287 P.2d 349 (1955).

*In re. Estate of John T. Wilbur*, 44 P.262 (Wash. 1896).

**Miscellaneous Documents**

*H. Joint Memorial No. 8*, 17th sess. (1921).

**United States Congress**

**Bills, House**

U.S. Congress. House. *A Bill Granting to Women Married to Foreigners the Right to Retain their Citizenship*. 65th Cong., 2nd sess., 1917. H.R. 4049.

U.S. Congress. House. A *Bill to Regulate the Citizenship of Married Women*. 65th Cong., 2nd sess., 1918. H.R. 12335.

U.S. Congress. House. *A Bill Relative to the Citizenship and Naturalization of Married Women*. 67th Cong., 2nd sess., 1922. H.R. 5525.

U.S. Congress. House. *A Bill to Provide a Uniform Rule of Naturalization and to Amend and Codify the Laws Relating to the Acquisition and Loss of Citizenship to Equalize the Citizenship Stats of Men and Women; to Establish a Method for the Registration of Aliens for Their Better Guidance and Protection; and for Other Purposes*. 67th Cong., 2nd sess., 1922. H.R. 10860.

U.S. Congress. House. *A Bill Relative to Naturalization and Citizenship of Married Women*. 67th Cong., 2nd sess., 1922. H.R. 11773.

U.S. Congress. House. A Bill Relative to the Naturalization and Citizenship of Married Women. 67th Cong., 2nd sess., 1922, H.R. 12022.

**Bills, Senate**

U.S. Congress. Senate. *A Bill Granting to American Women Married to Foreigners the Right to Retain their Citizenship*. 66th Cong. 2nd sess., 1918. S. 3308.

U.S. Congress. *Senate. An Act to Amend Section 3 of An Act Entitled, "An Act to Regulate the Immigration of Aliens to, and the Residence of Aliens in, the United States," Approved February 5, 1917*. 66th Cong. 2nd sess., 1920. S. 3566.

U.S. Congress. Senate. *A Bill Relating to Married Women Intermarried with Aliens*. 66th Cong. 2nd sess., 1920. S. 3945.

U.S. Congress. Senate. *A Bill Relative to the Citizenship and Naturalization of Married Women*. 67th Cong. 2nd sess., 1921. S. 2828.

## Enacted Laws

34 Stat. 1228, sec. 3 (1907).
39 Stat. 874 (1917).
41 Stat. 153 (1924).
42 Stat. Li, cxii (1922).

## Hearings

U.S. Congress. House. Committee on Immigration and Naturalization. *Proposed Changes in Naturalization Laws, 1920: Hearings on H.R., 10374, H.R., 10435, and H.R. 12749*. 66th Cong., 2nd sess., 28 February 1920.

U.S. Congress. House. Committee on Immigration and Naturalization. *Immigration, 1921: Hearings on Conditions Among Migrants in Europe Operation of Three Percentum Immigration act Monthly Quota Tables, etc*. 67th Cong., 2nd sess., 13 December 1921.

U.S. Congress. House. Committee on Immigration and Naturalization. *To Provide a Uniform Rule of Naturalization and to Amend and Codify the Laws Relating to the Acquisition and Loss of Citizenship; to Equalize the Citizenship Status of Men and Women; to Establish a Method or the Registration of Aliens for Their Better Guidance and Protection; and for Other Purposes.* Hearings on H.R., 10860, 67th Cong., 2nd sess. 3. 1922.

U.S. Congress. House. Committee on Immigration and Naturalization. *Naturalization and Citizenship of Married Women, 1921: Hearings on H.R. 11773*. 67th Cong., 2nd sess., 8 June 1922.

## House Reports

U.S. Congress. House. Committee on Immigration and Naturalization. *Return of Certain Filipinos to Philippine Islands. Report No. 127*, 73rd Cong., 1st sess. (c. 1935).

U.S. Congress. House. *Committee on Immigration and Naturalization. Naturalization and Citizenship of Married Women. Report No. 1110*. 67th Cong., 2nd sess., 16 June 1922.

U.S. Congress. House. Committee on Immigration and Naturalization. *To Amend Section 4067, Revised Statutes. Report No. 285*. 65th Cong., 2nd sess., 5 February 1918.

## Senate Reports

U.S. Congress. Senate. Committee on Immigration and Naturalization. *Statements and Recommendations Submitted by So-*

*cieties and Organizations Interested in the Subject of Immigration.* 61st Cong., 3rd sess., 1910.

**Congressional Record**

40 *Congressional Record* 1485 (1907).
62 *Congressional Record* 9, 8740 (1922).
62 *Congressional Record* 12, 12322 (1922).

**THESES AND DISSERTATIONS**

Dahlie, Jorgen. "A Social History of Scandinavian Immigration, Washington State, 1895-1910." Ph.D. diss, Washington State University, 1967.

Gold, Gerald. "The Development of Local Number 7 of the Food, Tobacco, Agricultural and Allied Workers of America-C.I.O." M.A. thesis, University of Washington, 1949.

Lee, David Kwang. "Why Washington State Did Not Have an Anti-Miscegenation Law." M.A. thesis, Washington State University, 1998.

Nelson, Judy. "The Chinese in Spokane, 1860-1915." M.A. thesis, Eastern Washington University, 1995.

**INTERNET**

horluck.com
androsdance.tripod.com
umich.edu
bartleby.com
cwu.edu
engr.washington.edu
historlink.org
lib.washington.edu
lummi-island.com
portorchard.com
students.washington.edu
sanjuanproperty.com

**MISCELLANEOUS SOURCES**

Alice Y. Chai, "A Picture Bride from Korea: The Life History of a Korean American Woman in Hawaii," paper presented at the 6th Annual Conference on Ethnic and Minority Studies, La Crosse, Wisconsin, 19-22 April, 1978.

"The ILWU Story: The Development of Militant Unionism" 2nd ed. San Francisco, CA: Information Department of International Warehouse-men's Union, 1963.

# Index

# About the Author

Michael Serizawa Brown is an attorney based in Seattle Washington, where he also teaches courses on history and law as adjunct faculty at various postsecondary institutions in the Puget Sound area.

He was born in Tachikawa Japan of a Japanese mother and an Euro-American father and has thus lived, from his earliest memories, with the knowledge and realities of being both of and not of any particular race, culture, or heritage. It was this knowledge, along with firsthand awareness of the realities of racial hierarchies and their perpetuation in often unconscious, subtle ways that led him to decide to write a biography of an Asian male's experience in the United States, which today often parallels the experience of African Americans in terms of living with the realities of race-based prejudices during the 19th century and early 20th century. A particular inspiration has been the parallels between the experience of Asian males during Velasco's life and of the author's own times. In the latter period, unlike in Velasco's lifetime, there are no formal mechanisms regulating social relations, such as job opportunities and interracial romantic relationships. However, time has proven that informal social mechanisms perpetuated by commonly accepted, race-based, negative images of Asian men in the United States today have proven to be just as effective in replicating for Asian males of today experiences that hounded Velasco's in his lifetime, including the existence of a cadre of overqualified Asian males who cannot find employment commensurate with their qualifications and who, in their personal lives, are predestined to form today's equivalent of the "bachelor society" because of continuing negative images about Asian male sexuality. The author thus seeks to elucidate the realities of our own times by opening up a window into the past and, hopefully, encourage his readers to critically examine the parallels between the past and the present.